Classifying Educational Programmes

Manual for ISCED-97 Implementation in OECD Countries

1999 Edition

ORGANISATION FOR ECONOMIC CO-OPERATION AND DEVELOPMENT

**ORGANISATION DE COOPÉRATION
ET DE DÉVELOPPEMENT ÉCONOMIQUES**

En vertu de l'article 1er de la Convention signée le 14 décembre 1960, à Paris, et entrée en vigueur le 30 septembre 1961, l'Organisation de Coopération et de Développement Économiques (OCDE) a pour objectif de promouvoir des politiques visant :

- à réaliser la plus forte expansion de l'économie et de l'emploi et une progression du niveau de vie dans les pays Membres, tout en maintenant la stabilité financière, et à contribuer ainsi au développement de l'économie mondiale ;
- à contribuer à une saine expansion économique dans les pays Membres, ainsi que les pays non membres, en voie de développement économique ;
- à contribuer à l'expansion du commerce mondial sur une base multilatérale et non discriminatoire conformément aux obligations internationales.

Les pays Membres originaires de l'OCDE sont : l'Allemagne, l'Autriche, la Belgique, le Canada, le Danemark, l'Espagne, les États-Unis, la France, la Grèce, l'Irlande, l'Islande, l'Italie, le Luxembourg, la Norvège, les Pays-Bas, le Portugal, le Royaume-Uni, la Suède, la Suisse et la Turquie. Les pays suivants sont ultérieurement devenus Membres par adhésion aux dates indiquées ci-après : le Japon (28 avril 1964), la Finlande (28 janvier 1969), l'Australie (7 juin 1971), la Nouvelle-Zélande (29 mai 1973), le Mexique (18 mai 1994), la République tchèque (21 décembre 1995), la Hongrie (7 mai 1996), la Pologne (22 novembre 1996) et la Corée (12 décembre 1996). La Commission des Communautés européennes participe aux travaux de l'OCDE (article 13 de la Convention de l'OCDE).

Also available in English under the title:

CLASSIFYING EDUCATIONAL PROGRAMMES
MANUAL FOR ISCED-97 IMPLEMENTATION IN OECD COUNTRIES – 1999 EDITION

© OCDE 1999
Les permissions de reproduction partielle à usage non commercial ou destinée à une formation doivent être adressées au Centre français d'exploitation du droit de copie (CFC), 20, rue des Grands-Augustins, 75006 Paris, France, Tél. (33-1) 44 07 47 70, Fax (33-1) 46 34 67 19, pour tous les pays à l'exception des États-Unis. Aux États-Unis, l'autorisation doit être obtenue du Copyright Clearance Center, Service Client, (508)750-8400, 222 Rosewood Drive, Danvers, MA 01923 USA, or CCC Online: http://www.copyright.com/. Toute autre demande d'autorisation de reproduction ou de traduction totale ou partielle de cette publication doit être adressée aux Éditions de l'OCDE, 2, rue André-Pascal, 75775 Paris Cedex 16, France.

Foreword

As the structure of educational systems varies widely between countries, a framework to collect and report data on educational programmes with a similar level of educational content is a clear prerequisite for the production of internationally comparable education statistics and indicators. In 1997, a revised International Standard Classification of Education (ISCED-97) was adopted by the UNESCO General Conference. This multi-dimensional framework has the potential to greatly improve the comparability of education statistics – as data collected under this framework will allow for the comparison of educational programmes with similar levels of educational content – and to better reflect complex educational pathways in the OECD indicators. The purpose of *Classifying Educational Programmes: Manual for ISCED-97 Implementation in OECD Countries* is to give clear guidance to OECD countries on how to implement the ISCED-97 framework in international data collections.

First, this manual summarises the rationale for the revised ISCED framework, as well as the defining characteristics of the ISCED-97 levels and cross-classification categories for OECD countries, emphasising the criteria that define the boundaries between educational levels. The methodology for applying ISCED-97 in the national context that is described in this manual has been developed and agreed upon by the OECD/INES Technical Group, a working group on education statistics and indicators representing 29 OECD countries. The OECD Secretariat has also worked closely with both EUROSTAT and UNESCO to ensure that ISCED-97 will be implemented in a uniform manner across all countries. Selected programmes in OECD countries that meet specific classification criteria are also presented as examples of how the criteria can be properly applied.

Secondly, the manual contains detailed proposals for the allocation of national educational programmes to ISCED-97 levels for all 29 OECD countries in a tabular format. These proposals have been developed by Member countries, in consultation with the OECD Secretariat, and represent the starting point for a process of consultation within the OECD/INES Technical Group, with the aim of working towards an internationally agreed upon allocation of national educational programme to ISCED-97 in the OECD. The national programme allocations presented here have been reviewed and approved by the OECD/INES Technical Group and will form the basis of data reporting in the 1999 UNESCO/OECD/EUROSTAT (UOE) Data Collection on Education Statistics. These country allocations will also guide the implementation of ISCED-97 in all future OECD data collections, including the alignment of levels of educational attainment data collected in national Labour Force Surveys and the categorisation of both students' educational aspirations and teachers' educational qualifications in the Programme for International Student Assessment (PISA).

The primary goal of OECD's work in the ISCED-97 implementation process is that the allocation of national education programmes to the revised ISCED framework be perfectly transparent and jointly agreed upon by all Member countries. The Technical Group will continue to serve as a forum for discussing and evaluating individual country's ISCED-97 allocations. Particular programme allocations that do not match the criteria laid out in this manual, and thereby do not lead to comparable education statistics, will be brought up and discussed in the Technical Group. In cases where this manual does not make it clear how a programme with particular characteristics should be mapped to ISCED-97, proposals for modifying the manual will be developed and discussed within the Technical Group. The implementation of ISCED will be both an iterative and interactive process, with both Member countries and international organisations reviewing countries' assignments of programmes to ISCED categories and recommending adjustments to enhance international comparability.

The OECD foresees that the implementation instructions for ISCED-97, as well as ISCED itself, will need to be updated as education systems evolve and additional comparability issues are identified. The publication of this manual is an important step forward in a long-term consultative process designed to improve the comparability of educational statistics.

The book is published on the responsibility of the Secretary-General of the OECD.

Table of contents

Introduction 7

Coverage and structure of ISCED-97 11

Other dimensions not accounted for ISCED-97 17

Level structure of ISCED-97 and corresponding classification criteria 21

ISCED 0 – Pre-primary level of education 25

ISCED 1 – Primary level of education 29

ISCED 2 – Lower secondary level of education 33

ISCED 3 – Upper secondary level of education 39

ISCED 4 – Post-secondary non-tertiary 47

ISCED 5 – First stage of tertiary education 51

ISCED 6 – Second stage of tertiary education 63

Proposed allocation of national educational programmes to ISCED-97 65

ISCED-97 levels for each OECD country

AUSTRALIA	67
AUSTRIA	68
BELGIUM (FLEMISH COMMUNITY)	70
BELGIUM (FRENCH COMMUNITY)	74
CANADA	76
CZECH REPUBLIC	78
DENMARK	80
FINLAND	81
FRANCE	82
GERMANY	84
GREECE	86
HUNGARY	87
ICELAND	89
IRELAND	92
ITALY	93
JAPAN	94
KOREA	96
LUXEMBOURG	98
MEXICO	99
NETHERLANDS	100
NEW ZEALAND	101
NORWAY	102
POLAND	103
PORTUGAL	104
SPAIN	106
SWEDEN	108
SWITZERLAND	109
TURKEY	111
UNITED KINGDOM	112
UNITED STATES	113

Introduction

♦ The need to revise ISCED

The structure of education and learning systems has changed dramatically over the last 25 years. The increasing complexity of education systems, often reflecting more choice both between types of programmes and modes of attendance, has imposed new difficulties for the international comparability of education statistics. New forms of education have appeared and the boundaries that have traditionally separated different types of education programmes have blurred. Many of these changes could no longer be adequately reflected in data collected under the original International Standard Classification of Education (ISCED), which was first implemented in the mid-1970s. These structural changes in national education systems have driven the need to revise ISCED, the classification system underlying the mapping of national data to policy-oriented international indicators of education systems.

ISCED is significant for educational policy making in OECD countries, as it provides the essential basis for collecting the data underlying OECD's set of policy-guided indicators on education systems. It provides the metric through which the level of educational content underlying different educational programmes is assessed and aligned. Although the INES project (Indicators of Education Systems) has advanced significantly in developing internationally comparable education indicators, a conceptually adequate and operational definition of levels of education has been the essential missing element, without which the usefulness of the indicator set for policy purposes is compromised. Particularly affected by the current problems of ISCED are indicators on costs and resources, graduation rates and level of educational attainment in the population and indicators on labour market outcomes.

The purpose of ISCED is to provide an *integrated* and *consistent* statistical framework for the collection and reporting of *internationally comparable* education statistics. The coverage of ISCED-97 extends to all organised and sustained learning opportunities for children, youth and adults, including those with special educational needs, irrespective of the institutions or organisations providing them or the form in which they are delivered.

In the remainder of this section the key problems with the original ISCED framework (referred to in this document as ISCED-76) are summarised and OECD's priorities for the revised ISCED framework are reviewed. As the revised ISCED framework is broadly compatible with OECD's priorities, the ultimate success of the ISCED revision rests on the uniformity of its implementation across Member countries. This manual provides a methodology for the uniform implementation of the revised ISCED framework in OECD countries.

♦ The necessary components of a revised ISCED

An international taxonomy for classifying levels of education must take variations in national education structures explicitly into account. The objective of any taxonomy is to represent diverse structures satisfactorily within a single set of international categories. How such variations in structures are handled by the classification system is critically important for achievement of the comparability goal. A lack of comparability between countries in various education indicators was introduced in data collected under ISCED-76 for three main reasons: 1) the ISCED categories did not adequately reflect the diversity in structure of national education systems; 2) ISCED provided few guidelines for how to classify programmes that did not neatly fit into the taxonomy framework; and 3) countries were left to interpret the ISCED level taxonomy on their own.

With each country deciding separately how to portray its system in terms of ISCED levels, the responses have been of two main kinds: some countries simply identified their own national institutional stages with seemingly corresponding ISCED categories, without consideration of the starting points or lengths of programmes; others have deviated deliberately from national structures in attempts to conform their statistics at least partly to the ISCED model. Not surprisingly, given the lack of a co-ordinating mechanism, these modes of response have not always yielded internationally consistent programme groupings.

To resolve this unsatisfactory situation, is critical that explicit and detailed operational specifications become an integral part of the revised ISCED framework – that is, inseparable from the basic taxonomy. Without specific instructions that are internationally agreed upon, a particular country, despite the best of intentions, will not be in a position to determine whether its methods of assigning programmes to international categories are compatible with those of other countries.

It is critical that any framework used for empirically describing national educational systems be capable of reflecting existing variations and complexities. Such a framework needs to incorporate multiple statistical dimensions that allow for a more complete description of national educational programmes. Among these are the duration of programmes, typical starting ages, the programme orientation (general/vocational/pre-vocational), programme prerequisites, the characteristics of degrees or certificates awarded upon completion, etc. A multi-dimensional taxonomy of educational programmes that contains these elements will make it possible to aggregate statistics along various dimensions of the classification, according to analytical and policy requirements. Graduation rate statistics could, for example, respect the institutional structure of educational systems, while enrolment data, on the other hand, could ensure that programmes of comparable duration and orientation are being compared.

The establishment of an internationally comparable set of categories for the levels of education involves the "valuation" of educational activities in very different educational systems in an internationally comparable way. A prerequisite for this is to find international consensus on the criteria that are used to describe and classify national educational programmes as well as on the statistical formulation of these criteria.

Most importantly, it has been critical that the revised ISCED will lead countries to depart from current institutionally based reporting practices. Only in this way can it be ensured that the content of educational activities serve as the baseline of international comparisons. It was generally agreed upon by OECD countries that the revised ISCED must be built on three components: 1) internationally agreed concepts and definitions; 2) a classification system that strikes a careful balance between the faithful representation of national education systems and the possibility of aggregating data according to dimensions that are interpretable; and 3) operational instructions and a well-defined implementation process.

The ISCED-76 framework is also limited in the extent to which it captures learning opportunities in modern education systems. The skill and qualification requirements of labour markets have changed considerably since ISCED-76 was developed. New demands on education and training systems have lead to new types of learning opportunities for both children and adults, as well as those with special needs, which cannot be captured adequately under ISCED-76. Particular deficiencies are evident at the higher levels of education and, specifically, in the domain of continuing education and training outside institutional settings. It has been a clear priority for the OECD throughout the revision process that the revised ISCED address these new learning opportunities, and to reflect the multiple pathways through education systems.

◆ OECD contribution to the revision of ISCED

At the third INES General Assembly in Lahti (June 1995), Member countries recommended that OECD make a contribution towards the revision of ISCED currently being undertaken by UNESCO. This co-operation was initiated with an exchange of letters between the Secretary-General of OECD and the Director-General of UNESCO in October 1995. In his letter, the Secretary-General of OECD suggested that the OECD would focus its work on the further elaboration of the taxonomy of the levels of education and on the definition of the scope and coverage of ISCED for the purpose of reporting.

Four basic principles were advocated by OECD in the revision of ISCED, namely that: 1) the level concept should be defined on the basis of the content of the underlying education activities and operationalised on the basis of multiple auxiliary criteria; 2) the uni-dimension ladder system of ISCED (1976) should be replaced by a flexible multi-dimensional taxonomy; 3) the coverage of ISCED should be expanded in order to better capture the higher levels of education, in particular the domains of continuing education and training outside institutional settings; and 4) the revised ISCED should have an empirical foundation, reflecting the complexities and structures of national educational systems.

Following this General Assembly, a proposal for a survey of national education programmes was prepared by the Secretariat and circulated to Member countries for comment. This Taxonomy Survey of National Educational Programmes, which was undertaken in January 1996, collected information on national educational programmes and their various attributes, including: the national level and type of the educational programme, theoretical and typical ages of attendance, minimum and typical entrance requirements, theoretical and typical duration, qualifications awarded and degree of access to further educational programmes. This study has provided the empirical basis for OECD's contribution to the revision of ISCED, through the UNESCO ISCED Task Force, in an effort to ensure that the new framework would more accurately reflect the complexities of national education systems in the international comparative framework of the OECD education indicators. As a result, the revised ISCED has developed as a multi-dimensional framework, able to capture the complexities of modern education systems.

In October 1997, the 29th Session of the UNESCO General Conference reviewed and approved a revised framework for the International Standard Classification of Education (ISCED). This framework proposes a methodology for translating national educational programmes into an internationally comparable set of categories for the levels of education. The revised ISCED framework (henceforth referred to as ISCED-97) provides the potential for significant improvement in the coverage and comparability of international education indicators, and thus for their relevance to educational policy.

The general framework of the revised ISCED is detailed in UNESCO document 151 EX/8 Annex II (March 1997).

The successful implementation of ISCED-97 is a crucial next step in the improvement of international statistics on education. This multi-dimensional framework has the potential to greatly improve the comparability of educational statistics, as data collected under this framework will allow for the comparison of educational programmes with similar levels of educational content, and to better reflect complex educational pathways in the OECD indicators.

♦ Purpose of this manual and the next steps in the implementation of ISCED-97

The purpose of this ISCED-97 implementation manual is to give clear guidance to OECD countries on how to implement the ISCED-97 framework in international data collections. The methodology for applying ISCED-97 in the national context that is described below has been developed and agreed upon by the OECD/INES Technical Group, a working group on education statistics and indicators representing 29 OECD countries. The OECD Secretariat has also worked closely with both EUROSTAT and UNESCO to ensure that ISCED-97 will be implemented in a uniform manner across all countries.

First, this manual summarises the defining characteristics of the ISCED-97 levels and cross-classification categories in OECD countries, emphasising the criteria that define the boundaries between levels. Selected programmes in OECD countries that meet specific classification criteria are also presented as examples of how the criteria can be properly applied.

Secondly, this manual contains the mapping of national educational programmes to ISCED-97 for all 29 OECD countries in a tabular format. The allocations of national programmes to ISCED-97 have been developed by Member countries, in consultation with the OECD Secretariat. These proposals represent the starting point for a process of consultation within the Technical Group, with the aim of working towards an internationally agreed upon allocation of national educational programme to ISCED-97 in the OECD. These mappings will form the basis of data reporting in the 1999 UOE Data Collection on Education Statistics. These country allocations will also guide the application of ISCED-97 in all future OECD data collections, including the alignment of levels of educational attainment data collected in national Labour Force Surveys and the categorisation of both students' educational aspirations and teachers' educational qualifications in the Programme for International Student Assessment (PISA).

The primary goal of OECD's work in the implementation process is that the mapping of national education programmes to the revised ISCED be perfectly transparent and jointly agreed upon by all Member countries. The Technical Group will continue to serve as a forum for discussing and evaluating individual country's ISCED-97 allocations. Particular programme allocations that do not match the criteria laid out in this manual, and thereby do not lead to comparable education statistics, will be brought up and discussed amongst the Technical Group. In cases where this manual does not make it clear how a programme with particular characteristics should be mapped to ISCED-97, proposals for modifying the manual will be developed and discussed within the Technical Group. The implementation of ISCED will be both an iterative and interactive process, with both Member countries and international organisations reviewing countries' assignments of programmes to ISCED categories and recommending adjustments to enhance international comparability.

The OECD Secretariat foresees that the implementation instructions for ISCED-97, as well as ISCED itself, will need to be updated as education systems evolve and additional comparability issues are identified. While this document primarily deals with institutional structures for which data are currently collected, it will be expanded as data development expands.

Coverage and structure of ISCED-97

The purpose of ISCED is to provide an *integrated* and *consistent* statistical framework for the collection and reporting of *internationally comparable* education statistics.

While it is widely recognised that learning can occur in situations that are not formally organised (*e.g.* reading a newspaper article or watching a particular educational television programme) and in activities of short duration (*e.g.* a one-off lecture or visit to a museum), the requirement that instruction be organised and sustained facilitates the collection of comparable data across countries. In the ISCED-97 framework, "organised" activities include those planned with explicit or implicit educational aims. They involve a providing agency that establishes both the learning environment and the method of instruction. For a learning activity to be "sustained", it must contain the elements of duration and continuity. While ISCED-97 does not explicitly state a minimum duration for inclusion, an individual data collection certainly would. For example, an international data collection on enrolment in educational programmes, based primarily on institutional level data, might limit coverage to programmes leading towards an educational qualification, while a sample survey designed to measure participation in continuing education and training might seek much broader coverage.

♦ The content of educational activities as the key to the level concept

The definition of the level concept and the establishment of an internationally comparable set of categories for the levels of education is far from trivial since it involves the "valuation" of educational activities in very different educational systems in an international comparable way. A precondition for improving the comparability of educational statistics was to find international consensus on the criteria that should be used to describe and classify national educational programmes, as well as on the statistical formulation of these criteria. Consensus for the overall framework of ISCED-97 was built throughout the ISCED revision process, with a number of diverse countries participating in the UNESCO ISCED Task Force and a larger number in the ISCED Reference Group. It was important that classification criteria for ISCED-97 fit the wide diversity in educational programmes in both OECD and non-OECD countries in order for data collected under this framework to meet the standards of comparability that today's policy makers are using to access the validity of education indicators.

A departure from a purely institutionally based reporting practice is critical if any level taxonomy is to make the level of the content of educational activities the baseline of statistical comparisons. It is recognised that the use of institutional categories facilitates the reporting and the interpretation of the level categories in the context of national education systems. It is also evident that institutional categories continue to be an integral component of ISCED, not least because they relate to important transition characteristics of education systems. However, the sole reliance on such criteria sacrifices the goal of international comparability for a wide range of comparisons, simply because institutional structures are not comparable in terms of non-institutionally bound criteria (for example, entrance qualifications or theoretical and typical ages or typical programme durations). From a practical standpoint, transition points of national education systems will often need to be used as criteria for allocating programmes to the education levels because of the way in which data are collected at the national level. It must be ensured, however, that the selection of national transition points for matching the classification categories in ISCED-97 is determined by the content and structural attributes of the underlying educational programmes. Allocating a programme to an international category simply because its national name matches the name of the international reporting category must be avoided.

♦ The educational programme remains the basic unit of classification in ISCED-97

In the general absence of individualised data on participants in educational activities, international educational comparisons rely on taxonomies in which aggregates of educational activities – referred to as educational programmes – provide the basis for comparisons. ISCED-97, as was the original ISCED, is such a programme-based taxonomy. ISCED-97 works through the reduction of complex national educational structures along certain classification criteria into defined international categories. It thus provides the possibility of transforming detailed national education statistics on recipients, providers and sponsors of education, which were compiled on the basis of national concepts and definitions, into aggregate categories that are deemed to be internationally comparable and that can be meaningfully interpreted from an international comparative perspective.

The basic unit of classification in ISCED-97 is the educational programme. Educational programmes are defined on the basis of their educational content as an array or sequence of educational activities which are organised to accomplish a pre-determined objective or a specified set of educational tasks. Objectives can, for example, be preparation for more advanced study, qualification for an occupation or range of occupations, or simply an increase of knowledge and understanding. ISCED-97 is intended to cover both initial education at the early stages of a person's life prior to entry into the world of work, as well as continuing education throughout a person's life.

The term "educational activity" implies a broader meaning than the terms "course" or "class," which is important because education at a given level comprises not only courses organised into programmes but also free-standing courses and a variety of non-course activities as well. Programmes sometimes include major components not normally characterised as courses – for example, interludes of work experience in enterprises, research projects, and preparation of dissertations.

It must be recognised, however, that ISCED has natural limitations for the direct classification and assessment of competencies and qualifications of the participants in educational activities. This is because there is no close and universal relationship between the programmes a participant is enrolled in and actual educational achievement. The educational programmes an individual has participated in or even successfully completed are, at best, a first approximation of the skills and competencies he or she has actually obtained. Furthermore, for a programme-based taxonomy it is very difficult to capture educational activities that are not organised in the form of educational programmes.

♦ Proxies for educational content

As discussed above, the only concept that can meaningfully underlie an international level taxonomy is the educational content of the educational activities involved. This implies, for instance, that whether the instruction a country provides to its 11-year-olds should be called primary or lower secondary education would be determined by an assessment of what 11-year-olds are expected to learn.

It is clearly not possible, however, to directly assess and compare the content of the educational programmes in an international comparative way. Curricula are far too diverse, multi-faceted, and complex to permit unambiguous determinations that one curriculum for students of given age or grade belongs to a higher level of education than another. The kind of international curricular standards that would be needed to support such judgements do not exist. It is therefore necessary to establish auxiliary criteria as proxies for the content, including:

- Typical starting ages of participants and theoretical and typical durations of the programmes.
- Typical entrance qualifications and minimum entrance requirements.
- Type of certifications, diplomas, or qualifications awarded upon successful completion of the programme.
- Types of subsequent education for which completers are eligible.
- The degree to which the programme is specifically oriented towards a specific class of occupations or trades and is generally oriented towards the immediate transition into the labour market.

Each of these criteria serves as classifying criteria for ISCED-97. When a national programme has programme options or paths of study that differ with respect to one or more of such criteria, then – depending on the level of education and the education system concerned – it should be broken apart and reported as separate programmes under ISCED-97. For example, if in a country it takes four years to train a teacher and seven years to train a medical doctor, then the corresponding activities should be reported as separate programmes under ISCED-97, even if they are considered from a national perspective as one type of programme (*e.g.* university education).

A fundamental aspect of these criteria is that they complement, rather than exclude, each other. For example, while some students may be classified to the "primary level of education" on the basis of their ages, other classification criteria may be utilised for classifying participants in adult literacy programmes.

Similarly, neither the duration of an educational programme nor the theoretical and typical starting ages should be the sole criterion for its level attribution. Australia, New Zealand, and the United Kingdom are examples of countries where the final years of secondary education and the first years of the tertiary level of education are organised according to a qualifications framework based on a recognition of competencies. This organisational framework implies that the mapping of programmes at the boundary between these educational levels cannot be solely based on either the typical entry ages of participants or the theoretical duration of the programmes. In the area of vocational education and training, the Australian National Framework for Recognition of Training includes provisions for the recognition of prior learning, competency-based articulation of courses and credit transfer between them, accreditation of courses, registration of private providers and mutual recognition among states of qualifications obtained by individuals through accredited courses. The National Vocational Qualification (NVQ) in the United Kingdom provides a similar competency-based model. For these types of programmes, multiple classification criteria must be utilised to map them to ISCED-97.

To the extent that data availability forces transition points in national education systems to be used as the main criteria for allocating educational programmes to a particular ISCED-97 level, it will be necessary to ensure that these transition points are consistent with the classification criteria set forth in this document. It is expected that the ISCED-97 framework will not match perfectly the data reporting framework in all countries and that estimation procedures may need to be employed to either combine or divide national programmes for reporting under ISCED-97.

♦ Comparison of ISCED-97 with ISCED-76

The biggest change between ISCED-97 and ISCED-76 is the introduction of a multi-dimensional classification framework, allowing for the alignment of the educational content of programmes using multiple classification criteria. These dimensions include: 1) the type of subsequent education or destination to which the programme leads; 2) the programme orientation (whether it be general education or pre-vocational education or vocational education); 3) the programme duration (for the ISCED Levels 3, 4 and 5, where programmes that vary widely in duration exist); and 4) position in the national degree and qualification structure. In ISCED-1976, there was no such provision.

In the revised version of ISCED, a new level, *Level 4*, has been introduced to cover programmes which straddle the boundary between upper secondary and post-secondary education from an international point of view, even though some of them might be either upper secondary or post-secondary programmes in the national context. In ISCED 1976, such programmes belonged either to Level 3 or Level 5.

Tertiary education now comprises only two levels, Level 5 or Level 6, instead of the previous three Levels 5 to 7. The new *Level 5* consists of programmes that do not lead directly to an advanced research qualification while Level 6 is now reserved for programmes leading to advanced research qualifications. Level 5 is subdivided into two categories, ISCED 5A and 5B. While ISCED 5A covers more theoretically-based programmes that give access to advanced research qualifications or professions with high skill requirements, ISCED 5B is meant for more practically oriented or occupationally specific programmes that provide participants with a labour-market relevant qualification. Level 5 in ISCED 1997 corresponds approximately to Levels 5 and 6 of ISCED-76, as well as graduate programmes (*e.g.* those leading to the Master's degree) in countries with an undergraduate/graduate split that were previous part of 7, and advanced research qualifications are now covered exclusively in the new Level 6.

	ISCED 1976		ISCED 1997
0	Education preceding the first level	0	Pre-primary level of education
1	Education at the first level	1	Primary level of education
2	Education at the second level, first stage	2	Lower secondary level of education (2A, 2B and 2C)
3	Education at the second level, second stage	3	Upper secondary level of education (3A, 3B, 3C)
		4	Post-secondary, non-tertiary education (4A, 4B, 4C)
5	Education at the third level, first stage, of the type that leads to an award not equivalent to a first university degree		
		5	First stage of tertiary education 5B,1st, 2nd qualifications (short or medium duration)
6	Education at the third level, first stage, of the type that leads to a first university degree or equivalent		5A, 1st degree (medium duration)
7	Education at the third level, second stage of the type that leads to a post-graduate university degree or equivalent		5A, 1st degree (long) 5A, 2nd degree
		6	Second stage of tertiary education (leading to an advanced research qualification)
9	Education not definable by level		

Level 9 of ISCED 1976, which was reserved for the educational programmes that could not be allocated to any other level, has been eliminated in ISCED-97. It is presumed that all educational programmes can be classified in one of the proposed seven levels (0 to 6).

The correspondence between the level classifications of ISCED 1976 and ISCED 1997 is shown in the table above.

◆ Classification of programmes that do not easily fit into the ISCED level taxonomy

Some educational activities cannot be easily mapped to a particular level of education even though they clearly involve organised and sustained communication designed to bring about learning. As countries move towards more flexible provision of education, modelled on a lifelong learning approach, characteristics such as typical entry ages, entry requirements, and programme duration may not be very useful criteria for classifying some programmes.

All such educational activities should be classified based on the degree of equivalence of their educational content with programmes that can be mapped to ISCED-97 using the classification criteria detailed below. For some programmes, the equivalence of the qualifications or certifications awarded upon successful completion can help to classify an educational activity. For example, the level of educational content of a distance education programme might be classified based on the type of qualifications that are awarded upon its successful completion.

Another example of educational programmes that are typically organised outside of the regular education system are those organised by the military. As with other types of programmes, military education and training programmes should be mapped to ISCED according to the similarity of the content of these programmes to other educational programmes. For example, if a military college awards an engineering degree that has similar academic content to an engineering degree awarded by a civilian university, then the military qualification should be mapped to the same ISCED level as the civilian qualification. It should be noted, however, that since many countries do not report military qualifications in international data collections, the reporting of military degrees by only some countries can lead to data incomparability. This is an issue that must be taken up when defining the coverage of an individual data collection.

Enterprise-based education is another type of programme that can be difficult to classify under ISCED. While some enterprise training courses may have minimum entrance requirements that can be easily identified in ISCED, many will not. One option would be to assess what minimum level of skills are required to benefit from participation in a particular programme, along with the typical level of educational attainment that the typical participant in this programme might have. Another consideration would be whether or not the programme prepares participants for entry into a programmes in the regular education system. By considering these three criteria jointly, and relating them to the criteria for programmes that can more easily be mapped to ISCED, the enterprise-based programme can be mapped to a particular ISCED level.

Other dimensions not accounted for ISCED-97

The dimensions listed below were not taken up in the first stage of the revision of ISCED, although they are relevant for classifying educational programmes. Detailed definitions and classification categories for these dimensions have not yet been developed, although further developmental work is intended.

♦ Institutional and structural arrangements

The main distinctions under this heading could be among services offered in educational institutions, in other types of education or training facilities, and in workplaces (as under apprenticeship programmes). A distinction between school-based, work-based, and mixed school/work-based programmes could be made.

School-based and combined school- and work-based programmes

Although not specifically detailed in ISCED-97, ISCED 3 and ISCED 4 programmes can be divided into "school-based programmes" and "combined school- and work-based programmes" on the basis of the amount of training that is provided in-school as opposed to training at the workplace. The following definition is used for this distinction:

- In *school-based programmes* instruction takes place (either partly or exclusively) in educational institutions. These include special training centres for vocational education run by public or private authorities or enterprise-based special training centres if these qualify as educational institutions. These programmes can have an on-the-job training component, *i.e.* a component of some practical experience at the workplace.
- In *combined school- and work-based programmes* instruction is shared between school and the workplace, although instruction may take place primarily at the workplace.

In distinguishing between school-based and combined school- and work-based programmes, classification should be made according to the amount of training provided in school. Programmes should be classified as *school-based* if at least 75% of the curriculum is presented in the school environment (covering the whole educational programme) where distance education is included.

Programmes are classified as *combined school- and work-based* if less than 75% of the curriculum is presented in the school environment or through distance education. The 75% cut-off point should be regarded as a general guideline that may need to be operationalised differently in different countries.

Dual-system apprenticeship programmes are examples of combined school and work-based educational programmes. They typically involve alternating between learning in an educational institution (ordinary or specialised) and learning through work experience programmes, which may include highly organised training in a firm or with a craftsperson. Even though only a part of the training occurs in schools, it is considered as a full-time activity, because it covers both theoretical and practical training.

Service provider

This embraces classification both by type of institution and by auspices or control, specifically for the setting of objectives and/or the design and content of the programme. It does not necessarily coincide with the institution actually delivering the education. The principal distinction with respect to institutional type is between educational institutions – meaning institutions with education as their principal function – and institutions that exist mainly for other purposes but also provide educational services. The latter include government non-education agencies, various non-profit organisations, business firms, and more generally, employers engaged in training their own employees. The main distinction with respect to auspices is between public and private providers, with public providers further sorted by level of government, and private providers divided into enterprises and other private entities.

Categories that would need to be considered in this dimension are: Ministries of Education or institutions at the national level which are delegated authority by the Ministry of Education (national school boards, chambers, etc.); other ministries at the national level; regional government authorities; local government authorities; institutional providers of education or training; trade unions; professional bodies; employer associations; enterprises (*e.g.* dual system or apprenticeship employers); or religious organisations.

Mode of service provision

This dimension refers to the methods and, especially, the technologies used to deliver educational services. For instance, it could involve distinctions among conventional (classroom) instruction, correspondence education, various forms of telecommunications-based education (*e.g.* distance learning via television), and computer-based education.

Type of participant

This heading covers possible distinctions among programmes serving persons in different age ranges, persons with different labour-force status, and students with various special needs (handicapped students, immigrants, etc.). These attributes generally have not been treated as dimensions of programmes in the past but have been reflected in specific statistics (*e.g.* enrolment data are routinely broken down by age). By using them selectively to classify programmes, it might be possible to bring out certain distinctions lost in the current classification by level – *e.g.* the difference between primary programmes for children and basic literacy programmes (also classified as primary) serving adults.

Mode of participation

Mode refers mainly, in this instance, to intensity or time commitment – whether the programme is designed for full-time or part-time or for full-year or part-year students. These attributes currently are taken into account in enrolment statistics but have not been used to distinguish among programmes. Their usefulness depends on the extent to which they reflect attributes of the programme rather than attributes of the individual participants. A completely different aspect of mode of participation concerns on-site versus remote involvement in instruction. Its usefulness would depend on whether the potentially overlapping dimensions of educational setting and mode of service provision are to be included in the taxonomy.

Level structure of ISCED-97 and corresponding classification criteria

ISCED-97 facilitates the transformation of detailed national education statistics on participants, providers and sponsors of education, compiled on the basis of national concepts and definitions, into aggregate categories that are internationally comparable and that can be meaningfully interpreted. In ISCED-97, a "level" of education is broadly defined as the gradations of learning experiences and the competencies built into the design of an educational programme. Broadly speaking, the level is related to the degree of complexity of the content of the programme. This does not, however, imply that levels of education constitute a ladder, where the access of prospective participants to each level necessarily depends on having successfully completed the previous level. It also does not preclude the possibility that some participants in educational programmes at a given level may have previously successfully completed programmes at a higher level.

Empirically, ISCED assumes that there exists several main and auxiliary criteria which can help point to the level of education into which a given educational programme should be classified (typical or minimum ages for entry, typical entrance qualifications, minimum entrance requirements, educational properties of the programme, duration of programmes, types of educational or labour market activities that programmes are designed to prepare students for, staff qualification requirements, etc.). These criteria are introduced in the following table for each ISCED-97 level and are discussed in detail for the specific ISCED level that they relate to in the remainder of this manual.

It should be noted that the degree of detail in which the ISCED-97 levels, classification categories, and sub-categories are described below reflect the greatest degree of detail in which it is envisaged that ISCED-97 will be utilised in international data collections. Although, in theory, a greater number of cross-classification categories can be created using the ISCED-97 framework, the presentation in this manual reflects a collapsing of categories to a manageable number in order to be useful to both the designers of data collections, and the suppliers of data.

Description of ISCED-97 levels, classification criteria, and sub-categories

0	PRE-PRIMARY LEVEL OF EDUCATION	Main criteria	Auxiliary criteria	Sub-categories	
	Initial stage of organised instruction, designed primarily to introduce very young children to a school-type environment.	Should be centre or school-based, be designed to meet the educational and development needs of children at least 3 years of age, and have staff that are adequately trained (*i.e.* qualified) to provide an educational programme for the children.	Pedagogical qualifications for the teaching staff; implementation of a curriculum with educational elements.		

1	PRIMARY LEVEL OF EDUCATION	Main criteria	Auxiliary criteria		
	Normally designed to give students a sound basic education in reading, writing and mathematics.	Beginning of systematic studies characteristic of primary education, e.g. reading, writing and mathematics. Entry into the nationally designated primary institutions or programmes.	In countries where the age of compulsory attendance (or at least the age at which virtually all students begin their education) comes after the beginning of systematic study in the subjects noted, the first year of compulsory attendance should be used to determine the boundary between ISCED 0 and ISCED 1.		
		The commencement of reading activities alone is not a sufficient criteria for classification of an educational programmes at ISCED 1.			

2	LOWER SECONDARY LEVEL OF EDUCATION	Main criteria	Auxiliary criteria	Destination for which the programmes have been designed to prepare students		Programme orientation	
	The lower secondary level of education generally continues the basic programmes of the primary level, although teaching is typically more subject-focused, often employing more specialised teachers who conduct classes in their field of specialisation.	Programmes at the start of Level 2 should correspond to the point where programmes are beginning to be organised in a more subject-oriented pattern, using more specialised teachers conducting classes in their field of specialisation.	If there is no clear break-point for this organisational change, however, then countries should artificially split national programmes into ISCED 1 and 2 at the end of 6 years of primary education.	A	Programmes designed to prepare students for direct access to Level 3 in a sequence which would ultimately lead to tertiary education, that is, entrance to ISCED 3A or 3B.	1	Education which is not designed explicitly to prepare participants for a specific class of occupations or trades or for entry into further vocational/technical education programmes. Less than 25% of the programme content is vocational or technical.
		If this organisational transition point does not correspond to a natural split in the boundaries between national educational programmes, then programmes should be split at the point where national programmes begin to reflect this organisational change.	In countries with no system break between lower secondary and upper secondary education, and where lower secondary education lasts for more than 3 years, only the first 3 years following primary education should be counted as lower secondary education.	B	Programmes designed to prepare students for direct access to programmes at Level 3C.	2	Education mainly designed as an introduction to the world of work and as preparation for further vocational or technical education. It does not lead to a labour-market relevant qualification. Content is at least 25% vocational or technical.
			Programmes primarily designed for direct access to the labour market at the end of this level (sometimes referred to as "terminal" programmes).	C		3	Education which prepares participants for direct entry, without further training, into specific occupations. Successful completion of such programmes leads to a labour-market relevant vocational qualification.

3	UPPER SECONDARY LEVEL OF EDUCATION	Main criteria	Modular programmes	Destination for which the programmes have been designed to prepare students		Programme orientation	
	The final stage of secondary education in most OECD countries. Instruction is often more organised along subject-matter lines than at ISCED Level 2 and teachers typically need to have a higher level, or more subject-specific, qualification than at ISCED 2.	National boundaries between lower secondary and upper secondary education should be the dominant factor for splitting Levels 2 and 3.	An educational qualification is earned in a modular programme by combining blocks of courses, or modules, into a programme meeting specific curricular requirements.	A	ISCED 3A: programmes at Level 3 designed to provide direct access to ISCED 5A.	1	Education which is not designed explicitly to prepare participants for a specific class of occupations or trades or for entry into further vocational/technical education programmes. Less than 25% of the programme content is vocational or technical.
		Admission into educational programmes usually requires the completion of ISCED 2 for admission, or a combination of basic education and life experience that demonstrates the ability to handle ISCED 3 subject matter.	A single module, however, may not have a specific educational or labour market destination or a particular programme orientation.	B	ISCED 3B: programmes at Level 3 designed to provide direct access to ISCED 5B.	2	Education mainly designed as an introduction to the world of work and as preparation for further vocational or technical education. It does not lead to a labour-market relevant qualification. Content is at least 25% vocational or technical.
	There are substantial differences in the typical duration of ISCED 3 programmes both across and between countries, typically ranging from 2 to 5 years of schooling.		Modular programmes should be classified at Level "3" only, without reference to the educational or labour market destination of the programme.	C	ISCED 3C: programmes at Level 3 not designed to lead directly to ISCED 5A or 5B. Therefore, these programmes lead directly to labour market, ISCED 4 programmes or other ISCED 3 programmes.	3	Education which prepares participants for direct entry, without further training, into specific occupations. Successful completion of such programmes leads to a labour-market relevant vocational qualification.

Description of ISCED-97 levels, classification criteria, and sub-categories (cont.)

4	POST-SECONDARY NON-TERTIARY	Main criteria	Types of programmes that can fit into Level 4		Destination for which the programmes have been designed to prepare students		Programme orientation
	These programmes straddle the boundary between upper secondary and post-secondary education from an international point of view, even though they might clearly be considered as upper secondary or post-secondary programmes in a national context.	Students entering ISCED 4 programmes will typically have completed ISCED 3.	The first type are short vocational programmes where either the content is not considered "tertiary" in many OECD countries or the programme did not meet the duration requirement for ISCED 5B -- at least 2 years FTE since the start of Level 5.	A	Programmes at Level 4, designed to provide direct access to ISCED 5A.	1	Education which is not designed explicitly to prepare participants for a specific class of occupations or trades or for entry into further vocational/technical education programmes. Less than 25% of the programme content is vocational or technical.
	They are often not significantly more advanced than programmes at ISCED 3 but they serve to broaden the knowledge of participants who have already completed a programme at Level 3. The students are typically older than those in ISCED 3 programmes.	Programme duration: ISCED 4 programmes typically have a full-time equivalent duration of between 6 months and 2 years.	These programmes are often designed for students who have completed Level 3, although a formal ISCED Level 3 qualification may not be required for entry.	B	Programmes at Level 4, designed to provide direct access to ISCED 5B.	2	Education mainly designed as an introduction to the world of work and as preparation for further vocational or technical education. It does not lead to a labour-market relevant qualification. Content is at least 25% vocational or technical.
			The second type of programmes are nationally considered as upper secondary programmes, even though entrants to these programmes will have typically already completed another upper secondary programme (i.e. second-cycle programmes).	C	Programmes at Level 4 not designed to lead directly to ISCED 5A or 5B. These programmes lead directly to labour market or other ISCED 4 programmes.	3	Education which prepares participants for direct entry, without further training, into specific occupations. Successful completion of such programmes leads to a labour-market relevant vocational qualification.
5	FIRST STAGE OF TERTIARY EDUCATION	Classification criteria for level and sub-categories (5A and 5B)			Cumulative theoretical duration of tertiary		Position in the national degree and qualifications structure
	ISCED 5 programmes have an educational content more advanced than those offered at Levels 3 and 4.	Entry to these programmes normally requires the successful completion of ISCED Level 3A or 3B or a similar qualification at ISCED Level 4A or 4B.					
5A	ISCED 5A programmes that are largely theoretically based and are intended to provide sufficient qualifications for gaining entry into advanced research programmes and professions with high skills requirements.	The minimum cumulative theoretical duration (at tertiary level) is of three years (FTE). The faculty must have advanced research credentials. Completion of a research project or thesis may be involved.	The programmes provide the level of education required for entry into a profession with high skills requirements or an advanced research programme.	A	Duration categories: Medium: 3 to less than 5 years; Long: 5 to 6 years; Very long: more than 6 years.	A	Categories: Intermediate; First; Second; Third and further.
5B	ISCED 5B programmes that are generally more practical/technical/occupationally specific than ISCED 5A programmes.	Programmes are more practically-oriented and occupationally specific than programmes at ISCED 5A and they do not prepare students for direct access to advanced research programmes. They have a minimum of two years' full-time equivalent duration.	The programme content is typically designed to prepare students to enter a particular occupation.	B	Duration categories: Short: 2 to less than 3 years; Medium: 3 to less than 5 years; Long: 5 to 6 years; Very long: more than 6 years.	B	Categories: Intermediate; First; Second; Third and further.
6	SECOND STAGE OF TERTIARY EDUCATION (LEADING TO AN ADVANCED RESEARCH QUALIFICATION)						
	This level is reserved for tertiary programmes that lead to the award of an advanced research qualification. The programmes are devoted to advanced study and original research.	The level requires the submission of a thesis or dissertation of publishable quality that is the product of original research and represents a significant contribution to knowledge. It is not solely based on course-work.	It prepares recipients for faculty posts in institutions offering ISCED 5A programmes, as well as research posts in government and industry.				

ISCED 0
Pre-primary level of education

♦ Definitions and classification criteria

Pre-primary education (ISCED 0) is defined as the initial stage of *organised instruction*, designed primarily to introduce very young children to a school-type environment, that is, to provide a bridge between the home and a school-based atmosphere.

Boundary between education and child care

Some countries define pre-primary or early childhood education more broadly than others. Thus, the comparability of international statistics on pre-primary education depends on each country's willingness to report data for this level according to a standard international definition, even if that definition diverges from the one that the country uses in compiling its own national statistics. The distinction between programmes that would fall into ISCED 0 and programmes that would be outside of the scope of ISCED-97 rests primarily on the educational properties of the programme. As the educational properties are difficult to assess directly, several proxy measures should be utilised to determine whether or not a programme should be classified at this level. ISCED Level 0 programmes should be centre or school-based, be designed to meet the educational and developmental needs of children at least 3 years of age, and have staff that are adequately trained (*i.e.* qualified) to provide an educational programme for the children.

Centre-based

For a programme to be considered as pre-primary education, it must be school-based or centre-based. These terms are used to distinguish activities in organised educational settings from services provided in households or family settings, which would generally not be included at this level. These centres may come under the jurisdiction of a public or private school or other education service provider.

Age range

Programmes at this level are typically designed for children at least 3 years old and not older than 6. Most OECD countries consider the *typical starting age* of pre-primary education to be three years or older and do not include children younger than three in their own national statistics on pre-primary education. In some cases, however, programmes that are considered "educational" by the country concerned serve children as young as two or two-and-a-half. An educational programme cannot be considered as belonging to Level 0 if it is primarily designed to serve children aged two years or less.

The upper age limit depends in each case on the typical age for entry into primary education, typically age 6 or 7.

Staff qualifications and educational content in the curriculum

As it is very difficult to specify precisely where child care ends and education begins, it is necessary to rely on proxy criteria. The requirement of pedagogical qualifications for the teaching staff can be a good proxy criterion for distinguishing an educational programme from a non-educational programme. It serves to distinguish pre-primary education from child care for which para-medical or no qualifications are required. In countries where the government does not closely regulate pre-primary education (*e.g.* there are no qualification requirements for staff), this criterion cannot be, however, the sole factor determining whether or not a programme has sufficient educational content to be classified at ISCED 0.

Formal implementation of a curriculum with educational elements is also a useful criterion for distinguishing between programmes that meet the educational content requirements of ISCED 0 and programmes with little or no educational content.

Special needs education

Organised instruction for children with special needs should also be included at this level if either the participants are the same age as other students enrolled in pre-primary education or if the content of the instruction is significantly lower than that of the first years of primary education. This education may be also provided in hospitals or in special schools or training centres.

Programmes that combine education and child care

In some countries, institutions providing pre-primary education also provide extended day or evening child care. In the interest of international comparability, a country whose institutions provide these extended day or evening services should attempt to exclude the cost of such services from any reported expenditure statistics relating to ISCED 0. Personnel data should also be pro-rated. This does not preclude, however, the collection of participation, personnel, or finance data on early childhood programmes that fall outside of the boundary of ISCED 0.

∇ Examples

→ *Long Day Care centre* (Australia). Pre-school programmes will be classified at 0. Pre-school education meets all the main and subsidiary criteria. Programmes at formal Long Day Care centres are a "grey area" because the programmes generally have some educational content, they are centre based, many of the children fall into the appropriate age range (though a large proportion do not), and some staff have teaching qualifications. The Australians will exclude children enrolled in Long Day Care centre programmes from ISCED 0. This is because they only partially meet the ISCED 97 criteria in that:

- Many children attending are aged under 3 years.
- Only a minority of staff have teaching qualifications.
- The educational properties of programmes at child care centres are considered insufficient.

→ *Day care in private homes* (Denmark). In Denmark, young children can attend programmes that are offered either in educational institutions or private homes. The "day care" offered in private homes is paid by the public authorities and controlled by them. As these programmes are not centre-based, however, they do not meet the criteria to be classified at ISCED 0.

ISCED 1
Primary level of education

♦ Definitions and classification criteria

Primary education usually begins at age 5, 6, or 7 and generally lasts for 4 (*e.g.* Germany) to 6 years (the mode of the OECD countries being six years). Programmes at the primary level generally require no previous formal education, although it is becoming increasingly common for children to have attended a pre-primary programme before entering primary education.

Level of educational content

Programmes at ISCED 1 are normally designed to give students a sound basic education in reading, writing and mathematics along with an elementary understanding of other subjects such as history, geography, natural science, social science, art and music. The commencement of reading activities alone is not a sufficient criterion for classification of an educational programme at ISCED 1.

Boundary between ISCED 0 and ISCED 1

The boundary between pre-primary and primary education is typically the beginning of systematic studies characteristic of primary education, *e.g.* reading, writing and mathematics. It is common, however, for children to begin learning basic literacy and numeracy skills at the pre-primary level.

An additional proxy criterion for classification at ISCED Level 1 is the stage when children enter into the primary institutions or programmes, although in countries where primary education starts at an early age (*e.g.* age 4 or 4-and-a-half), children enrolled in these grades should be classified at ISCED 1 only if the duration of the school day, the qualifications of the staff, and the level of content of the programme are similar to the grades where children of age 6 are enrolled.

Although the start of compulsory education is also laid out as a subsidiary criterion for determining the boundary between ISCED 0 and 1, this criterion is not particularly useful in many OECD countries, as the start of compulsory schooling is often not related to either the beginning of systematic studies or the typical age of entry of children. In countries where the age of compulsory attendance (or at least the age at which virtually all students begin their education) comes after the beginning of systematic study in the subjects noted above, the first year of compulsory attendance should be used to determine the boundary between ISCED 0 and ISCED 1. This latter criterion is imposed to emphasise that the start of ISCED 1 should reflect the point at which systematic studies in the above subjects start for all students, not just a select few.

In most countries, ISCED 1 will correspond to nationally designated primary education. In countries where "basic education" covers the entire compulsory school period (*i.e.* where there is no systems break between primary and lower secondary education) and where in such cases "basic education" lasts for more than 6 years, only the first 6 years following pre-primary education should be counted as primary education.

Special needs education

Organised instruction for children with special needs should also be included at this level if the content of the instruction is broadly similar to that of other ISCED 1 programmes.

Adult literacy programmes

Literacy or basic skills programmes within or outside the school system which are similar in content to programmes in primary education for those considered too old to enter elementary schools are also included at this level because they require no previous formal education.

▽ Examples of international variability in the length of primary programmes

- → 4 years: Austria, Germany and Hungary.
- → 5 years: Czech Republic, France and Italy.
- → 6 years: Belgium, Denmark, Finland, Greece, Japan, Mexico, Poland, Spain and the United Kingdom.
- → 7 years: Iceland
- → 7 or 8 years: Australia (depending on the state/territory).
- → As duration varies across regions, the first 6 years will be reported as ISCED 1: Canada and the United States.
- → Since full basic education ranges from 9 to 10 years, the first 6 years will be reported as ISCED 1: Denmark, Norway and Sweden.

▽ Examples of countries with national variability in the length of primary programmes

- → *Elementary/primary schools* (Canada and the United States). Primary and secondary education form a continuum, with the duration of elementary or primary school primarily based on institutional characteristics that can differ by province/state or locality (ranging from 3 grades to as many as 8). In these countries, the elementary-secondary continuum will be split at the end of grade 6 for reporting at ISCED Level 1, so that the grades contained in each level facilitate cross-country comparability. This method of reporting programme data will ensure that, in a national context, comparable programmes are allocated at each level as the level of content is broadly similar at a particular grade across the states/provinces.

- → *Primarschule, école primaire, scuola elementare* (Switzerland). The entry age to primary education is either 6 (4 cantons), 6.5 (2 cantons) or 7 (17 cantons). One canton leaves the decision whether to start school at the age of 6 or 7 to the communes (local authorities). Since the length of the primary and lower secondary levels combined is a uniform 9 years, the differences in the beginning ages translate into different beginning ages all through the school careers of the students. Primary education lasts between 4 and 6 years (depending on the canton). Reforms under way will reduce the fraction of students in four-year programmes. For comparability purposes, the first 6 years of primary/lower secondary education will be allocated to ISCED Level 1.

▽ Examples of programmes for individuals outside of the typical age of primary schooling

→ *Adult basic academic upgrading* (Canada). Less than one-year programme to upgrade basic skills. Results in a certificate of achievement.

→ *Enseñanzas Iniciales de Educación Básica para personas en edad adulta* (Spain). Adult education programme at the primary level.

→ *Svenska för vuxna invandrare* (Sweden). This one-year programme teaches Swedish to adult immigrants.

♦ Unresolved issue of incomparability at ISCED 1

In neither the Technical Group nor the OECD Expert Group on the Implementation of ISCED-97 was there a consensus to standardise the number of years allocated to ISCED 1 across countries. Countries felt strongly that the ISCED 1/2 boundary should correspond to national boundaries between primary and lower secondary education – that the boundary should reflect the transition point in national educational structures where the way in which instruction is organised begins to change (discussed further below). As the theoretical duration of ISCED 1 can range from 4 to 8 years, and the duration of ISCED 2 is correspondingly longer or shorter, many forms of comparisons at the primary level will remain problematic. For example, comparisons of the percentage of GDP spent on ISCED 1 or the percentage of total expenditure spent at ISCED 1 will not be comparable across countries. Even comparisons of pupil/teacher ratios or expenditure per student could be affected if the quantity of resources allocated to older students (*e.g.* through class sizes) differs from resources allocated to younger students. Users of data collected under the ISCED-97 taxonomy will need to take these differences in the duration of programmes at ISCED 1 into account when analysing results.

ISCED 2
Lower secondary level of education

♦ Definitions and classification criteria

The lower secondary level of education generally continues the basic programmes of the primary level, although teaching is typically more subject-focused, often employing more specialised teachers who conduct classes in their field of specialisation. Lower secondary education may either be "terminal" (*i.e.* preparing the students for entry directly into working life) and/or "preparatory" (*i.e.* preparing students for upper secondary education). This level can range from 2 to 6 years of schooling (the mode of OECD countries is 3 years).

Entry requirements

Entry to an ISCED 2 programme typically requires the completion of primary education or its equivalent; that is, a demonstrable ability to handle ISCED 2 content through a combination of basic education and life experience.

Duration of ISCED 2

Entry to ISCED 2 is typically after 6 years of primary education, and the end of this level is typically after 9 years of schooling since the beginning of primary education. In many OECD countries, the end of lower secondary education is a major educational, and in some cases labour market, transition point. For this reason, the end of ISCED 2 should generally conform to the end of lower secondary or "basic" education.

Boundary between ISCED 1 and ISCED 2

The boundary between ISCED 1 and ISCED 2 coincides with the transition point in national educational structures where the way in which instruction is organised begins to change. Programmes at the start of Level 2 should correspond to the point where programmes are beginning to be organised in a more subject-oriented pattern, using more specialised teachers conducting classes in their field of specialisation. If this organisational transition point does not correspond to a natural split in the boundaries between national educational programmes, then countries should split their programmes for international reporting at the point where national programmes begin to reflect this organisational change. If there is no clear break-point for this organisational change, however, then countries should artificially split national programmes into ISCED 1 and 2 at the end of 6 years of primary education.

◆ Sub-categories at this level

Type of subsequent education or destination

ISCED Level 2 programmes are sub-classified according to the destination for which the programmes have been designed to prepare students:

- ISCED 2A: programmes designed to prepare students for direct access to Level 3 in a sequence which would ultimately prepare students to attend tertiary education, that is, entrance to ISCED 3A or 3B.
- ISCED 2B: programmes designed to prepare students for direct access to programmes at Level 3C.
- ISCED 2C: programmes primarily designed for direct access to the labour market at the end of this level (sometimes referred to as "terminal" programmes).

Programme orientation[1]

Programmes at Level 2 can also be subdivided into three categories based on the degree to which a programme is specifically oriented towards a specific class of occupations or trades and leads to a labour-market relevant qualification:

- Type 1 (general): education which is not designed explicitly to prepare participants for a specific class of occupations or trades or for entry into further vocational or technical education programmes. Less than 25% of the programme content is vocational or technical.
- Type 2 (pre-vocational or pre-technical): education which is mainly designed to introduce participants to the world of work and to prepare them for entry into further vocational or technical education programmes. Successful completion of such programmes does not lead to a labour-market relevant vocational or technical qualification. For a programme to be considered as pre-vocational or pre-technical education, at least 25% of its content has to be vocational or technical.
- Type 3 (vocational or technical): education which prepares participants for direct entry, without further training, into specific occupations. Successful completion of such programmes leads to a labour-market relevant vocational qualification.[2]

In some cases the first few months or first year of a Type 3 programme has Type 2 elements. For the purpose of mapping to ISCED-97, however, only whole programmes that meet the above criteria for Type 2 should be classified in that category.

---

1. ISCED-97 explicitly uses the terms general, pre-vocational, and vocational to describe the different programme orientations. As these terms have different national applications in OECD countries, differences that have lead to much confusion and incomparability of data, they are not utilised in this document. The definitions underlying these categories, which are more universal than the terms themselves, have been numbered Type 1, 2, and 3 in this manual, an ordering that corresponds to general, pre-vocational, and vocational in the UNESCO ISCED-97 framework.
2. ISCED-97 also allows for the subdivision of Type 3 (vocational) programmes into two types: 1) those which are primary theoretically oriented; and 2) those which are primarily practically oriented. As these categories are unlikely to be utilised in any OECD data collection, they are not elaborated on here.

◆ Specific classification issues

Use of Type 2 (pre-vocational) for special education programmes

Countries should attempt to classify and report programmes that are specifically designed to provide a basic labour market orientation to students with special educational needs as Type 2 (pre-vocational) if the programme meets the classifying criteria of pre-vocational programmes, that is, education which is mainly designed to introduce participants to the world of work and to prepare them for entry into further vocational or technical education programmes. If a country has such a programme for special needs students but cannot separate it from data reported as Type 1 (general) or Type 3 (vocational), the country should note this in its mapping of the corresponding programme to ISCED-97.

Boundary between ISCED 2 and ISCED 3

National boundaries between lower secondary and upper secondary education should be the dominant factor for splitting Levels 2 and 3. As a result, the completion of lower secondary education can occur after 8, 9, or 10 years of schooling and at 15, 16, or even 17 years of age. For countries that have two major transition points in or around these grades and age spans (*e.g.* the United Kingdom at ages 14 and 16), the allocation of these will be decided on a case by case basis in consultation with the Secretariat. In countries with no system break between lower secondary and upper secondary education, and where lower secondary education lasts for more than 3 years, only the first 3 years following primary education should be counted as lower secondary education.

Bridging programmes

Short programmes that follow completion of ISCED 2, but have a level of content similar to programmes at Level 2, should be also categorised at Level 2. For example, in Denmark, Finland, and Switzerland there is a 10th year which follows the end of lower secondary that students can use to change streams, that is, to prepare for entry into a different type of programme at Level 3 than which they prepared for at Level 2. These programmes will be classified at Level 2.

Special needs and adult education

This level includes special needs education programmes and all adult education which are similar in content to the education given at this level, *e.g.* the education which gives to adults the basic skills necessary for further learning.

▽ Examples

ISCED 2A – Type 1 (general)
→ Canada and the United States will apportion their elementary-secondary programmes in a manner that will result in grades 7 through 9 being reported in this category.
→ *Secondary school: 1st stage* (Australia). The first stage of secondary school lasts for 3 or 4 years, depending on the length of primary school in the state concerned, and ends with the award of the Year 10 Certificate. Students follow a general school programme, offering the opportunity for further academic progression.
→ *Lower secondary schools, access to general* (Germany). Programme (grades 5 to 10) following the 4 years of primary school which is marked by the beginning of subject presentation. Successful completion leads to *Realschulabschluß* (*Gymnasium, Integrierte Gesamtschule, Freie Waldorfschule*). Successful graduates are entitled to enter studies at upper secondary general schools which qualify for ISCED 5A programmes.

- → *Almen voksenuddannelse (AVU) (General adult education 9th-10th grade)* (Denmark). Certificates correspond to certificates for single courses in grades 9 and 10 in basic school.
- → *Lower secondary evening schools* (Germany). Programme (of 1 to 2 years of duration) especially intended for adults with no or lower level ISCED 2 qualification (*e.g. Hauptschulabschluß*) who want to obtain a higher qualification at lower secondary level (mostly *Realschulabschluß*).
- → *Schuljahr, Vorkurs, préapprentissage, corsi preparatori* (Switzerland). These programmes last one year, are general in content and prepare the students mainly for vocational education in the dual system (by "upgrading" the skills of students coming from lower secondary programmes with basic demands, for instance). The specific vocational content is too low to warrant their classification as Type 2. This group of programmes is nationally considered to be part of the lower secondary or the upper secondary level according to its institutional affiliation.

ISCED 2A – Type 2 (pre-vocational or pre-technical)
- → *Berufsvorbereitungsjahr* (Germany). One-year pre-vocational programme designed for students with 9 or 10 years of general education who did not obtain a contract in the dual system. It prepares students for vocational training (ISCED 3B).
- → *Muvészeti általános iskola* (Hungary). Lower secondary education with additional music, dance, or sports teaching in preparation for higher studies in these areas (National Core Curriculum Key Stage Grade 8).

ISCED 2B – Type 1 (general)
- → *Felzárkóztató általános iskolai programok* (Hungary). Remedial programme for drop-outs and poor learners to provide a second chance for further education. Typically attended by late maturers and low achievers. Provides entry to ISCED 3C programmes.

ISCED 2B – Type 2 (pre-vocational or pre-technical)
- → *Basic Education and Basic Employment Skills (Stream 2100)* (Australia). Courses classified to Stream 2100 provide remedial education or involve preparatory activities to enable participation in subsequent education or social settings. They are of a type which aims to achieve basic skills and standards and completion can be a foundation to entering more advanced vocational education and training (VET) courses and can also assist in gaining employment. For example, one Stream 2100 course, equivalent to about one-year full-time, is designed to provide Aboriginal adults with the skills necessary to manage further vocational study or raise their prospects towards base grade employment.
- → *Voorbereidend beroepsonderwijs* (Netherlands). Pre-vocational education (VBO) is for 4 years; in content – general and vocational courses – it is designed as basic training leading to further vocational training. The VBO is aimed at young people aged 12 to 16.

ISCED 2B – Type 3 (vocational or technical)
- → *Secundair onderwijs voor sociale promotie – LSBL en LSTL* (Flemish Community of Belgium). Social advancement secondary education is divided into 2 cycles: the lower and the higher secondary level. The lower level includes the following programmes: lower secondary vocational courses (LSBL: *lagere secundaire beroepsleergangen*) and lower secondary technical courses (LSTL: *lagere secundaire technische leergangen*).

ISCED 2C – Type 1 (general)
- → *Zvláštní škola – 3. stupen* (Czech Republic). Remedial school – 3rd stage. Programme for children with learning difficulties (including those that are socially disadvantaged). Results in a school leaving certificate (*vysvedcení*).

ISCED 2C – Type 2 (pre-vocational or pre-technical)
- → *Youth Reach* (Ireland). Results in a basic skills training certificate.

ISCED 2C – Type 3 (vocational or technical)

→ *Buitengewoon secundair onderwijs – opleidingsvorm 1 en 2* (Flemish Community of Belgium). Special secondary education – training form 1 and 2. This programme is for students with a physical or mental handicap who cannot enter the normal streams of education and training. It is tailored to their abilities and prepares them for integration into a protected environment and work situation.

→ *Szakiskola alapfokú iskolai végzettség nélküli szakmákra* (Hungary). NVQL (National Vocational Qualification List) training in programmes requiring less than 10 years of completed general education.

→ *Capacitación para el trabajo (lower secondary job training)* (Mexico). The typical duration of these programmes is 4 years, although there are also shorter programmes. Students in this programme are commonly adults. The programme is oriented to train persons (15 years and over) for introducing them to the world of work.

ISCED 3
Upper secondary level of education

♦ Definitions and classification criteria

ISCED 3 corresponds to the final stage of secondary education in most OECD countries. Instruction is often more organised along subject-matter lines than at ISCED Level 2 and teachers typically need to have a higher level, or more subject-specific, qualifications that at ISCED 2. The entrance age to this level is typically 15 or 16 years. There are substantial differences in the typical duration of ISCED 3 programmes both across and between countries, typically ranging from 2 to 5 years of schooling. ISCED 3 may either be "terminal" (*i.e.* preparing the students for entry directly into working life) and/or "preparatory" (*i.e.* preparing students for tertiary education).

Entry requirements

Admission into ISCED 3 educational programmes usually requires the completion of ISCED 2 (typically 8 or 9 years of full-time education since the beginning of Level 1), or a combination of basic education and life experience that demonstrates the ability to handle ISCED 3 subject matter.

Special needs and adult education

This level includes special needs education programmes and all adult education which are similar in content to the education given at this level.

♦ Sub-categories at this level

Type of subsequent education or destination

ISCED Level 3 programmes are sub-classified according to the destination for which the programmes have been designed to prepare students:

– ISCED 3A: programmes at Level 3 designed to provide direct access to ISCED 5A.

- ISCED 3B: programmes at Level 3 designed to provide direct access to ISCED 5B.
- ISCED 3C: programmes at Level 3 designed to prepare students for direct entry into the labour market, although they also provide access to ISCED 4 programmes or other ISCED 3 programmes. Upper secondary apprenticeship programmes would fall into this category unless the programme was primarily designed to prepare students to enter ISCED 5.

Direct access should not be interpreted as either a strict legal definition of the destination of programmes (which might be far from the reality) or by looking at the actual destination of students (which might be strongly influenced by the current labour market situation). Programmes should be mapped to A, B, and C based on the orientation of *the design of the curriculum*, that is, what type of Level 5 programmes (A or B) does the curriculum of the Level 3 programme prepare students to attend or is the programme primarily designed to prepare students for direct labour market entry. For example, in France, the *baccalauréat technologique* is designed to prepare students to enter 5B programmes [primarily the *enseignement en institut universitaire de technologie* (IUT) or the *sections de techniciens supérieurs* (STS) and not 5A (university) programmes, even though all students holding the *baccalauréat technologique* are legally entitled to enter universities]. Therefore, the *baccalauréat technologique* would be classified at Level 3B.

Some programmes offered at this level provide access to multiple educational and labour market destinations. Programmes primarily designed to provide access (as defined above) to 5A (even if most students go to 5B or the labour market) should be classified as 3A; programmes primarily designed to provide access to 5B should be classified as 3B; and programmes that are primarily designed for either direct labour force entry or to prepare students to enter another programme at Level 3 or a programme at Level 4 should be classified as 3C.

Can ISCED 3C programmes provide access to ISCED 5?

It was not originally intended in the ISCED revision that ISCED 3C would include programmes that have been designed to provide access to ISCED 5. According to ISCED-97, ISCED 3C programmes are designed to prepare students for direct access to the labour market or access to either ISCED 4 or other programmes at ISCED 3. This distinction does not fully capture the degree of openness of the education system in many countries, however. In several Nordic countries, for example, there are ISCED Level 3 programmes that have been primarily designed to prepare students for direct labour market entry, although they also serve as minimum entry requirements for ISCED 5B programmes. Programmes should be mapped to ISCED 3C if they are primarily designed to equip students with the skills needed for direct transition into the labour market. If, however, a programme is designed both to prepare students for further study at ISCED 5B and for students to directly enter the labour market, they should be classified at ISCED 3B.

Programmes that span the boundary between ISCED 3 and ISCED 5

Primary teacher education in Switzerland is an example of a programme that spans the boundary of education Levels 3 and 5B. This programme requires a lower secondary qualification for entry, has 5 years duration, and awards a qualification that is nationally deemed as equivalent to other qualifications at the ISCED 5B level. For programmes of this type, the enrolment should be apportioned across the two levels and the number of students that would have received an ISCED Level 3 qualification, had the programme given this option at the midway point, should be estimated for the calculation of graduates.

Programme orientation

Programmes at Level 3 can also be subdivided into three categories based on the degree to which the programme is specifically oriented towards a specific class of occupations or trades and leads to a labour-market relevant qualification:

- Type 1 (general): education which is not designed explicitly to prepare participants for a specific class of occupations or trades or for entry into further vocational or technical education programmes. Less than 25% of the programme content is vocational or technical.
- Type 2 (pre-vocational or pre-technical): education which is mainly designed to introduce participants to the world of work and to prepare them for entry into further vocational or technical education programmes. Successful completion of such programmes does not lead to a labour-market relevant vocational or technical qualification. For a programme to be considered as pre-vocational or pre-technical education, at least 25% of its content has to be vocational or technical.
- Type 3 (vocational or technical): education which prepares participants for direct entry, without further training, into specific occupations. Successful completion of such programmes leads to a labour-market relevant vocational qualification.

In some cases the first few months or first year of a Type 3 programme has Type 2 elements. For the purpose mapping to ISCED-97, however, only whole programmes that meet the above criteria for Type 2 should be classified in that category.

♦ Specific classification issues

Modular programmes

An educational qualification is earned in a modular programme by combining blocks of courses, or modules, into a programme meeting specific curricular requirements. A single module, however, may not have a specific educational or labour market destination or a particular programme orientation. Educational and labour market options are determined, at least in part, by how an individual combines different modules into a coherent programme. For example, in Denmark it is possible for students to combine different modules at Level 3 into a programme that could meet the criteria of 3A, 3B, or 3C. The students themselves, however, may never be enrolled in programme with a particular destination *per se*, since it is how the modules they take are combined that determines their further educational or labour market access. This issue is similar to the case in many secondary institutions in Canada and the United States, where the educational and labour market access of students is determined by course or credit selection rather than a formal programme selection.

Modular programmes should not be classified as ISCED 3A, 3B or 3C simply because there is not enough information regarding what a particular student is doing at a particular point in time. For the purpose of reporting enrolment, programmes of this type should be classified at Level "3" only, without reference to the educational or labour market destination of the programme. Countries with modular systems at Level 3 should make every attempt, however, to report graduates and educational attainment according to the educational or labour market destination that completion of a particular series of modules (or courses) prepares a student to enter.

Successful completion of Level 3

As widely acknowledged, difficulty in interpreting what signifies a Level 3 completion under the old ISCED has led to many problems in the comparability of education data on both graduates and the educational attainment of the population. Because of the wide variability in the duration and level of content in ISCED 3 programmes, both within and between countries, ISCED-97 has specified a requirement for Level 3 programmes that are considered to be of insufficient duration to count as a Level 3 "completion" (see paragraph 74 of the UNESCO document 151 EX/8 Annex II, March 1997). The criterion for completion at Level 3 in ISCED-97 requires either the successful completion of a 3A or 3B programme (completion of a programme that is designed to provide access to a Level 5 programme) or the successful completion of a 3C programme with a cumulative theoretical duration of 3 years full-time equivalent (FTE).

After examining the preliminary results of the mapping of national programmes to ISCED 3 in OECD countries, and to ISCED 3C in particular, it is clear that the above duration requirement for 3C will do little to decrease the heterogeneity of ISCED 3 qualifications that might be aggregated into an aggregate ISCED 3 completion rate. In fact, this distinction may lead to even more comparability problems. For example, while both ISCED 3A and 3C programmes in Ireland have 2 years cumulative duration at ISCED 3, in the United Kingdom the cumulative duration (at ISCED 3) of an ISCED 3A completion is 4 years, while the cumulative duration of an ISCED 3C completion would be 2 years. In Iceland, a student can complete an ISCED 3C programme of 1, 2, 3 or 4 years, while an ISCED 3A programme takes 4 years. A strict application of the duration requirement would lead to the exclusion of ISCED 3C completers in both Ireland and the United Kingdom, even though students completing ISCED 3C programmes in Ireland have completed a similar number of years of education as ISCED 3A completers. Completers of 3-year programmes in Iceland would be counted as ISCED 3 completions, even if they have completed one year of schooling less than their ISCED 3A counterparts.

Both of the following options will be employed for the 1999 UOE data collection, although the option selected for reporting in *Education at a Glance – OECD Indicators* will depend on whether or not country reclassification of ISCED 3C programmes under option 2 will in fact lead to meaningful comparisons:

- *Option 1.* In addition to collecting data on first-time ISCED 3 graduates (unduplicated) in the UOE, we will also collect data on first-time ISCED 3A or 3B graduates (unduplicated). Comparisons of graduates in *Education at a Glance – OECD Indicators* will focus primarily on first-time ISCED 3A or 3B graduates, although the number of ISCED 3C graduates would be discussed separately as well (assuming that total graduates minus first-time ISCED 3A or 3B graduates roughly equals ISCED 3C graduates). We would, then, be admitting that ISCED 3C is a wide mix of different programmes in different countries, with some leading directly to the labour market, some leading to vocational programmes at Levels 3 and 4, while others are simply the first 2 years of the 4 or 5 years that have been designated as upper secondary (ISCED 3).
- *Option 2.* The duration breakdown for ISCED 3C programmes has been revised in the 1999 UOE. The distinction between ISCED 3C less than 3-year programmes and ISCED 3C programmes of 3 years or more will be dropped. This distinction will be replaced, instead, by a distinction that would separate ISCED 3C programmes into those of a similar length (in cumulative years at ISCED 3), at the national level, as ISCED 3A and 3B programmes from those that are significantly shorter (*e.g.* more than 1 year). Cumulative duration is used as a means to roughly assess the similarity in the level of educational content between ISCED 3A/B

programmes and ISCED 3C programmes. We may then decide to define an ISCED 3 completion (for the purposes of reporting in *Education at a Glance – OECD Indicators*) as successful completion of an ISCED 3A or 3B programmes or successful completion of an ISCED 3C programmes that is no more than 1 year (FTE) duration shorter than the country's ISCED 3A or 3B programmes. The change will allow for us to control for the wide variability in the number of years being mapped to ISCED Level 3, as well as for national differences in the lengths of ISCED 3A/B programmes and ISCED 3C programmes.

∇ Examples

ISCED 3 (no classification by destination or programme orientation)

→ Both Canada and the United States will apportion their elementary-secondary programmes in a manner that will result in Grade 10 to the end of secondary schooling (Grade 12 in the United States and most Canadian provinces and Grade 13 in Ontario) being reported at this category. As most of these programmes are modular in nature, that is, students combine different course offerings in order to prepare for entry into higher education or a specific trade, enrolments will be reported as ISCED 3 – all. To the extent to which student transcripts or records can be evaluated to determine the type of subsequent education or destination and programme orientation of graduates, these sub-categories should be estimated when reporting graduate data.

ISCED 3A – Type 1 (general)

→ *Upper secondary schools, general* (Germany). Three-year upper secondary general programme, comprising grades 11 to 13, which leads to the *Abitur (Hochschulreife)*. It is attended by students who have earned the *Realschulabschluß (Gymnasium, Integrierte Gesamtschule, Freie Waldorfschule)*. Successful graduates of this programme are entitled to enter ISCED 5A programmes.

→ *Eniaio Lykeio* (Greece). In school year 1997-98, the institution of Eniaio Lykeio (Comprehensive Lyceum) was established and is gradually being applied from the first class of Lyceum. This programme is designed to provide a high standard of general education; to develop the pupils skills, initiatives, creativity and critical thought; to provide the pupils with the essential knowledge and adequately equip them for the advancement of their studies at the higher education level; and to help pupils to develop those skills which will enable them to access the labour market through further specialisation or training. Graduates have access to tertiary education (at ISCED 5A and 5B) and to the labour market through the Institutes for Vocational Training (IEK), an ISCED 4C programme.

ISCED 3A – Type 2 (pre-vocational or pre-technical)

→ *Szakközépiskola nappali képzés 9-12. évfolyam* (Hungary). Upper level secondary education with pre-vocational elements, designed to prepare pupils for the Maturity Examination.

→ *Leaving Certificate Vocational Programme* (Ireland). This programme prepares people for the employment-targeted *Leaving Certificate* and combines general and vocational subjects. It is one of three streams leading up to the *Leaving Certificate*. Participants must learn a living European language and take three compulsory modules: familiarity with the workplace, vocational preparation and work experience.

ISCED 3A – Type 3 (vocational or technical)

→ *Gewoon secundair onderwijs – 2de graad en 1ste en 2de leerjaar van de 3de graad TSO* (Flemish Community of Belgium). Regular secondary education – 2nd stage and 1st and 2nd year of the 3rd stage TSO. TSO (technical secondary education) essentially concentrates on general and technical/theoretical subjects. This programme consists of practical and general courses. Young people emerging from TSO can join the labour market or continue their studies in higher education.

→ *Istituto tecnico* (Italy). Certain technical colleges train young people for technical and administrative work at intermediate level in agriculture, industry, commerce and tourism. At the end of 5 years' training, students take an examination to obtain the certificate of upper secondary education for their chosen field, which enables them to embark up a career or go on to university.

→ *Berufsmaturität, maturité professionnelle, maturità professionale* (Switzerland). The programme combines an apprenticeship of 3 or 4 years duration with additional schooling in general subjects. It gives unconditional access to the newly created *Fachhochschulen*, classified at Level 5A.

→ *General National Vocational Qualification Advanced Level* (United Kingdom). These programmes are essentially aimed at young people aged 16 to 19 in full-time education (in secondary education establishments and colleges), but they also offer part-time training for adults. They are more or less equivalent to GCE (General Certificate of Education) at grade A or a Level 3 NVQ (National Vocational Qualification). The key skills include communication, mathematics and computer skills and the development of "employability". The objective is to develop knowledge, skills and understanding in general vocational fields such as commerce, the manufacturing industry, retailing and distribution. These programmes can lead to a job or to post-secondary and higher education. They are usually for two years full-time.

ISCED 3A or C (depending on the particular programme) – Type 3 (vocational or technical)

→ *Secondary vocational schools* (Czech Republic). These technical/vocational programmes combine school and work-based elements, although the majority of instruction is given in schools. The schools prepare their students directly for entry into an occupation. They also offer a longer study for 4 years ending with the maturita exam enabling the graduate the entry to the university (this will be classified at 3A). These schools specialise mostly in engineering and technical areas, more recently also in management. They also provide general education, including mother tongue, history, mathematics and sciences. Study at secondary vocational schools is completed with a final exam and is classified at ISCED 3C, Type 3. Graduates of four-year curricula take both the final exam and the maturita exam and will be classified at ISCED 3A, Type 3.

ISCED 3B – Type 2 (pre-vocational or pre-technical)

→ *Felnottek szakközépiskolája 9-12.* (Hungary). Upper level part-time, secondary education programme preparing pupils for the Maturity Examination. This programme has pre-vocational programme elements.

→ *Listnám á framhaldsskólastigi* (Iceland). Fine and applied arts programme at the upper secondary level. Designed to provide access to fine arts programmes at ISCED 5B.

ISCED 3B – Type 3 (vocational or technical)

→ *Skilled Courses for Recognised Trades* (Australia). Complete Trade Courses (Stream 3212) provide initial education and training for entry to a specific trade. Such vocations require a high degree of skill, usually in a wide range of related activities, performed with minimal direction and supervision. In contrast to operatives, persons in such vocations are competent to carry out a broad range of related tasks. The skill level for such vocations is less than that required of a para-professional within the same industry. These courses can lead to more advanced technician and supervisory courses, though only a minority of graduates currently proceed to further studies.

→ *Lehre (Duale Ausbildung)* (Austria). In this 3-year programme, learning takes place alternatively at the workplace and in a vocational education school (dual system). The apprentices are expected to attend a vocational school for further general education, study of the theoretical technical aspects of an occupation and for practical training. They are employed and paid by the enterprise. Education in part-time vocational schools takes place throughout the school year, in one- or two-day periods. Apprenticeship training is open to all young people who have completed their 9 years of compulsory schooling.

→ *Baccalauréat professionnel* (France). This programme prepares for a vocational *baccalauréat*. It takes place mainly in an educational/training institution but includes training periods in an enterprise and aims at helping participants to enter working life. It is also possible to earn the *baccalauréat professionnel* by apprenticeship, with instructional time shared between an education/training institutions and an enterprise. The professional *baccalauréat* allows an immediate labour force entry. A minority of graduates continues to higher studies however, mainly to earn the *Brevet de technicien supérieur* (BTS) at ISCED 5B.

→ *Berufsschulen/Duales System* (Germany). Special form of apprenticeship which comprises education and training both at a vocational school and in an enterprise. Students must have completed ISCED 2. Graduates qualify for entry into *Fachschulen* (5B) or into the labour market.

ISCED 3C – Programmes with a cumulative duration similar to ISCED 3A and 3B programmes – Type 2 (pre-vocational or pre-technical)

→ *Leaving Certificate Applied* (Ireland). This 2-year programme is intended to meet the needs of those students who are not adequately catered for by other Leaving Certificate programmes or who chose not to opt for such programmes. It includes theoretical and practical vocational modules. It does not provide direct access to tertiary education. This new programme was set up in 1995.

ISCED 3C – Programmes with a cumulative duration similar to ISCED 3A and 3B programmes – Type 3 (vocational or technical)

→ *Stredni odborná škola, studium bez maturity* (Czech Republic). Secondary technical school without a *maturita* examination. This 3-year programme provides both general education and practical vocational training. Students do not have access to higher education unless they take the *maturita* examination, which can be sat after taking a 2-year ISCED 4A programme.

→ *Erhvervsfaglige uddannelser* (Denmark). Primary vocational youth programme which includes training for carpenters, blacksmiths, electricians, etc. There are 86 different courses in trade and technical fields, and more than 20 specialities. Most courses last between 3 and 4 years.

→ *Szakiskolai szakképzo évfolyamok és programok* (Hungary). One- to two-year vocational programmes preparing for National Vocational Qualification List (NVQL) examinations. Entry requirement: the completion of Grade 10 and/or the Basic Secondary Examination (an ISCED 3C, general programme). The typical starting ages are 16 and 17 and the cumulative years of schooling at ISCED 3 would be 3-4 years.

ISCED 3C – Programmes with a cumulative duration less (more than one year) than ISCED 3A and 3B programmes – Type 1 (general)

→ *Entry to Employment or Further Education: Educational Preparation, Stream 2200* (Australia). A one-half-year course designed to provide remedial education or teach other preparatory activities to enable participation in subsequent education or social settings. The typical starting age is 15 or older.

→ *Általános iskola, szakiskola általánosan képzo 9-10. évfolyamai* (Hungary). Basic education programme of the vocational school. Grade 9-10 general subject courses preparing pupils for entrance to NVQL programmes with an entrance requirement of 10 years of general education. The typical starting age is between 14 and 15.

ISCED 3C – Programmes with a cumulative duration less (more than one year) than ISCED 3A and 3B programmes – Type 2 (pre-vocational or pre-technical)

→ *Polytechnische Schule, pre-vocational year* (Austria). One-year programme in the last year of compulsory education which introduces into broad occupational fields. It is often followed by apprenticeship (ISCED 3B). The typical starting age is 14.

→ *General National Vocational Qualification Foundation Level* (United Kingdom). These programmes are essentially targeted at 16-19 year-olds in full-time education (secondary education establishments and colleges), although they also offer part-time training for adults. They are more or less equivalent to four GCSE (General Certificate of Secondary Education) D to G passes or a Level 1 NVQ (National Vocational Qualification). The key skills include communication, mathematics, computer skills and the development of "employability". The aim is to develop information, skills and understanding in general vocational fields such as commerce, the manufacturing industry, retailing and distribution. These programmes may lead to employment or to post-secondary or higher education or training. They are full-time for a year, and there are no specific admission conditions.

ISCED 3C – Programmes with a cumulative duration less (more than one year) than ISCED 3A and 3B programmes – Type 3 (vocational or technical)

→ *Enseignement de second cycle professionnel du second degré (sous statut scolaire)* (France). This 2-year programme prepares for an intermediate vocational diploma *(Brevet d'études professionnelles/*BEP) leading to a job or to further vocational education and training (at ISCED 3A or 3B). It is mainly provided in an education/training institutions but includes training periods in an enterprise. The typical starting ages are between 15 and 17.

→ *Formazione professionale regionale post-obbligo* (Italy). This 2-year programme, which comes after the end of compulsory education, offers a basic qualification and trains skilled workers in various sectors of the economy. Each region is in charge of setting the objectives and designing the programme. The typical starting ages are between 14 and 18.

ISCED 4
Post-secondary non-tertiary

♦ Definitions and classification criteria

Level 4 was introduced in ISCED-97 to cover programmes that straddle the boundary between upper secondary and post-secondary education from an international point of view, even though they might clearly be considered as upper secondary or post-secondary programmes in a national context. According to ISCED-97 (paragraph 72), Level 4 programmes cannot, considering their content, be regarded as tertiary programmes. They are often not *significantly* more advanced than programmes at ISCED 3 but they serve to broaden the knowledge of participants who have already completed a programme at Level 3. The students are typically older than those in ISCED 3 programmes.

Programme duration

ISCED 4 programmes typically have a full-time equivalent duration of between 6 months and 2 years.

Entry requirements

The typical entry requirement for ISCED 4 programmes is successful completion of ISCED 3. As described above, successful completion of any programme at Level 3A or 3B counts as a Level 3 completion. If a course requires the completion of an ISCED 3A or 3B course for entry, it would meet the minimum entry requirements for being classified at ISCED 4. ISCED 3C programmes that have a similar duration and level of educational content to ISCED 3A or 3B programmes also serve as the minimum entry requirements for ISCED 4. In cases where ISCED 3C programmes are of significantly shorter duration than ISCED 3A or 3B programmes (*e.g.* more than one year), then the criterion of successful completion of ISCED 3 should be interpreted in the context of the cumulative duration of programmes spanning both Level 3 and Level 4. For example, if a 2-year programme under consideration for classification at ISCED 4 has a 2-year ISCED 3C programme as a minimum entry requirement and corresponding ISCED 3A and 3B courses also have 2 years cumulative duration at ISCED Level 3, then the minimum cumulative duration requirement is met (2 years at ISCED 3C + 2 years at ISCED 4 = 4 years cumulative duration). If, however, a 6-month programme under consideration for classification at ISCED 4 has a 2-year ISCED 3C programme as a minimum entry requirement, where comparable ISCED 3A and 3B courses have a cumulative duration of 4 or more years, then the minimum cumulative duration requirement would not be met (2 years at ISCED 3C + 0.5 years at ISCED 4 = 2.5 years cumulative duration – less than the comparable ISCED 3A and 3B courses). The programme in the second example would not meet the criteria for being classified at ISCED 4 and should be classified at ISCED 3.

◆ Sub-categories at this level

Type of subsequent education or destination

Level 4 programmes are sub-classified according to the destination for which the programmes have been designed to prepare students.

- ISCED 4A: programmes at Level 4, designed to provide direct access to ISCED 5A.
- ISCED 4B: programmes at Level 4, designed to provide direct access to ISCED 5B.
- ISCED 4C: programmes at Level 4 designed to prepare students for direct entry into the labour market, although they also provide access to other ISCED 4 programmes. Apprenticeships that are designed for students who have already completed an ISCED 3 (upper secondary programme) would fall into this category unless the programme was primarily designed to prepare students to enter ISCED 5.[3]

Programme orientation

Programmes at Level 4 can also be subdivided into three categories based on the vocational emphasis of the programme:

- Type 1 (general): education which is not designed explicitly to prepare participants for a specific class of occupations or trades or for entry into further vocational or technical education programmes. Less than 25% of the programme content is vocational or technical.
- Type 2 (pre-vocational or pre-technical): education which is mainly designed to introduce participants to the world of work and to prepare them for entry into further vocational or technical education programmes. Successful completion of such programmes does not lead to a labour-market relevant vocational or technical qualification. For a programme to be considered as pre-vocational or pre-technical education, at least 25% of its content has to be vocational or technical.
- Type 3 (vocational or technical): education which prepares participants for direct entry, without further training, into specific occupations. Successful completion of such programmes leads to a labour-market relevant vocational qualification.

∇ Examples

Several types of programmes can fit into Level 4. The first type are short vocational programmes for which either the content would not be considered "tertiary" in many OECD countries or the programme does not

---

3. In the "Levels of Education" framework approved by the UNESCO Executive Board (151 EX/8 Annex II, March 1997), Level 4 is divided into two sub-categories: 4A and 4B. In order to maintain parallel structure to the educational and labour market destinations at Level 3, it is proposed that Level 4 be split into 3 categories: 4A, programmes designed to provide direct access to ISCED 5A; 4B, programmes designed to provide direct access to ISCED 5B; and 4C, programmes not designed to lead directly to ISCED 5A or 5B. Programmes at Level 4C, then, lead directly to labour market or other ISCED 4 programmes.

meet the duration requirement for ISCED 5B (at least 2 years FTE since the start of Level 5). These programmes are often designed for students who have completed Level 3, although a formal ISCED Level 3 qualification may not be required for entry. The second type of programmes are nationally considered as upper secondary programmes, even though entrants to these programmes will have typically already completed another upper secondary programme (*i.e.* second-cycle programmes).

Post-secondary, but not tertiary programmes from an international perspective

ISCED 4B – Type 3 (vocational or technical)

→ *Trade Technician/Trade Supervisory* (Australia). Programmes classified nationally to Stream 3300 which provide initial education and training in skills at a level higher than trade or trade-equivalent skills (which would be learned in an ISCED Level 3 programme). Stream 3300 courses may include skills needed for supervision, but do not provide the level of breadth of specialisation that is provided through courses for para-professionals. Examples of Stream 3300 courses are Advanced Certificates in Plumbing and other trades, Advanced Certificates in Laboratory Technology. Most courses require completion of a trade certificate course (ISCED 3), though some programmes allow for entry following completion of upper secondary (general).

→ *Schulen für Gesundheits- und Krankenpflege* (Austria). A three-year programme consisting of theoretical and practical courses leading to a nursing diploma. Training comprises fields such as nursing, medical and various related subjects such as law and psychology. These programmes are open to pupils who have successfully completed the tenth year of education (ISCED 3C). Upon completion of this programme, a student will have completed one more year of schooling than graduates from ISCED 3A programmes.

→ *Ausbildung für Krankenpflege, formation pour les professions de la santé* (Switzerland). Vocational programmes for the health professions which have a minimum entrance age of 18. Not all schools require a completed ISCED Level 3 programme as an entrance condition and there is a lively national debate on whether the content of these programmes would allow them to be classified as tertiary.

ISCED 4C – Type 3 (vocational or technical)

→ *Mittlere Speziallehrgänge* (Austria). One-year specialised courses designed for people who have completed initial vocational education. They aim at imparting specialised theoretical and practical knowledge. The minimum entry requirement is an ISCED 3B qualification and the typical entry age is 17.

→ *Trade and vocational certificates* (Canada). Trade/vocational certificate (1 year), trade/vocational certificate (1-2 years), vocational certificate programme (less than 1 year). These programmes are allocated to this level, as they do not meet the duration criteria associated with Level 5B. They are pre-employment and apprenticeship programmes, as well as skill upgrading programmes designed for people already working who would like to improve or develop new skills in their occupational areas.

→ *Vocational preparation and training II (PLC) Yr 1 & 2* (Ireland). These courses offer a range of one-year and two-year vocational training programmes directed towards upper secondary completers. These programmes lead to the NCVA Level 2 Award.

→ *Formazione professionale (post-maturità) regionale o scolastica* (Italy). This programme, which follows on upper secondary education, is a preparation for highly skilled jobs in various sectors of the economy. The courses are mainly practical in content. On completion of this variable-length programme students may obtain a certificate of attendance or, if they pass an examination, they are awarded a certificate of vocational qualification. This programme is not part of the national educational system. The typical entry ages are between 19 and 21.

→ Vocational Certificate (United States). Programmes of up to two years duration offered in for-profit, private institutions, community colleges and universities that lead to an occupationally specific vocational certificate. Typical entry ages for the programme are between 18 and 30.

Upper secondary, second-cycle programmes

ISCED 4A – Type 1 (general)

→ *Upper secondary evening schools* (Germany). Three-year general programme for adults. Admission requirements include: minimum age 19, completion of vocational training or at least 3 years work experience. Successful graduates of this programme earn the *Abitur (Hochschulreife)* and are entitled to enter ISCED 5A programmes.

→ *Berufsmaturität nach der Lehre, maturité professionnelle après l'apprentissage* (Switzerland). Programmes offering the additional general subjects required for the *maturité professionnelle*. They can only be attended by students with a completed three- or four-year apprenticeship and last one year giving a complete duration of four or five years after the beginning of ISCED Level 3.

ISCED 4A – Type 2 (pre-vocational or pre-technical)

→ *TIF-kurser/værkstedskurser* (Denmark). Half-year practical admittance courses for programmes at ISCED 5B.

ISCED 4A – Type 3 (vocational or technical)

→ *Gewoon secundair onderwijs - 3de leerjaar van de 3de graad BSO* (Flemish Community of Belgium). The 3rd year of the 3rd stage of vocational secondary education. This specialisation year gives access to higher education under certain conditions.

→ *Nástavbové studium* (Czech Republic). Follow-up courses. The student who completed vocational education in a 3-year programme in order to enter the labour market can re-enter the secondary school for a secondary education with *maturita* exam. The student has, therefore, a higher level of education in the labour market and this qualification also enables him/her to enter, after passing an entrance examination, into higher education institutions.

ISCED 4B – Type 3 (vocational or technical)

→ *Berufsschulen/Duales System* (Germany). Special form of apprenticeship (second cycle) which comprises education and training both at a vocational school and in an enterprise. Students must have completed an ISCED 3B programme for entry. Graduates qualify for *Fachoberschulen* (4A), *Fachschulen* (5B) or for entry into the labour market.

→ *Berufliche Zweitausbildung auf Sekundarstufe II – Second vocational programmes at upper secondary level (1 year)* (Switzerland). Short vocational programmes are offered for holders of the *maturité gymnasiale* (mainly in business administration) and the final exam is considered to be equivalent to a vocational education at ISCED Level 3B.

ISCED 4C – Type 3 (vocational or technical)

→ *Erikoisammattitutkinto* (Finland). Specialist vocational qualifications. A demonstration examination is taken usually after some years of work experience (for example in crafts and technical skills). Participants must have completed ISCED 3 or have equivalent skills.

ISCED 5
First stage of tertiary education

ISCED 5 programmes have an educational content more advanced than those offered at Levels 3 and 4. Entry to these programmes normally requires the successful completion of ISCED Level 3A or 3B or a similar qualification at ISCED Level 4A or 4B. Programmes at Level 5 must have a cumulative theoretical duration of at least 2 years from the beginning of Level 5 and do not lead directly to the award of an advanced research qualification (those programmes are at Level 6). Programmes are subdivided into 5A, programmes that are largely theoretically-based and are intended to provide sufficient qualifications for gaining entry into advanced research programmes and professions with high skills requirements, and into 5B, programmes that are generally more practical/technical/occupationally specific than ISCED 5A programmes.

♦ ISCED 5A – Definitions and classification criteria

The curriculum of programmes at this level has a strong theoretical foundation, emphasising the liberal arts and sciences (history, philosophy, mathematics, etc.) or preparing students for professions with high skills requirements (*e.g.* medicine, dentistry, architecture, etc.). As the organisational structure of tertiary education programmes varies greatly across countries, no single criterion can be used to define boundaries between ISCED 5A and ISCED 5B. The following criteria are the minimum requirements for classifying a programme as ISCED 5A, although programmes not satisfying a single criterion should not be automatically excluded.

Programmes at Level 5A:

− Have a minimum cumulative theoretical duration (at tertiary level) of *three* years' full-time equivalent, although they are typically 4 or more years. If a programme has 3 years' full-time equivalent duration, it is usually preceded by at least 13 years of previous schooling at the primary and secondary levels. For systems in which degrees are awarded by credit accumulation, a comparable amount of time and intensity would be required.
− Provide the level of education required for entry into a profession with high skills requirements or an advanced research programme.
− Typically require that the faculty have advanced research credentials. This criterion is not meant to draw an institutional boundary, that is, 5A programmes do not have to take place in the same institutions in which advanced research degrees are awarded (*e.g.* universities). In general, the

faculty in 5A programmes should be qualified to teach students at a level that can prepare them to enter an advanced research programme or into a profession with high skills requirements.
- May involve completion of a research project or thesis.

When programmes meeting the above criteria are organised and provide sequential qualifications, it is often the case that only the last qualification gives direct access to Level 6, although each of the programmes in this sequence should be allocated to Level 5A. For example, although many Ph.D. programmes in the United States may require that a student earn a Master's degree prior to entry, the Bachelor's degree would still count as an ISCED 5A qualification.

♦ ISCED 5A – Sub-categories

Cumulative theoretical duration

ISCED 5A programmes can be sub-classified by the theoretical cumulative duration of programmes. For initial programmes at tertiary level, the cumulative theoretical duration is simply the theoretical full-time equivalent duration of those programmes from the beginning of Level 5. For programmes that require completion of other tertiary programmes prior to admission (see national degree and qualification structure below), cumulative duration is calculated by adding the minimum entrance requirements of the programme (*i.e.* full-time equivalent years of tertiary education prerequisites) to the full-time equivalent duration of the programme. For degrees or qualifications where the full-time equivalent duration is unknown (*i.e.* courses of study designed explicitly for flexible or part-time study), cumulative duration is calculated based on the duration of more traditional degree or qualification programmes with a similar level of educational content.

Duration categories[4]

- Short: 2 to less than 3 years.
- Medium: 3 to less than 5 years.
- Long: 5 to 6 years.
- Very long: more than 6 years.

As "short" programmes would not meet the minimum duration requirement for classification at ISCED 5A, this category is only appropriate for intermediate programmes in the national qualification and degree structure (see below). That is, less than 3-year programmes must be a component or a stage of a longer programme in order to be classified at Level 5A. Individuals who complete these intermediate programmes would not be counted as 5A graduates, however.

Theoretical versus typical duration

In some countries, the theoretical duration of a programme does not accurately reflect the amount of time that the typical student studying full-time should take to complete the programme. This is particularly the case where theoretical duration has a legal basis (*e.g.* it is tied to the amount of time during which a student receives a subsidy) rather than a credit or course hour requirement. In cases where the theoretical duration is thought to be distortionary, that is, it reflects a requirement that is laid

---

4. These duration categories differ slightly from the categories described in ISCED-97, which are 2 and less than 3 years; 3 and less than 4 years; 4 and less than 5 years; 5 and less than 6 years; 6 years and more. The categories described here have been designed to group ISCED 5 programmes with similar levels of educational content and are considered to be the categories that would most likely be employed in a data collection.

out in law but does not reflect the reality of the design of today's programmes, the typical duration may be used as a proxy for theoretical duration in assigning a programme to the above duration categories.

National degree and qualification structure

This dimension cross-categorises ISCED 5A and 5B qualifications by their position in the national qualification structure for tertiary education within an individual country. The main reason why the national degree and qualification structure is included as a separate dimension is that the timing of these awards mark important educational and labour market transition points within countries. For example, in Australia, Canada, New Zealand, and the United Kingdom a student who completes a three-year Bachelor's degree programme will have access to a wide range of occupations and opportunities for further education, whereas a student studying in Austria or Germany will only obtain a labour market relevant qualification after the completion of a full five-year degree programme, even though the level of content of the latter programme may be similar to that of a second (Master's) degree programme in many English-speaking countries.

The "position" of a degree or qualification structure is assigned (intermediate, first, second, third, etc.) based on the internal hierarchy of awards within national education systems. For example, a first theoretically-based degree or qualification (cross-classifying the "theoretically-based" type of programme 5A with the "first" position in the national degree and qualifications structure) would necessarily meet all of the criteria listed above for a theoretically-based programme and lead to the first important educational or labour market qualification within this type of programme. It is only by combining national degree structure with other tertiary dimensions, such as cumulative theoretical duration and programme orientation, that enough information is available to group degrees and qualifications of similar education content.

Categories for the degree and qualification structure

- Intermediate.[5]
- First.
- Second.
- Third and further.

Bachelor's degrees in many English-speaking countries, the *Diplom* in many German-speaking countries, and the *Licence* in many French-speaking countries meet the content criteria for the first theoretically-based programmes. Second and higher theoretically-based programmes (*e.g.* Master's degree in English-speaking countries and *Maîtrise* in French-speaking countries) would be classified in ISCED 5A separately from advanced research qualifications, which would have their own position in ISCED 6.

♦ ISCED 5A – Specific classification issues

ISCED 5A intermediate qualifications – where do they go?

ISCED-97 requires that ISCED 5A first degrees have a minimum 3 years full-time equivalent duration. ISCED 5A intermediate was developed explicitly because some countries have shorter

---

5. Although ISCED-97 does not specifically mention "intermediate" qualifications at ISCED 5A, it is introduced in this document as a means of classifying ISCED 5A programmes that do not meet the duration requirements for their completion to be counted as an ISCED 5A graduation.

programmes in the 5A trajectory, which were not considered long enough to be comparable to the majority of 5A qualifications – including the DEUG in France, *Laurea Breve* in Italy and the University Transfer Programme in Canada. Qualifications that are awarded for less than 3 years FTE study at ISCED 5A are, from an international perspective, to be considered intermediate qualifications. No information on the award of intermediate qualifications will be collected in the UOE data collection, and thus, no 2-year awards should be included in the graduate data (*e.g.* the DEUG should not be included). In principal, we could collect and report 5A intermediate graduates, although the reporting might get a bit confusing, as most countries do not have intermediate qualifications and, in most cases, the intermediate qualifications are often not required for progressing on to earn the 1st 5A degree.

This procedure will not be sufficient, however, for classifying individuals by their level of educational attainment. From a human capital perspective, individuals who have earned a 5A intermediate qualification are likely to have a higher level of skill than an ISCED 3 completer. It would also be quite strange, from the point of view of similar programme content, for them to be placed in either ISCED 5B (even though this might be considered the point at which most are nationally "equivalent") or at ISCED 4. From an educational attainment perspective, there are at least two main options:

- Classification at ISCED 3 (reflecting the last completed level of educational attainment in the ISCED framework).
- Specific classification in a category for intermediate 5A qualifications (which could then be combined with either ISCED 3, 4, 5B, or 5A, depending on analytical purpose).

The Technical Group concluded that the latter solution be recommended for the collection of educational attainment data by ISCED-97.

Post-graduate diplomas

ISCED-97 states that ISCED Level 5A programmes are tertiary programmes that are largely theoretically-based and are intended to provide sufficient qualifications for gaining entry into advanced research programmes and professions with high skills requirements. Post-graduate diplomas are qualifications that are earned in some countries after the successful completion of a 5A programme. The programmes are often geared to broaden or specialise one's knowledge at a particular level (*e.g.* pedagogy, urban planning), although they do not directly lead to an advanced research programme. For example, in Canada, post-graduate certificate programmes are for students who have already completed a Bachelor's degree (1st ISCED 5A qualification of medium duration) or higher academic certificate. The content covered in this programme includes 3rd and 4th year undergraduate courses as well as graduate courses. Depending on the institution offering the programme and the subject field being pursued, completion of this programme may involve a research project. Its completion leads to the awarding of a certificate or diploma that is subsequent to a first degree at Level 5A. These qualifications should be counted as ISCED 5A if they require a 5A qualification for entry and build on the knowledge gained in the 5A programme. It is not necessary that these programmes lead directly to an advanced research qualification.

Requirements for classification at ISCED 5A, second programmes

The preliminary ISCED-97 country mappings indicate that their is a wide variability in the length of programmes being classified as ISCED 5A (2nd). For example, in Australia Graduate Certificate (0.5 years FTE), Bachelor's Graduate Entry (1-year FTE), Graduate Diplomas (1.5 years) and Master's degrees (2 years FTE) are all proposed to be classified as ISCED 5A (2nd) programmes. This variability in duration can lead to wide variation in the cumulative duration of programmes at ISCED 5 leading to a second qualification.

In order to improve the comparability of data reported under ISCED-97, the following criteria for classification at ISCED 5A 2nd are introduced:

- ISCED 5A 2nd programmes require an ISCED 5A first qualification (or an equivalent level of educational content) for entry. The programme should be at a significantly higher level of educational content than ISCED 5A first programmes. Programmes that are designed to allow students to earn a qualification in a different field from their first 5A qualification should not be classified as ISCED 5A 2nd programmes if the level of the curriculum is broadly similar to the curricular offered in first programmes. For example, if the programme content of graduate certificate in accounting is generally similar to the level of curriculum offered in a 1st 5A course in accounting, then the certificate programme should be mapped to 5A, 1st rather than to 5A 2nd.
- If a country cannot separately report ISCED 5A (2nd) degrees by cumulative duration, second programmes that are less than 1-year FTE duration should be excluded from the UOE data collection on graduates. This second recommendation would also pertain to the collection of data on educational attainment.

Example: Higher education "postgraduate" in Australia follow the structure below:

Higher degree:
- Higher Doctorate
- Doctorate by research
- Doctorate by coursework
- Master's by research
- Master's by coursework

Other Postgraduate:
- Postgraduate qualifying or preliminary (for Master's, Ph.D. or Higher Doctorate)
- Graduate diploma/postgraduate diploma
- Graduate Certificate

As the "Other Postgraduate" courses are designed to widen a student's education rather than to educate the student to a significantly higher level, Australia has proposed to allocate the "Other Postgraduate" to ISCED 5A 1st programmes. The "Master's by research" and "Master's by coursework" would remain as 2nd programmes.

Degrees in medicine, dentistry, and veterinary medicine

First degrees in medicine, dentistry, and veterinary medicine should be classified at Level 5A, unless they meet the research requirements at ISCED Level 6. It is unlikely, however, that many first degrees in these fields will meet the advanced research requirements of ISCED 6.

Advanced qualifications (or "specialist" degrees) in these fields should also be classified at Level 5A, unless they meet the research requirements at Level 6. There is wide variability in the degree to which programmes of this type have a substantial research component. There also appears to be wide variability in the degree to which qualifications of this type would come under the coverage of the collection of education statistics. For example, in Germany these specialist qualifications would be considered professional qualifications (rather than educational qualifications) and would not be counted in educational statistics, while in France and Switzerland these would be considered as educational qualifications and would be counted. For individual data collections, it will need to be considered whether or not the collection of specialist degrees in these fields can lead to comparable results across countries. In general, however, these qualifications should only be classified at ISCED Level 6 if they meet the advanced research guidelines outlined for ISCED 6. In most cases, specialist degrees in these fields would be classified at Level 5A.

Research degrees at ISCED 5A

ISCED-97 also allows for the separate categorisation of programmes leading to the award of a research qualification at the 5A Level. This category is intended for the countries which have a sub-doctoral research qualification, designed explicitly to prepare recipients to conduct original research. These programmes will often meet many of the same criteria as an ISCED 6 programme, although they tend to be of shorter duration (5 to 6 years cumulative FTE duration from the start of tertiary) and typically lack the level of independence required of students seeking an advanced research qualification. Examples of 5A research degrees include the Master's degree by Research in Australia, Ireland, New Zealand, and the United Kingdom. As many long ISCED 5A programmes will have a research component, even if they are not explicitly designed to prepare participants for research positions, it is likely that 5A research qualifications and long 5A programmes would be grouped for analytical purposes.

∇ Examples

ISCED 5A – Short, Intermediate

→ *University Transfer Programmes* (Canada). These are programmes of one- or two-year duration offered by non-university institutes under special arrangements with the universities whereby the college offers the first year(s) of a university degree programme. Students who complete the programmes at the colleges can then transfer their credits to university Bachelor's degree programmes. Although enrolments in these programmes count at ISCED 5A, students who complete these programmes are not counted as ISCED 5A graduates.

ISCED 5A – Medium, 1st degree

→ *Ammattikorkeakoulu (programmes in polytechnics)* (Finland). Programmes (3.5 to 4.5 years) prepare for occupations with high skill requirements. These programmes combine theoretical studies (basic and professional studies) with work and practical training. Programmes involve completion of a large research project or thesis. Students must have completed ISCED 3A prior to entry.

→ *Licence* (France). This programme (one year), follows the 2 years of the *Diplôme d'études universitaires générales* (DEUG). For the purpose of ISCED classification, the DEUG is considered an intermediate qualification and all three years of the combined programmes are allocated to the *licence*. Students can also enter the *licence* year, however, after completing a *Diplôme universitaire de technologie* (DUT) at a University Institute of Technology (IUT) or after completing the *classes préparatoires aux grandes écoles* (CPGE). As the DUT is primarily designed to prepare students for direct labour market entry, and not for transferring to a university, enrolment in DUT programmes are classified at ISCED 5B. The *licence* is earned in a university.

→ *Hoger beroepsonderwijs* (Netherlands). In these four-year higher vocational education (HBO) programmes, teaching is of a more practical nature than in the universities. The most common fields studied are economics, engineering, agriculture, teacher education, social work and community education, health care and the arts.

→ *Høgre utd. lavere grad* (Norway). These are 4-year degree programmes leading to *Candidatus magisterii*, *allmennlærer*, or *siviløkonom*. They can serve as the first part of a longer degree programme or as a more vocationally-aimed independent education.

→ *Diplomatura Universitaria* (Spain). Three-year university programme leading to the *Diplomado Universitario*,

Arquitecto Técnico or *Ingeniero Técnico* in a particular field. The holder of these qualifications may enter professional practice or obtain admission to second-stage higher education.

→ *Fachhochschule, haute école spécialisée* (Switzerland). This type of programme was officially inaugurated in 1998. The programmes will demand a *Berufsmaturität/maturité professionnelle* (ISCED 3A vocational education of three or four years duration with a substantially enlarged general education part) as entry requirement, last three or four years and prepare for highly skilled professions such as architecture, engineering, business administration or design. The areas mentioned are the ones in which the first *Fachhochschulen* will be created, but others will follow suit.

→ *Bachelor's degree programme* (United Kingdom). First degree, awarded usually after three year's study (although 5 years is common in medicine and related fields). There are two kinds of Bachelor's degrees. The first type is the honours degree, which is at a higher level than the second type and usually comprises the study on one main and one subsidiary subject only. The second type is the ordinary or pass degree, study for which may included several subjects (often three) and which the depth of studies is not carried to the degree of specialisation required for the honours degree. Students usually have to satisfy examiners in a series of annual examinations or by a system of continuous assessment, as well as sit for a final degree examination.

→ *Bachelor's degree programme* (United States). Typically a 4-year programme undertaken at colleges or universities. These undergraduate programmes typically require a high school diploma or equivalent for entry. Bachelor's degree recipients can enter the labour force or continue their education in graduate (Master's or Ph.D.) or first-professional (law, medicine, dentistry) degree programmes.

ISCED 5A – Medium or Long, 1st degree

→ *Enseignement des écoles de commerce* leading to the *Diplôme d'ingénieur commercial* (France). There are different types of commercial and business *grandes écoles*. They recruit from the *classes préparatoires aux grandes écoles* (CPGE) or from the universities (*licence, maîtrise*). Enrolment in the CPGE should also be classified as ISCED 5A.

→ *Corsi di Laurea* (Italy). University-level studies generally last from four to six years, depending on the field of study. At the end of the course, successful candidates in the final examination (*esame di laurea*) become holders of the *laurea* diploma and are awarded the title of *dottore* (Dott.).

→ *Daigaku Gakubu* (Japan). A university undergraduate programme. The *gakushi* is the first qualification awarded after four years' study in most subjects (six years in medicine, veterinary medicine and dentistry). In addition to study in a specialised field, general education (which includes humanities, social and natural sciences) is obligatory for every student. At the end of each semester, candidates must take an examination in each subject, usually in the form of written tests, and sometimes as research progress reports.

→ *Bachelor's degree programmes* (Mexico). The requirement for entering into this programme is the successful completion of 12 years of schooling. Bachelor's degrees can be earned in universities, technological institutes, or teacher training schools. The duration depends on field of education: 4 to 5 years (6 years in some cases, like medicine). Four-year Bachelor's degree programmes should be allocated to ISCED 5A medium and 5- to 6-year programmes allocated to ISCED 5A long.

ISCED 5A – Medium and Long, 1st and 2nd degrees

→ *University programmes* (Czech Republic). The typical length of university programmes has traditionally been 5 years (the first qualification being the Master's). Recently, a shorter Bachelor's programme has been introduced, which is either more practically oriented or serves as a first stage of a university programme. In principle, both the Bachelor's and the Master's degree can be first qualifications, as not all students get the Bachelor's degree prior to earning the Master's degree. Studies for training teachers for basic school, 1st stage (primary level) last four years (on average). University study ends with a defence of a thesis and the passing of state exams.

ISCED 5A – Long, 1st degree

→ *Bachelor's degrees in professional areas* (Australia). Undergraduate studies lasting between 5 years (veterinary science, dentistry, architecture) and 7 years (medicine and surgery), leading to a Bachelor's degree.

→ *Fachhochschulen* (Germany). Programme (4 or 5 years) at the university level which prepares for occupations which require the application of scientific findings and methods. Students must at least have completed *Fachoberschule* (ISCED 3A or 4A) or equivalent. Leads to a first degree, *Diplom* (FH).

ISCED 5A – Long or Very long (depending on particular programme), 1st degree

→ *Universitäten* (Germany). First degree programme at universities (*i.e.* in academic disciplines) of 5 to 7 years which prepares for occupations which require the application of scientific knowledge and methods. Students must have completed ISCED 3A. Graduates may enter ISCED 6.

ISCED 5A – Long and Very Long, 2nd degree

→ *Master's degree* (Australia). Higher degree, obtained after a period of typically two years following upon a Bachelor's degree (honours). Following upon a Bachelor's degree (pass), entry to a Master's degree may be obtained by completing a Master's qualifying course of one year. Master's degrees may be obtained by research (usually entered after a period of employment) culminating in the submission of a thesis or by course-work often undertaken in conjunction with professional employment.

→ *Daigakuin Shushi katei* (Japan). A university graduate programme leading to the *shushi* (Master's degree). Completion of the *shushi* degree requires two years' full-time study (at least 6 years cumulative at the tertiary level) following the *gakushi*, including 30 credit hours and a substantial amount of research culminating in a thesis.

→ *Master's degree programmes* (Mexico). This programme involves advanced research and complete knowledge about specific subjects and fields of study. The duration of the programme is commonly 2 years. The entry requirement is a 4- or 5-year Bachelor's degree programme.

→ *Universität Nachdiplom, troisième cycle, diplôme postgrade* or *Fachhochschule Nachdiplom, haute école spécialisée diplôme postgrade* (Switzerland). After the first degree, universities offer specialisation programmes not leading to a research degree. They generally last one or two years. Some examples are specialisation in urban planning, in health care management or in environmental studies. The *Fachhochschulen* also offer programmes for specialisation after the first degree. They typically last one year. Examples include business administration for engineers or specialisation in environmental aspects for chemical engineers. The cumulative duration at ISCED 5 ranges from 4 to 6.5 years, depending on the specific programme.

→ *First Professional degree programmes* (United States). Completion of these programmes signifies both completion of the academic requirements for beginning practice in a given profession and a level of professional skill beyond that normally required for a Bachelor's degree. These degree programmes typically require at least two years at ISCED 5A prior to entrance (although most require a 4-year Bachelor's degree) and a cumulative total of between 6 and 8 years of full-time equivalent study at ISCED 5A to be completed. First Professional degrees are awarded in dentistry, medicine, optometry, pharmacy, veterinary medicine, law and theological professions.

♦ ISCED 5B – Definitions and classification criteria

ISCED 5B programmes are generally more practical/technical/occupationally specific than ISCED 5A programmes. Qualifications in category 5B are typically shorter than those in 5A and focus on occupationally-specific skills geared for direct entry into the labour market, although some theoretical foundations may be covered in the respective programmes.

A 5B programme typically meets the following criteria:

- It is more practically oriented and occupationally specific than programmes at ISCED 5A and does not prepare students for direct access to advanced research programmes.
- It has a minimum of *two* years' full-time equivalent duration. For systems in which qualifications are awarded by credit accumulation, a comparable amount of time and intensity would be required.
- The programme content is typically designed to prepare students to enter a particular occupation.

◆ ISCED 5B – Sub-categories

Cumulative theoretical duration

Like ISCED 5A programmes, 5B programmes can be subdivided based on the cumulative theoretical full-time equivalent duration from the beginning of Level 5. Calculation of the cumulative theoretical duration is done in a manner similar to 5A programmes (see above).

Duration categories

- Very short: less than 2 years.
- Short: 2 to less than 3 years.
- Medium: 3 to less than 5 years.
- Long: 5 to 6 years.
- Very long: more than 6 years.

As "very short" programmes would not meet the minimum duration requirement for classification at ISCED 5B, this category is only appropriate for intermediate programmes in the national qualification and degree structure (see below). That is, less than 2-year programmes must be a component or a stage of a longer programme in order to be classified at Level 5B. Individuals who complete these intermediate programmes would not be counted as 5B graduates, however. Most ISCED 5B programmes would fall into the short and medium categories.

National qualification structure

As with 5A programmes, this dimension cross-categorises 5B qualifications by their position in the national qualification structure for tertiary education within an individual country.

Categories for the qualification structure

- Intermediate.
- First.
- Second.
- Third and further.

▽ Examples

ISCED 5B – Short, 1st qualification

→ 3400 *Initial Vocational Courses: Paraprofessional/Technician* (Australia). Paraprofessional/Technician courses classified to Stream 3400 are designed to provide initial education and training to develop the breadth of specialised skills required for employment in para-professional vocations. Common awards are Associate

Diploma or Advanced Certificate, and entry requirements usually specify that entrants hold a certificate in the relevant field. Courses are generally of the order of 2 years full-time equivalent duration.

→ *Kollegs* (Austria). Two-year, post-secondary courses in technical and vocational education (TVE). This programme is primarily designed to provide the holders of a long type secondary education diploma (ISCED 3A) with vocational qualifications similar to those acquired in secondary technical and vocational colleges.

→ *Ammatillinen opisto (vocational colleges)* (Finland). Advanced vocational programmes (2 to 3 years) leading to the Diplomas or the title of Technician Engineer.

→ *Enseignement en institut universitaire de technologie (IUT)* (France). A two-year programme in technology leading to the *Diplôme universitaire de technologie* (DUT). Holders of a DUT may continue in university studies to earn the *licence* (a 1st ISCED 5A qualification), although the programme is primarily designed to prepare students for direct labour market entry. The entry qualification is the *baccalauréat*, complemented by an academic record submitted for assessment by the admissions board.

→ *Enseignement des classes des sections de techniciens supérieur (sous statut scolaire)* (France). A two-year programme leading to the *Brevet de technicien supérieur* (BTS). The admission requirement is the *baccalauréat* or the *brevet de technicien* complemented by a satisfactory school record. Holders of a BTS may, under certain conditions, continue their studies at university or in higher schools. This qualification is at the same level as the DUT, although it is more specialised and offers fewer opportunities for further studies.

→ *Vocational Associate's Degree Programmes* (Mexico). These programmes are offered in Technological Universities. Graduates from these 2-year programmes are considered qualified technicians.

→ *Ciclos Formativos de Formación Profesional de Grado Superior* (Spain). Specific Vocational Training-Advanced Level leading to the qualification *Técnico Superior*. This programme offers structured training through which the skills, abilities and knowledge needed in a specific occupation can be acquired. The qualifications obtained on completion of training are equivalent to those of a skilled technician in that occupation. Admission is based on successful completion of the *bachiller* (ISCED 3A).

→ *Höhere Fach- und Berufsschule, école technique* (Switzerland). Programmes lasting at least two years of full-time school. The typical prerequisite is a vocational education of at least three years or an equivalent general education at ISCED Level 3. The programmes prepare for a variety of skilled professions such as technician, manager in tourism or the lower echelons of upper business management.

→ *Higher National Diploma* (United Kingdom). To be admitted to this programme, participants must be at least 18 and have an appropriate national qualification awarded by Edexcel or equivalent or a GCE A level. The aim is to develop skills and provide training that will lead to many vocational activities. The training is designed to meet employers' needs. It is provided by colleges, certain universities and some training centres and generally leads to the level of senior technician or junior management. The duration is either two years full-time or three years part-time.

ISCED 5B – Short and Medium, 1st qualification

→ *2-3 year college; 3-4 year college; Occupational/Technology programmes; Vocational Diploma (27 months)* (Canada). These are technical programmes designed to prepare students for direct entry into the labour force and last two, three or four years. These programmes do not provide access to advanced research programmes. The admission requirements for eligibility into these college programmes are completion of high school (ISCED 3), eligibility as a mature student or the completion of a certain level of adult upgrading programmes.

→ *Fachschulen – 2 bis 4 jährig* (Germany). Advanced vocational programmes of 2 to 4 years duration. Attended after completion of the dual system and several years of work experience to obtain Master's/technician's qualifications or to qualify for occupations in the social sector.

ISCED 5B – Medium, 1st qualification

→ *Bakalářské univerzitní studium* (Czech Republic). Three-year university programmes leading to the *bakalář* (Bachelor's degree). Programmes that do not give direct access to Master's or Engineer programmes are classified at ISCED 5B, while programmes providing direct access to Master's or Engineer programmes are classified at ISCED 5A.

- → *Hogescholenonderwijs van 1 cyclus* (Flemish Community of Belgium). One-cycle higher education provided by *hogescholen*. These 3- to 4-year programmes lead to a final diploma which qualifies the holder for immediate employment. Qualifications are awarded in industry, commerce, agriculture, health and rehabilitation, social work, teaching, informatics, applied arts or the media.

- → *Verwaltungsfachhochschulen/College of public administration* (Germany). Special type of *Fachhochschulen* run by the public administration to provide training for medium-level, non-technical careers within the public sector. Entrants hold a qualification that would also allow them to enter ISCED 5A. Designed for direct entry into civil service.

- → *Schulen des Gesundheitswesens – 3 jährig* (Germany). School-based vocational education (3 years) for nurses, midwives, etc. Often these schools are associated with hospitals where training is provided in theory and practice. Designed for direct labour market entry.

- → *Diploma programmes* (New Zealand). Vocationally oriented 2- to 3-year (cumulative) programmes leading to Diplomas and National Diplomas (Levels 5, 6).

- → *Nauczycielskie kolegium jêzyków obcych (foreign language teacher training college)* (Poland). A three-year programme leading to a qualification to teach West European languages (English, German and, to a limited degree, Spanish) at pre-school institutions, primary schools and secondary schools. Requires the secondary school leaving certificate, *matura*, for entry.

ISCED 5B – Medium, 2nd qualification

- → *Stream 3600 – Initial Vocational Courses – Professional* (Australia). Initial Vocational Courses – Professional are classified to Stream 3600 and provide initial education and training at a higher level than paraprofessional courses, and include courses which lead to employment in vocations comparable to those entered by graduates of Diploma (UG2) courses. Awards are typically Advanced Diploma and entry requirements are usually completion of a Diploma or equivalent course. Courses are commonly about 2 years full-time equivalent duration in addition to the prerequisites. Examples include Advanced Diplomas in Information Technology or in Rural Management.

ISCED 6
Second stage of tertiary education
(leading to an advanced research qualification)

♦ Definitions and classification criteria

This level is reserved for tertiary programmes that lead directly to the award of an advanced research qualification. The theoretical duration of these programmes is 3 years full-time in most countries (for a cumulative total of at least 7 years FTE at the tertiary level), although the actual enrolment time is typically longer. The programmes are devoted to advanced study and original research.

For a programme to be classified at ISCED 6, it:

– For successful completion, requires the submission of a thesis or dissertation of publishable quality that is the product of original research and represents a significant contribution to knowledge.
– Is not solely based on course-work.
– Prepares recipients for faculty posts in institutions offering ISCED 5A programmes, as well as research posts in government and industry.

Although most countries would only have a "first" advanced research qualification (*e.g.* the Ph.D. in the United States), some countries do award an "intermediate" advanced research qualification [*e.g.* the *Diplôme d'études approfondies* (DEA) in France] and others award a "second" advanced research qualification (*e.g. Habilitation* in Germany and *doktor nauk* in the Russian Federation). Accounting for these intermediate and second awards in the classification scheme is important for defining the boundary around the first advanced research qualifications, although they might be ignored in a data collection.

Programmes leading to intermediate research qualifications should either be counted as 1st stage component of Level 6 programmes (where completing this component would not count as a Level 6 completion) or as Level 5A programmes. This allocation decision should be based on the degree to which the programme is designed to lead directly to the award of an advanced research qualification. Programmes that are primarily designed to prepare students for direct labour market entry with either basic or intermediate research skills should be classified at ISCED 5A, even if these programmes also allow students to continue towards an advanced research degree.

▽ Examples

ISCED 6 – Intermediate stage, no qualification

→ *Diplôme d'études approfondies (DEA)* (France). Qualification awarded after the first year of preparation for research work, which is obligatory in preparing for a *doctorat*. Enrolment for the DEA is open to holders of the *maîtrise*. While enrolments in the DEA year are included at ISCED 6, the DEA does not count as an ISCED 6 completion.

ISCED 6 – 1st qualification

→ *Doctor's degree or doctorate* (Australia). These are degrees obtained after a Bachelor's degree (high honours) or a Master's degree and usually three years' full-time study devoted to preparing a thesis based on an original research project resulting in a significant contribution knowledge or understanding and/or the application of knowledge within the field of study.

→ *Doctorat* (France). The *doctorat* is awarded after three years of study following the DEA (8 years of tertiary) in the humanities, science, economics, law, pharmacy and dentistry, after the submission of a thesis based on original research acceptable to the *responsable de l'école doctorale* or the *conseil scientifique* of the university. Candidates carry out personal research work constituting an original contribution to the subject.

→ *Promotion* (Germany). Doctoral studies programme (2 to 5 years). In most cases students must have successfully completed programmes at universities. A doctoral degree is awarded to successful students on the basis of a thesis and oral examination.

→ *Dottorati di ricerca* (Italy). This diploma is the highest academic degree awarded. It is granted after a minimum of three years spent in a university department carrying out a specific research programme under the direction of university professors. Admission to the *Dottorati di ricerca* is restricted and is by competitive examination among holders of the *laurea*.

→ *Hakushi* (Japan). The highest degree, awarded to students who have completed a doctorate course at a postgraduate school or have been recognised as holding equivalent qualifications. The requirement for completion of the doctorate course is more than five years of study at a postgraduate school (in addition to 4 years undergraduate), with 30 or more credits, the submission of a dissertation and success in a final examination. Those who have completed highly qualified research work may be awarded the *hakushi* after three years' study at postgraduate school.

→ *Doctor of Philosophy (Ph.D.)* (United States). The Ph.D. is the highest academic degree and requires mastery within a field of knowledge and demonstrated ability to perform scholarly research (three to five years usually beyond the Master's degree – which is 8 to 10 years of tertiary study).

Proposed allocation of national educational programmes to ISCED-97

The following tables contain the proposed mapping of national educational programmes to ISCED-97 for all 29 OECD countries. The allocations of national educational programmes to ISCED-97 have been developed by Member countries, in consultation with the OECD Secretariat. These proposals represent the starting point for a process of consultation within the Technical Group, with the aim of working towards an internationally agreed upon allocation of national educational programme to ISCED-97 in the OECD. These mappings will form the basis of data reporting in the 1999 UOE Data Collection on Education Statistics. The goal of the ISCED-97 implementation process is that the mapping of national education programmes to the revised ISCED be perfectly transparent and jointly agreed upon by all Member countries.

The Technical Group will continue to serve as a forum for discussing and evaluating individual country's ISCED-97 allocations. Particular programme allocations that do not match the criteria laid out in this manual, and thereby do not lead to comparable education statistics, will be brought up and discussed amongst the Technical Group. In cases where this manual does not make it clear how a programme with particular characteristics should be mapped to ISCED-97, suggestions for modifying the manual will be sought. The implementation of ISCED will be both an iterative and interactive process, with both Member countries and international organisations reviewing countries' assignments of programmes to ISCED categories and recommending adjustments to enhance international comparability.

Table legend

NC	**ISCED-97 level** Not yet classified
General (G)/Type 1	**Programme orientation** Education which is not designed explicitly to prepare participants for a specific class of occupations or trades or for entry into further vocational/technical education programmes. Less than 25% of the programme content is vocational or technical.
Pre-vocational or pre-technical (P)/Type 2	Education which is mainly designed to introduce participants to the world of work and to prepare them for entry into further vocational or technical education programmes. Successful completion of such programmes does not lead to a labour-market relevant vocational or technical qualification. At least 25% of the content has to be vocational or technical.
Vocational or technical (V)/Type 3	Education which prepares participants for direct entry, without further training, into specific occupations. Successful completion of such programmes leads to a labour-market relevant vocational qualification.
Short (S) Medium (M) Long (L) Very long (VL)	**Cumulative duration at ISCED 5** Short: 2 to less than 3 years. Medium: 3 to less than 5 years. Long: 5 to 6 years. Very long: more than 6 years.
Intermediate 1st 2nd 3rd and +	**Position in the national degree/qualification structure** Intermediate degree/qualification. First degree/qualification. Second degree/qualification. Third and further degree/qualification.

Manual for ISCED-97 Implementation in OECD Countries – 1999 Edition

Australia

ISCED-97 level	Programme orientation	Cumulative duration at ISCED 5	Position in the national degree/qualification structure (intermediate, first, second, etc.)	Notes on programmes that span across ISCED levels or sub-categories	Descriptive name of the programme	Main diplomas, credentials or certifications	Typical starting ages	Theoretical length of the programme	Typical length of the programme	Cumulative years of education at the end of the programme	Minimum entrance requirement	Programme specifically designed for part-time attendance	Reported in the UOE	1995 enrolment year	Other relevant information
0					Pre-school/Kindergarten		4-5						No		
1A	G				Primary school		5-6	7.5	7.5	7.5				1834000	
2B	P			2B, 2C	2100 Entry to Employment or Further Education: Basic Education and Basic Employment Skills (Stream 2100)	Statement of Attainment, Certificate or not an award course	15-40	1	1	11.5	1	Yes		201639	Basic skills programmes (most likely in the Vocational Education and Training (VET) system) leading to other VET programmes or to labour market entry. In principle, they could qualify as either 2B or 2C.
2A	G				Secondary school: 1st stage	Year 10 Certificate	12-13	3.5	3.5	11	1			904000	
3C	V				2200 Entry to Employment or Further Education: Educational Preparation (Stream 2200)	Statement of Attainment, Certificate or not an award course	15-40	0.5	0.5	11.5	1	Yes		107032	Courses classified to Stream 2200 provide remedial education or involve other preparatory activities designed to enable participation in subsequent education or social settings.
3C	V				3100 Initial Vocational Courses: Operatives	Statement of Attainment, Certificate or not an award course	15-40	0.5	0.5	11.5	1	Yes		236301	Includes, for example, courses for plant and machine operators and for cleaners. Operatives are personnel who, after training, are able to perform a limited range of skilled operations.
3C	V				3211 Initial Vocational Courses: Skilled Courses for Recognised Trades – Partial Exemption to Recognised Trade Courses	Certificate or Statement of Attainment	17-20	0.5	0.5	11.5	2			27752	
3C	V				3221 Initial Vocational Courses: Other Skilled Courses – Partial Exemption to Other Skills Courses	Certificate or Statement of Attainment	17-30	0.5	0.5	11.5	2			74898	Stream 3221 courses belong in 3C because entrants generally have ISCED 2 Level qualifications and the courses lead either directly to the labour market or to other ISCED 3 Level courses.
3C	V				4100 Courses Subsequent to Initial Vocational Courses: Operative Level	Statement of Attainment, Certificate or not an award course	20-45	0.5	0.5	13.5	3B	Yes		29173	The short duration of these courses (even when added to a Stream 3100 course) is such that they do not meet the two-year minimum specified for ISCED 4 and 5.
3B	V				3212 Initial Vocational Courses: Skilled Courses for Recognised Trades – Complete Trade Courses	Certificate	17-22	4	4	15	2			104868	Similar to apprenticeship programmes in other countries. Post-trade courses at ISCED 5B are open to graduates.
3B	V				3222 Initial Vocational Courses: Other Skilled Courses – Complete Other Skills Courses	Certificate	17-30	4	4	15	2			106074	
3A	G				Secondary School: 2nd Stage	Higher School Certificate, Year 12 Certificate, (State) Certificate of Education	16-17	2	2	13	2			372000	
4B	V				3300 Initial Vocational Courses: Trade Technician/Trade Supervisory	Advanced Certificate	19-40	1.5	3	14	3B	Yes		109655	
4B	V				4300 Courses Subsequent to Initial Vocational Courses: Trade Technician/Trade Supervisory	Statement of Attainment	20-50	0.5	1	15	3B	Yes		13729	Courses are generally less than one year in duration, awards are often a statement of attainment, and completion of a Stream 3300 certificate is a common entrance requirement. Courses often involve advanced testing or supervision studies.
4B	V				4200 Courses Subsequent to Initial Vocational Courses: Skilled Level	Certificate or not an award course	20-45	0.5	1	17	3B	Yes		82074	These courses are too short to meet the duration requirements of ISCED 5 and are not truly tertiary in nature. They do, however, have ISCED 3 entry requirements and the cumulative 3-year duration makes them suitable for classification at ISCED 4.
5B		Short			3400 Initial Vocational Courses: Paraprofessional/Technician	Associate Diploma	17-40	2	4	15	2	Yes		20917	Because of the ISCED 3 entry requirement, course duration of over 2 years, the paraprofessional/technician nature of these courses and subsequent labour market destination, they appear to meet all the requirements of ISCED 5B.
5B		Short			3500 Initial Vocational Courses: Paraprofessional/Higher Technician	Associate Diploma (possibly a Diploma)	19-30	2	4	15	2	Yes		147062	Because of the ISCED 3 entry requirement, course duration of over 2 years, the paraprofessional/technician nature of these courses and subsequent labour market destination, they appear to meet all the requirements of ISCED 5B.
5B		Short			Undergraduate Diplomas awarded by universities	Associate Diploma, Diploma, Advanced Diploma	18-19	2	2	15	3A			14000	
5B		Short			4400 Courses Subsequent to Initial Vocational Courses: Paraprofessional/Technician	Statement of Attainment	20-50	0.5	1	16	5B	Yes		3227	These courses are generally less than one year in duration but typically have completion of an Advanced Diploma or Diploma as an entrance requirement, making the cumulative duration about three years. An example would be a Graduate Certificate in Packaging.
5B		Short			4500 Courses Subsequent to Initial Vocational Courses: Paraprofessional/Higher Technician	Statement of Attainment, Certificate or not an award course	20-50	0.5	1	16	5B	Yes		4153	Course length is generally less than one year and entry normally requires Diploma level qualifications, making the cumulative duration about three years. Examples are post-professional courses in real estate or teaching.
5B		Medium			3600 Initial Vocational Courses: Professional	Diploma	19-40	3	5	16	3B	Yes		6402	Courses are commonly about 2 years (FTE) in duration, in addition to the prerequisites. Examples include Advanced Diplomas in Information Technology or in Rural Management.
5A		Medium	1st		Bachelor (Pass)	Bachelor of Science, Bachelor of Arts, Bachelor of Economics, Bachelor of Applied Science	18-19	3	3	16	3A		No	478000	
5A		Medium	1st		Bachelor (Honours)	Bachelor Science (Hons), Bachelor of Arts (Hons), Bachelor of Economics (Hon)	18-19	4	4	17	3A			11000	
5A		Medium	2nd		Courses to Qualify Graduates for Further Study (Graduate Certificate)	Grad Certificate of Business, Accounting, Applied Science	30-40	0.5	0.5	16.5	5A (1st, M)	Yes		8000	
5A		Medium	2nd		Courses to Qualify Graduates for Further Study (Bachelor's Graduate Entry)	Bachelor's Graduate Entry in Business, Commerce, Applied Science, etc.	30-23	1	1	17	5A (1st, M)			7200	
5A		Medium	2nd		Graduate Diplomas	Graduate/Post-graduate Diploma (Arts, Applied Science, Science, Humanities, Business, Commerce, etc.)	21-23	1.5	1.5	17.5	5A (1st, M)			63000	
5A		Long	1st		Dentistry	Bachelor of Dentistry, Bachelor of Science (Dentistry)	18-19	5	5	18	3A			6000	
5A		Long	1st		Veterinary Science	Bachelor of Veterinary Medicine and Surgery, Bachelor of Veterinary Science	18-19	5	5	18	3A			6500	
5A		Long	1st		Medicine and Surgery	Bachelor of Medicine and Surgery	18-19	7	7	20	3A			66000	
5A		Long	2nd		Masters degree done by course work	Master of Arts	22-24	2	2	19	5A (1st, M)			49000	
5A		Long	2nd		Masters degree by thesis	Master of Arts	22-24	2	2	19	5A (1st, M)			11000	
5A		Long	2nd		Doctorate (by Course Work)	Doctor of Arts, Business, Science	22-24	2	2	19	5A (1st, M)			400*
6		Very Long			Doctorates	Doctor of Philosophy Science, Engineering, Business, Arts	22-24	3	3	20	5A (1st, M)			24000	
6		Very Long			Doctorates	Doctorates					6			200	

* The enrolments for the university-level are estimated.

Austria

ISCED-97 level	Programme orientation	Cumulative duration at ISCED 5	Position in the national degree/qualification structure (Intermediate, First, Second, etc.)	Notes on programmes that span across ISCED levels or sub-categories	Descriptive name of the programme	Main diplomas, credentials or certifications	Typical starting ages	Theoretical length of the programme	Typical length of the programme	Cumulative years of education at the end of the programme	Minimum entrance requirement	Programme specifically designed for part-time attendance	Reported in the UOE	Enrolment 1996-97	Other relevant information
0	G				Kindergarten		3-5	3	2					215820	
0	G				Vorschulstufe (pre-primary year)		6	1	1					9214	
1	G				Sonderschule (inkl. Heilstättenschulen), Schulstufen 1-4 (special school, stages 1-4)		6	4	4	4				6351	
1	G				Volksschule, 1-4. Schulstufe (primary school)		6	4	4	4				374486	Stages 1-4.
2A	G				Allgemeinbildende höhere Schule, Unterstufe (inkl. Übergangsstufe) (secondary academic school, stages 5-8)	Jahreszeugnis	10	4	4	8	1			102982	Stages 5-8.
2A	G				Volksschule, Oberstufe (primary school, stages 5-8)	Abschlußzeugnis	10	4	4	8	1			84	Stages 5-8.
2A	G				Sonderschule (inkl. Heilstättenschulen), Schulstufen 5-8 (special school, stages 5-8)	Jahreszeugnis	10	4	4	8	1			10202	
2A	G				Hauptschule (main general secondary school)	Abschlußzeugnis	10	4	4	8	1			263681	Stages 5-8.
2A	G				Realschule (programme similar to main general secondary school plus two additional years of education)	Abschlußzeugnis	10	6	6	10	1			2404	
				Levels 2/3/4, A/B, G/V	Externistenprogramme	Abschlußzeugnis, Abschlußprüfungszeugnis, Reifeprüfung, Reife- und Diplomprüfungszeugnis, Berufsreifeprüfung						Yes	No		
3C	P				Haushaltungs-, Hauswirtschaftsschulen (one-year and two-year home-economic schools)	Zeugnis	14	1	1	9	2			3554	Designed to bridge the gap between compulsory education and further education, mainly in the services and health sector.
3C	P				Land- und forstwirtschaftliche mittlere Schulen (1jährig, schulpflichtsentzend) (pre-vocational schools for agriculture and forestry)	Abschlußzeugnis	14	1	1	9	2			1000	One-year course in rural home economics in the last year of compulsory schooling.
3C	P				Polytechnische Schule (pre-vocational year)	Abschlußzeugnis	14	1	1	9	2			18965	One-year programme in the last year of compulsory education, provides an introduction into broad occupational fields; is often followed by apprenticeship.
3C	P				Sonderschule (inkl. Heilstättenschulen), Schulstufen 9 (special school, stages 9)		14	1	1	9	2			1018	Special education based on the curriculum of the pre-vocational year.
3C	V				Pflegehilfelehrgänge (training of auxiliary nurses)	Zeugnis	17	1	1	10	2			2000	Training in basic nursing topics.
3C	V				Schulen zur Ausbildung von Leibeserziehern und Sportlehrern (training of sports instructors)	"Staatlich geprüfter …", where … means an occupational specification; Trainer, Lehrwart	16	2	2	11	2		No	4000	Modular courses for training sports instructors.
3C	P				Berufsbildende Statut-Schulen (soweit nicht anders zugeordnet) (private schools of own statutory right)	Zeugnis	17	2	2	11	2			4000	Vocational or pre-vocational courses offered by private providers that run their own specific programmes (which do not fit into other programmes listed here).
3B	V				Land- und forstwirtschaftliche mittlere Schulen (weiterführend) (vocational schools for agriculture and forestry)	Abschlußzeugnis	14	3	3	11	2			9000	One- to 4-year course leading to a vocational qualification in the independent management of agriculture and forestry; also provides special professional training.
3B	V				Mittlere berufsbildende Schulen (secondary technical and vocational schools)	Abschlußzeugnis	14	3	3	11	2			33000	Full-time instruction providing complete vocational training.
3B	V				Lehre (Duale Ausbildung) (apprenticeship)	Lehrabschlußprüfung	15	3	3	12	2			125000	Vocational training taking place both at the apprentice's workplace and at a vocational school.
3A	G				Allgemeinbildende höhere Schulen, Oberstufe (secondary academic schools)	Reifeprüfung	14	4	4	12	2			77000	General education programme at the upper secondary level; offers access to tertiary programmes.
3A	V			Levels 3/4, completion 4A	Höhere berufsbildende Schulen für Berufstätige (secondary technical and vocational colleges for adults)	Reife- und Diplomprüfungszeugnis	17	4	4	13	2	Yes		6000	Provides adults with the opportunity to upgrade their qualifications.
3A	V				Allgemeinbildende höhere Schulen mit Berufsausbildung (secondary academic schools with vocational training)	Reifeprüfung	14	5	5	13	2			150	Secondary academic school, involving, at the same time, vocational training in the field of crafts.
3A	V			Levels 3/4, completion 4A	Höhere berufsbildende Schulen (secondary technical and vocational colleges)	Reife- und Diplomprüfungszeugnis, Reife- und Befähigungsprüfungszeugnis	14	5	5	13	2			100000	Designed to prepare students with the necessary skills and qualifications for immediate exercise of jobs on the executive level, as well as prepare them for university entry.
3A	G				Allgemeinbildende höhere Schule für Berufstätige (secondary academic schools for adults)	Reifeprüfung	17	4.5	4.5	13.5	2	Yes		3000	Provide adults with the opportunity to upgrade their level of attainment.

Austria (continued)

			Name	Certificate	Entry age	Duration		Exit age	ISCED		Enrol.	Description
4C	V		Mittlere Speziallehrgänge (specialised courses)	Zeugnis	17	1	1	12	3B		1500	Designed for people who have completed initial vocational education; aims at imparting specialised theoretical and practical knowledge.
4C	V		Universitätslehrgänge (Maturaniveau, kürzer als 2 Jahre)	Zeugnis	18	1	1	13	3A		No	Short vocationally oriented courses at the post-secondary level, held at higher education institutions.
4C	V		Höhere Speziallehrgänge (advanced-level specialised courses)	Zeugnis	19	2	2	15	4A		500	Aims at imparting or enhancing specialised theoretical and practical knowledge, target group: graduates of technical and vocational education (TVE) colleges.
4C	V		Sonderpädagogische Lehrgänge (courses for the teaching of children with special needs)	Diplomprüfungszeugnis	19	2	2	15	4A		200	Designed to enable educators and nursery school teachers to deal with all kinds of disabilities.
4B	V		Schulen für den medizinisch-technischen Fachdienst (secondary schools for medical services)	Diplom	17	2.5	2.5	12.5	3C		442	Designed to develop knowledge and skills in laboratory methods (basic), X-ray methods (basic), physiotherapy methods (basic).
4B	V		Schulen für Gesundheits- und Krankenpflege (secondary schools for nursing)	Diplom	16	3	3	13	3C		9564	Practical and theoretical training of nurses.
4A	V		Aufbaulehrgänge (add-on courses)	Reife- und Diplomprüfungszeugnis	17	2	2	14	3B		4000	Prepares graduates of secondary technical and vocational schools or of apprenticeship training for the school-leaving certificate of a secondary TVE college.
5B		Short	Berufspädagogische und land- und forstwirtschaftliche berufspädagogische Akademien (post-secondary colleges for the training of vocational teachers, post-secondary training college for teachers in the field of agriculture and forestry)	Lehramtsprüfung, Befähigungsprüfung	18	2	2	14	3B		766	
5B		Short	Meister- und Werkmeisterausbildung, Bauhandwerkerschulen (master craftsmen and foremen courses, courses for building workers)	Meister, Abschlußprüfungszeugnis	18	2	2	14	3B		5000	Advanced vocational training started after several years of practical experience. Some master courses are shorter than two years. The preparation courses for these programmes are outside the regular school system and are neither obligatory nor is data on enrolments collected.
5B		Short	Kollegs (post-secondary courses in TVE (Technical and Vocational Education)	Diplomprüfungszeugnis	18	2	2	14	3A		4000	Designed to provide graduates of a secondary academic school (or of a different TVE college) with the professional qualifications of a secondary technical and vocational college.
5B		Short	Universitätslehrgänge (Maturaniveau, mindestens 2jährig) (vocationally oriented courses at the post-secondary level, held at higher education institutions)	"akademisch geprüfter ..." plus name of an occupation	18	2	2	14	3A		No	
5B		Short	Kurzstudium an Universitäten und Universitäten der Künste (vocationally oriented studies at universities and universities of the arts which do not lead to a first academic degree but to a qualification similar to an intermediate degree)	"akademisch geprüfter ..." plus name of an occupation	18	3	4	15	3A		1962	
5B		Medium	Akademien zur Ausbildung von Lehrern für allgemeinbildende Pflichtschulen (post-secondary colleges for teacher training)	Lehramtsprüfungszeugnis	18	3	3	15	3A		7438	Teacher training for compulsory education teachers.
5B		Medium	Akademien des Gesundheitswesens (post-secondary colleges for medical services)	Diplom	18	3	3	15	3A		2600	Programmes designed to qualify graduates of secondary academic schools, TVE colleges or nursing schools for employment in the higher levels of the medical services.
5B		Medium	Akademien für Sozialarbeit (post-secondary colleges for social work)	Diplom	18	3	3	15	3A		1276	Programmes designed to qualify graduates of secondary academic schools or TVE colleges for employment in the area of social work.
5A		Medium	Fachhochschulstudium (university education)	Magister (FH), Diplomingenieur (FH)	18	4	4	16	3B		3756	Higher education programmes with a vocational focus.
5A		Long	1st	Diplomstudium und Studium nach alter Studienvorschrift an Universitäten und Universitäten der Künste (4-, 5-, 6jährig und länger) (studies at universities and universities of arts)	Magister, Diplomingenieur, Doktor (first degree)	18	5	7	17	3A		210000	
5A		Long or very long	1st										
5A		Long	2nd	Universitätslehrgänge (postgradual) (post-graduate studies)	Master of Business Administration, Master of Advanced Studies, Universitätsdiplom	23	2	2	19	5A (1st, L)		No	
5A		Long	2nd	Aufbau- und Ergänzungsstudium (post-graduate studies)	"Diplomierter ..." plus name of an occupation; internationales Magisterium	23	2	2	19	5A (1st, L)		2223	Post-graduate studies.
6				Doktoratsstudium (Zweitabschluß) (Doctorate)	Doktor	23	2	3	19	5A (1st, L)		21333	Post-graduate studies leading to a research degree.

Belgium (Flemish Community)

ISCED-97 level	Programme orientation	Cumulative duration at ISCED 5	Position in the national degree/qualification structure (Intermediate, First, Second, etc.)	Notes on programmes that span across ISCED levels or sub-categories	Descriptive name of the programme	Main diplomas, credentials or certifications	Typical starting ages	Theoretical length of the programme	Typical length of the programme	Cumulative years of education at the end of the programme	Minimum entrance requirement	Programme specifically designed for part-time attendance	Reported in the UOE	Enrolment 1996-97	Other relevant information
0					Gewoon kleuteronderwijs (regular nursery education)		2.5-3	3	3					251259	This level of education is not compulsory but free of charges. Nearly all children attend nursery school in Flanders. The staff requirement is a non-university tertiary education diploma (1-cycle).
0					Buitengewoon kleuteronderwijs (special nursery education)		2.5-3	3	3					1784	Enrolment in special education can only be allowed on the basis of the immatriculation report. This report is conducted by the PMS-centrum (guidance centre).
0				Also reported on ISCED 1, 2 and 3	Europese en internationale scholen (European and international schools)		2.5-3	3	3					Unknown	Included for the first time in the 1999 UOE (school year 1997-1998).
1					Gewoon lager onderwijs (regular primary education)	Getuigschrift Basisonderwijs (certificate of elementary education)	6	6	6	6				394248	In most cases, year class systems are used in primary education. Each class has its own teacher. In the first year the systematic apprenticeship of reading, writing and mathematics starts.
1					Buitengewoon lager onderwijs (special primary education)	Getuigschrift Basisonderwijs (certificate of elementary education)	6	6	6-7	6-7				23121	Enrolment in special education can only be allowed on the basis of the immatriculation report. This report is conducted by the PMS-centrum (guidance centre).
1				Also reported on ISCED 2 and 3	Huisonderwijs (home education)	These pupils must pass the examinations of the Examination Board of the Flemish Community								Unknown	The programme provides access to other programmes on the condition that they pass the examinations mentioned. For the first time in UOE 1999 (school year 1997-1998).
1				Also reported on ISCED 0, 2 and 3	Europese en internationale scholen (European and international schools)		6	6	6	6				Unknown	Included for the first time in the 1999 UOE (school year 1997-1998).
1					Basiseducatie (adult basic education)		18+	Variable	Variable			Yes	No	13590	Adult basic education offers education and training to poorly educated adults. The goals of this programme are the teaching and the improvement of basic knowledge, basic skills and attitudes necessary to function in society.
1					Deeltijds kunstonderwijs — lagere graad (part-time artistic education — lower degree)	In general, specific, certificates, complementary to elementary education are granted		4-6	4-6			Yes	No	75418	Part-time artistic education focusing on the 4 traditional forms of expression: image, dance, music and spoken word. The programmes are being offered on a part-time basis (evenings, Wednesday afternoons, weekends). These courses do not belong to compulsory education. Enrolment includes double counts within part-time artistic education and with regular education.
1				Also reported on ISCED 2 to 5B	VDAB-beroepsopleidingen [vocational training focused on the labour market (organised by the VDAB)]	Participants may obtain a certificate for certain courses they have attended. These certificates have no formal or legal value: they are not recognised as equivalent to certificates from the formal education sector	18+	Variable	Variable			Some	No	Unknown	The different initiatives of the VDAB include training students for the secondary and tertiary employment sectors, as well as other more specialised initiatives for unemployed people.
2C V					Buitengewoon secundair onderwijs – opleidingsvorm 1 en 2 (special secondary education – training form 1 and 2)		12-13			6				3932	Enrolment in special education can only be allowed on the basis of the immatriculation report. This report is conducted by the PMS-centrum (guidance centre). Pupils can stay in special secondary education until the age of 21.
2C V				Also reported on ISCED 1 to 5B	VDAB-beroepsopleidingen [vocational training focused on the labour market (organised by the VDAB)]	Participants may obtain a certificate for certain courses they have attended. These certificates have no formal or legal value: they are not recognised as equivalent to certificates from the formal education sector	18+	Variable	Variable			Some	No	Unknown	The different initiatives of the VDAB include training students for the secondary and tertiary employment sectors, as well as other more specialised initiatives for unemployed people.
2C V				Also reported on ISCED 3C	Sociaal-cultureel vormingswerk (social and cultural training)	None	18+	Variable	Variable			Yes	No	Unknown	Social and cultural training is organised by a few recognised associations and financed by the Welfare, Public Health and Culture Department (Ministry of the Flemish Community). Adults participate in this kind of training as leisure and hobby activities.
2B P					Buitengewoon secundair onderwijs – opleidingsvorm 3 – 1ste leerjaar (special secondary education – training form 3 – 1st year)		12-13	1	1	7				1910	Enrolment is for the school year 1997-98.
2B V					Secundair onderwijs voor sociale promotie – LSBL en LSTL (social advancement secondary education: lower secondary vocational courses and lower secondary technical courses)	Certificates are formally equivalent to those of ordinary secondary education		3-4	3-4		See remarks	Yes		51250	These courses can also be organised in a modular system. All persons who reached age 18 and who have completed the compulsory period are admitted. Generally speaking, the requirements are the same as for the corresponding levels of education. For those who have reached age 18 but have not obtained any certificate/diploma of primary or secondary education, admission to the programmes at the secondary level is allowed after successful participation of an entrance exam. Enrolment in language teaching (elementary knowledge) is also included.
2B V					Buitengewoon secundair onderwijs – opleidingsvorm 3 – 2de en 3de leerjaar (special secondary education – training form 3 – 2nd and 3rd year)		13-14	2	2	9-10	See remarks			4813	Enrolment is for the school year 1997-98. Minimum entrance requirement: 2B – P (Buitengewoon secundair onderwijs – opleidingsvorm 3 – 1ste leerjaar).
2A G					Gewoon secundair onderwijs – 1ste graad (regular secondary education – 1st stage)	Getuigschrift van de eerste graad	12	2	2	8	1			137489	

Belgium (Flemish Community) (continued)											
2A	G		Buitengewoon secundair onderwijs – opleidingsvorm 4 – 1ste graad (special secondary education – training form 4 – 1st stage)	Getuigschrift van de eerste graad	12	2	2	8	1		87	Enrolment in special education can only be allowed on the basis of the immatriculation report. This report is conducted by the PMS-centrum (guidance centre).
2A	G	Also reported on ISCED 1 and 3	Huisonderwijs (home education)	These pupils have to pass the examinations of the Examination Board of the Flemish Community							Unknown	This programme only gives access to other programmes when the pupils pass the examinations of the Examination Board of the Flemish Community. Data have been included for the first time in the 1999 UOE (school year 1997-98).
2A	G	Also reported on ISCED 0, 1 and 3	Europese en internationale scholen (European and international schools)		12	2	2	8	1		Unknown	Included for the first time in the 1999 UOE (school year 1997-98).
2A	G	Also reported on ISCED 3 and 5A	Afstandsonderwijs (distance learning)	These pupils/students have to pass the examinations of the Examination Board of the Flemish Community	Variable	Variable	Variable	Variable		Yes	25520	This kind of training is adapted to the needs and the level of the participants. Enrolment includes both general and vocational programmes. The enrolment figures refer to all levels of distance learning.
2A	V		Deeltijds kunstonderwijs – middelbare graad (part-time artistic education – middle degree)	In general, specific certificates, complementary to lower secondary education are granted	Youngsters and adults	3-6	3-6		See remarks	Yes	31699	Part-time artistic education focussing on the 4 traditional forms of expression: image, dance, music and spoken word. The programmes are being offered on a part-time basis (evenings, Wednesday afternoons, weekends). These courses do not belong to compulsory education. Enrolment includes double counts within part-time artistic education and with regular education. One cannot start a middle degree without sufficient training at a lower level (lower degree). Admission tests may be organised for the different classes.
3C	V		Gewoon secundair onderwijs – 2de graad en 1ste en 2de leerjaar van de 3de graad BSO (regular secondary education – 2nd stage and 1st and 2nd year of the 3rd stage BSO)	Studiegetuigschrift van secundair onderwijs after successful completion of the 2nd year in the 3rd stage BSO	14	4-5	4-5	12-13	2A		66560	A 3rd year in the 2nd stage of BSO is optional.
3C	V		Deeltijds beroepssecundair onderwijs (part-time vocational secondary education)	Studiegetuigschrift 2de graad of 3de graad	15-16	3-4	3-4		See remarks		4814	This programme is classified as full-time due to the fact that the pupil is part-time at school and part-time at the workplace. Minimum entrance requirement: age of 16 or 15 if the pupil has completed the 1st stage of secondary education.
3C	V		Experimenteel secundair onderwijs met beperkt leerplan voor sommige categorieën jongeren tussen 18 en 25 jaar (limited curriculum experimental secondary education)	Kwalificatiegetuigschrift	18-25				See remarks		535	This programme is classified as full-time due to the fact that the pupil is part-time at school and part-time at the workplace. Minimum entrance requirement: age between 18 and 25 and having a part-time job.
3C	V		Deeltijds zeevisserij-onderwijs (part-time offshore fishing secondary education)								12	This programme is classified as full-time due to the fact that the pupil is part-time at school and part-time at sea.
3C	V		Opleidingen in de leertijd georganiseerd door het VIZO (apprenticeship training courses organised by VIZO)	Getuigschrift in de leertijd	15	1-3	1-3		Age 15		9449	This programme is classified as full-time due to the fact that the pupil is part-time at a VIZO-centre and part-time at the workplace.
3C	V		Vormingsprogramma's voor de vervulling van de deeltijdse leerplicht (training programmes for compulsory education organised by recognized centres)		15-16				Age 15-16	Yes	Unknown	Included for the first time in the 1999 UOE (school year 1997-98).
3C	V		Buitengewoon secundair onderwijs – opleidingsvorm 3 – 4de en 5de leerjaar (special secondary education – training form 3 – 4th and 5th year)	Certificate	14	2		11-12	See remarks		4645	Enrolment is for the school year 1997-1998. Minimum entrance requirement: 2B - P (Buitengewoon secundair onderwijs – opleidingsvorm 3 – 2de en 3de leerjaar).
3C	V		Buitengewoon secundair onderwijs – opleidingsvorm 4 – 2de graad en 1ste en 2de leerjaar van de 3de graad BSO (special secondary education – training form 4 – 2nd stage and 1st and 2nd years of the 3rd stage BSO)	Studiegetuigschrift van secundair onderwijs after successful completion of the 2nd year in the 3rd stage BSO	14	4	4	12	2A		114	Enrolment in special education can only be allowed on the basis of the immatriculation report. This report is conducted by the PMS-centrum (guidance centre).
3C	V		Secundair onderwijs voor sociale promotie – HSBL en HSTL (social advancement secondary education: upper secondary vocational courses and upper secondary technical courses)	Certificates are formally equivalent to those of ordinary secondary education. In one particular case, there is no equivalency: a certificate of social advancement secondary education (upper cycle) does not give access to higher education as does the "Diploma van secundair onderwijs"		3-4	3-4	12	See remarks	Yes	75407	These courses can also be organised in a modular system. All persons who reached age 18 and who have completed the period of compulsory education are admitted. Generally speaking, the requirements are the same as for the corresponding levels of education. For those who have reached age 18 but have not obtained any certificate/diploma of primary or secondary education, admission to the programmes at the secondary level is allowed after successful participation of an entrance exam. Enrolment in language courses (practical knowledge and advanced knowledge) is included.
3C	G	Also reported on ISCED 0, 1 and 2	Europese en internationale scholen (European and international schools)		14	4	4	12	2A		Unknown	Education programmes in the European and international schools will be classified according to their similarity with the programmes in regular secondary education. Included for the first time in the 1999 UOE (school year 1997-98).
3C	V	Also reported on ISCED 1 to 5B	VDAB-beroepsopleidingen (vocational training focused on the labour market, organised by the VDAB)	Participants may obtain a certificate for certain courses they have attended. These certificates have no formal or legal value; they are not recognised as equivalent to certificates from the formal education sector	18+	Variable				Some	Unknown	The different initiatives of the VDAB include training students for the secondary and tertiary employment sectors, as well as other more specialised initiatives for unemployed people.

Manual for ISCED-97 Implementation in OECD Countries – 1999 Edition

ISCED-97 level	Programme orientation	Cumulative duration at ISCED 5	Position in the national degree/qualification structure (intermediate, first, second, etc.)	Notes on programmes that span across ISCED levels or sub-categories	Descriptive name of the programme	Main diplomas, credentials or certifications	Typical starting ages	Theoretical length of the programme	Typical length of the programme	Cumulative years of education at the end of the programme	Minimum entrance requirement	Programme specifically designed for part-time attendance	Reported in the UOE	Enrolment 1996-97	Other relevant information
Belgium (Flemish Community) (continued)															
3C	V			Also reported on ISCED 2C	Sociaal-cultureel vormingswerk (social and cultural training)	None	18+	Variable	Variable			Yes	No	Unknown	Social and cultural training is organised by a few recognised associations and financed by the Welfare, Public Health and Culture Department (Ministry of the Flemish Community). Adults participate in this kind of training because of leisure and hobby activities.
3A	G				Gewoon secundair onderwijs – 2de graad en 1ste en 2de leerjaar van de 3de graad ASO (regular secondary education – 2nd stage and 1st and 2nd years of the 3rd stage ASO)	Diploma van secundair onderwijs after successful completion of the 2nd year in the 3rd stage	14	4	4	12	2A			117079	
3A	G				Buitengewoon secundair onderwijs – opleidingsvorm 4 – 2de graad en 1ste en 2de leerjaar van de 3de graad ASO (special secondary education – training form 4 – 2nd stage and 1st and 2nd years of the 3rd stage ASO)	Diploma van secundair onderwijs after successful completion of the 2nd year in the 3rd stage	14	4	4	12-13	2A			25	Enrolment in special education can only be allowed on the basis of the immatriculation report. This report is conducted by the PMS-centrum (guidance centre).
3A	G			Also reported on ISCED 2 and 5A	Afstandsonderwijs (distance learning)	These pupils/students have to pass the examinations of the Examination Board of the Flemish Community	Variable	Variable	Variable	Variable	2A	Yes	No	25520	This kind of training is adapted to the needs and the level of the participants. Enrolment includes both general and vocational programmes. The enrolment figures refer to all levels of distance learning.
3A	G			Also reported on ISCED 0, 1 and 2	Europese en internationale scholen (European and international schools)		14	4	4	12	2A			Unknown	Education programmes in the European and international schools will be classified according to their similarity with the programmes in regular secondary education. Included for the first time in the 1999 UOE (school year 1997-98).
3A	V				Gewoon secundair onderwijs – 2de graad en 1ste en 2de leerjaar van de 3de graad TSO en KSO (regular secondary education – 2nd stage and 1st and 2nd year of the 3rd stage TSO and KSO)	Diploma van secundair onderwijs after successful completion of the 2nd year in the 3rd stage	14	4	4	12	2A			96020	
3A	V				Buitengewoon secundair onderwijs – opleidingsvorm 4 – 2de graad en 1ste en 2de leerjaar van de 3de graad TSO en KSO (special secondary education – training form 4 – 2nd stage and 1st and 2nd years of the 3rd stage TSO and KSO)	Diploma van secundair onderwijs after successful completion of the 2nd year in the 3rd stage	14	4	4	12-13	2A			24	Enrolment in special education can only be allowed on the basis of the immatriculation report. This report is conducted by the PMS-centrum (guidance centre).
3A	V				Deeltijds kunstonderwijs – hogere graad (part-time artistic education – higher degree)	In general, specific certificates, complementary to upper secondary education are granted	Youngsters and adults	3-5	3-5		See remarks	Yes	No	26064	Part-time artistic education focussing on the 4 traditional forms of expression: image, dance, music and spoken word. The programmes are being offered on a part-time basis (evenings, Wednesday afternoons, weekends). These courses do not belong to compulsory education. Enrolment includes double counts within part-time artistic education and with regular education. One cannot start a middle degree without sufficient training at a lower level (lower degree). Admission tests may be organised for the different classes.
4C	V				Gewoon secundair onderwijs – 3de leerjaar van de 3de graad TSO, KSO and BSO (regular secondary education – 3rd year of the 3rd stage TSO, KSO and BSO (BSO not giving access to higher education)	Studiegetuigschrift van het 3de leerjaar van de 3de graad		1	1	13	3C			11173	Enrolment includes the students in the 3rd year of the 3rd stage BSO that does not provide access to higher education.
4C	V				Gewoon secundair onderwijs – 4de graad BSO (regular secondary education – 4th stage BSO)	Several possibilities depending on the students' former education		2-3	2-3	15-16	3C (see remarks)			4417	Minimum entrance requirement: completion of the 2nd year of the 3rd stage of vocational secondary education or age 18 and having passed an entrance exam.
4C	V				Ondernemersopleiding georganiseerd door het VIZO (entrepreneurial training courses organised by VIZO)	Diploma ondernemersopleiding		2-3	2-3		See remarks	Yes		19744	Minimum entrance requirement: working in the field of study or former field of study.
4C	V				Secundair onderwijs voor sociale promotie – ASBL (social advancement secondary education: additional secondary vocational courses)	Certificates are formally equivalent to those of ordinary secondary education		3	3			Yes		593	Generally speaking, the requirements are the same as for the corresponding levels of education.
4C	V				Deeltijds kunstonderwijs – specialisatiegraad (part-time artistic education – specialisation degree)	Specific certificates, complementary to the 3rd year of the 3rd stage of artistic secondary education are granted	Youngsters and adults	2	2		See remarks	Yes	No	1736	Part-time artistic education focussing on the 4 traditional forms of expression: image, dance, music and spoken word. The programmes are being offered on a part-time basis (evenings, Wednesday afternoons, weekends). These courses do not belong to compulsory education. Enrolment includes double counts within part-time artistic education and with regular education. One cannot start a middle degree without sufficient training at a lower level (lower degree). Admission tests may be organised for the different classes.
4C	V			Also reported on ISCED 1 to 5B	VDAB-beroepsopleidingen (vocational training focused on the labour market (organised by the VDAB))	Participants may obtain a certificate for certain courses they have attended. These certificates have no formal or legal value; they are not recognised as equivalent to certificates from the formal education sector	18+	Variable	Variable			Some	No	Unknown	The different initiatives of the VDAB are grouped under three headings: training for the secondary and tertiary employment sectors and other more specialised initiatives for unemployed people.
4C	V				Landbouwopleidingen (agricultural training)		18+	Variable	Variable		Working in the field of study	Yes	No	Unknown	
4A	G				Gewoon secundair onderwijs – 3de leerjaar van de 3de graad ASO (regular secondary education – 3rd year of the 3rd stage ASO)	Attest van regelmatige lesbijwoning	18	1	1	13	3A		No	75	

Manual for ISCED-97 Implementation in OECD Countries – 1999 Edition

Belgium (Flemish Community) (continued)									
4A	G		Voorbereidende Divisie van de Koninklijke Militaire School (introductory/preparatory year for students at the Royal Military Academy)		18-24	1	1	13	See remarks		Unknown	Min. entrance requirements: 'Diploma van secundair onderwijs' + age between 18 and 24 + entrance exam.
4A	V		Gewoon secundair onderwijs – 3de leerjaar van de 3de graad BSO (regular secondary education – 3rd year of the 3rd stage BSO giving access to higher education)	Diploma van secundair onderwijs		1	1	13	3C		9137	Enrolment includes the students in the 3rd year of the 3rd stage BSO, which gives access to higher education.
5B		Medium	1st	Hogescholenonderwijs van 1 cyclus (1-cycle higher education provided by hogescholen)	Specific diplomas depending on the programme (e.g. social worker, teacher, physiotherapist, etc.)	18	3-4	3-4	15-16	3A		67135	Even though the programmes are not specifically designed as part-time programmes, part-time enrolment is possible.
5B		Medium	1st	Hoger onderwijs voor sociale promotie (social advancement higher education)	Certificates are formally equivalent to those of hogescholenonderwijs van 1 cyclus	18+	3-6	3-6		3A	Yes	13303	These courses can also be organised in a modular system. Admission to the higher education programmes always requires a certificate of schooling at the secondary level.
5B			1st	Also reported on ISCED 1 to 4C	VDAB-beroepsopleidingen (vocational training focused on the labour market, organised by the VDAB)	Participants may obtain a certificate for certain courses they have attended. These certificates have no formal or legal value: they are not recognised as equivalent to certificates from the formal education sector	18+	Variable				Some	Unknown	The different initiatives of the VDAB are grouped under three headings: training for the secondary and tertiary employment sectors and other more specialised initiatives for unemployed people.
5B		Long	2nd	Voortgezette opleidingen volgend op hogescholenonderwijs van 1 cyclus (advanced studies after 1-cycle higher education provided by hogescholen)	Gediplomeerde in de voortgezette studies		1+	1+		Diploma of higher education		Unknown	Even though the programmes are not specifically designed as part-time programmes, part-time enrolment is possible. Included for the first time in the 1999 UOE (school year 1997-98).
5A		Long	1st	Hogescholenonderwijs van 2 cycli (2-cycle higher education provided by hogescholen)	Licentiate or equivalent degrees (e.g. industrial engineer, etc.)	18	4-5	4-5	16-17	3A		27005	Even though the programmes are not specifically designed as part-time programmes, part-time enrolment is possible. In exceptional cases, an entrance exam is required (e.g. music and drama).
5A		Long	1st	Basisopleidingen aan de universiteiten (inclusief Open Universiteit en afstandsonderwijs) (basic academic education, 2 cycles, including Open University and distance learning)	Licentiate or equivalent degrees (e.g. civil engineer, physician, etc.)	18	4-7	4-7	16-19	3A		56416	Even though the programmes are not specifically designed as part-time programmes, part-time enrolment is possible. Enrolment figures included here do not include "Open University". "Open University" will be included for the first time in the 1999 UOE (school year 1997-98); distance learning will not be included.
5A		Long	2nd	Gediplomeerde in de aanvullende studies (complementary university education)	Gediplomeerde in de aanvullende studies		1+	1+		5A (1st)		2841	Even though the programmes are not specifically designed as part-time programmes, part-time enrolment is possible.
5A		Long	2nd	Gediplomeerde in de gespecialiseerde studies (advanced university education)	Gediplomeerde in de gespecialiseerde studies		1+	1+		5A (1st)		2271	Even though the programmes are not specifically designed as part-time programmes, part-time enrolment is possible.
5A		Long	2nd	Academische lerarenopleiding (academic teacher training)	Geaggregeerde voor het secundair onderwijs – groep 2		1	1				4259	Even though the programmes are not specifically designed as part-time programmes, part-time enrolment is possible. A qualified teacher's degree can be obtained concurrently with or after the Licentiate degree. Enrolment includes double counts with the basic academic studies.
5A		Long	2nd	Voortgezette opleidingen volgend op hogescholenonderwijs van 2 cycli (advanced studies after 2-cycle higher education provided by hogescholen)	Gediplomeerde in de voortgezette studies		1+	1+		Diploma of higher education		Unknown	Even though the programmes are not specifically designed as part-time programmes, part-time enrolment is possible. Included for the first time in the 1999 UOE (school year 1997-98).
5A		Long		Doctoraatsopleiding (doctoral training)	Certificaat van doctoraatsopleiding					5A (1st)+ additional requirements depending on the university		1693	Some universities require participation in this programme, covering a number of courses, seminars, congresses, etc., related to the chosen specialisation for the doctorate. Enrolment includes double counts with doctorates.
6				Doctoraat (doctorate)	Doctor in ...					5A (1st)+ additional requirements depending on the university		2073	Enrolment includes double counts with doctoral training.

73

MANUAL FOR ISCED-97 IMPLEMENTATION IN OECD COUNTRIES – 1999 EDITION

Belgium (French Community)

ISCED-97 level	Programme orientation	Cumulative duration at ISCED 5	Position in the national degree/qualification structure (intermediate, First, Second, etc.)	Notes on programmes that span across ISCED levels or sub-categories	Descriptive name of the programme	Main diplomas, credentials or certifications	Typical starting ages	Theoretical length of the programme	Typical length of the programme	Cumulative years of education at the end of the programme	Minimum entrance requirement	Programme specifically designed for part-time attendance	Reported in the UOE	Enrolment 1996-97	Other relevant information
0					Enseignement préscolaire (pre-school education)		2.5	3	3.5						This programme includes kindergarten and nursery classes.
1					Alphabétisation des adultes (adult literacy courses)		18+	Variable	Variable				No		This training is organised by ASBL, FOREM, CPAS, IBFFP.
1				Levels 1 to 3	Enseignement à domicile donné par la famille ou un précepteur et vérifié par un inspecteur de l'enseignement (home education)	CEB (ISCED 1), CESS (ISCED 3), CQ (ISCED 3)	6	12		12			No		Certificate is delivered by Examination Board of the French Community.
1				Levels 1 to 5B (excluding 5A)	Enseignement à distance (distance learning)							Yes	No		Certificate is delivered by Examination Board of the French Community.
1				Levels 1 to 4	Enseignement de promotion socio-culturelle (social and cultural training)								No		This programme provides music and drawing courses.
1					Cycle préparatoire de l'enseignement de promotion socio-culturelle; arts plastiques (artistic education – lower degree)		6	6	6	6			No		
1					Enseignement primaire ordinaire et spécial (regular and special education)	CEB (Certificat d'étude de base)	6	6	6	6					
1					Formations du FOREM et IBFFP, éducation des adultes – programmes non organisés par un ministère (ASBL, cours de langues, ...) (vocational training focused on the labour market)		18+	Variable	Variable				No		This programme aims to provide adults with labour-market relevant training and allows access to other vocational programmes.
2C	V				Enseignement spécial de forme 1 ou 2; CEFA inférieur, enseignement de promotion sociale secondaire inférieur (Régime 1 et 2) (special secondary education – training form 1 and 2)		12 years (special); 15 (CEFA) + 16 years PS	2-3			CEFA = minimum 2 years of secondary or age of 15	Yes			
2C				2C, 3C	Education permanente (continuing education)	None						Yes	No		This programme includes courses, conferences and training held by associations of continuing education (union, philosophical association, ...).
2B	V				Enseignement spécial de forme 3 Phase I (special secondary education – training form 3)	None		2		8					
2B	V				Enseignement professionnel secondaire ordinaire ou spécial de forme 4 (regular or special secondary education – training form 4)	None	12	2-3		8-9	Age of 12				
2A	V				Enseignement technique (dans l'enseignement secondaire traditionnel de type 2) (technical education, vocational training)	None	12	2-3		8-9	1				
2A	G				Enseignement secondaire général ordinaire ou spécial de forme 4 (regular or special secondary education, 4th form)	None	12	2-3		8-9	1				
3C	V				Enseignement spécial de forme 3 Phases II et III (special secondary education – training form 3)		15	Variable		12	2				
3C	V				Apprentissage des classes moyennes, formations du FOREM et IBFFP, éducation continue des adultes (vocational training focused on the labour market)		Variable	Variable							
3C	V				2e et 3e degrés de l'enseignement professionnel secondaire ordinaire ou spécial de forme 4 (regular or special secondary education – training form 4 – 2nd and 3rd level)	CQ	14	4		12	2				
3C	V				CEFA supérieur et CEFA 18-25; enseignement de promotion sociale secondaire supérieur (Régime 1 et 2) (social advancement secondary education)						2	Yes			

Belgium (French Community) (continued)								
3A	G		2e et 3e degrés de l'enseignement secondaire technique de transition ordinaire ou spécial de forme 4 (technical secondary education – 2nd and 3rd level)	CESS (Certificat d'enseignement secondaire supérieur)	14	4	12	2	
3A	G		2e et 3e degrés de l'enseignement général secondaire ordinaire ou spécial de forme 4 (regular or special secondary education – training form 4)	CESS (Certificat d'enseignement secondaire supérieur)	14	4	12	2	
3A	V		2e et 3e degrés de l'enseignement secondaire technique de qualification ou technique traditionnel ordinaire ou spécial de forme 4 (type 2) (technical secondary education, vocational training)	CESS or CQ	14	4	12	2	
4C	V		Formations des chefs d'entreprises; formation professionnelles des personnes travaillant dans l'agriculture (entrepreneurial training courses, agricultural training)			1-2	13-14	3	
4C	V		Education des adultes (adult education)						This programme provides complementary education on special topics (e.g., in the use of computer software). No
4C	V		La 7e année de l'enseignement professionnel secondaire ne permettant pas d'obtenir le CESS (secondary vocational education, 7th year, not giving access to CESS)	CQ	18	1	13	3	After a first qualification obtained in secondary education, this year of study allows students to acquire a complementary qualification in order to facilitate entry into the labour market.
4C	V		La 7e année de l'enseignement technique de qualification secondaire (secondary technical education, 7th year)	CQ	18	1	13	3	After a normal cycle of technical education, this year of study allows students to acquire a complementary qualification in order to facilitate entry into the labour market.
4C	V		Le 4e degré professionnel complémentaire; l'enseignement professionnel complémentaire de promotion sociale (Régime 2) (social advancement secondary education; additional secondary vocational courses)		18	3	15	3	This training is aimed at the student who has finished the second cycle of the secondary education. The programme does not award a diploma equivalent to higher education diploma. Yes and no
4A	V		La 7e année de l'enseignement professionnel secondaire permettant d'obtenir le CESS (secondary vocational education, 7th year, giving access to CESS)	CESS (Certificat d'enseignement secondaire supérieur)	18	1	13	3	Successful completion of this year, which follows the second cycle of vocational secondary education, allows succeed to access to higher education at ISCED 5B.
4A	G		La 7e année préparatoire à l'enseignement supérieur (pre-university education).	None	18	1	13	3A	This programme is organised in upper secondary institutions and while it requires completion of the secondary cycle for entry it is not required for access to higher education. During this year of study, a student can deepen their knowledge in four subject areas.
5B	Medium	1st	Enseignement de promotion sociale supérieur de type court; enseignement normal technique de promotion sociale (social advancement higher education)			3	15	3	Yes
5B	Medium	1st	Programmes permettant d'accéder au titre de gradué, régent ou instituteurs (higher educational programmes)		18	3	15	3	
5B	Medium	2nd	Diplômes complémentaires de l'enseignement de type court (complementary university education)		21	1	16	3	Specialisation in specific topics.
5A	Long	1st	Programmes permettant d'accéder au titre de licencié, ingénieur, docteur en médecine ou sciences vétérinaires, pharmacien; programmes de l'enseignement de promotion sociale de type long (university education, doctor's course of medicine, veterinary medicine	Licencié, ingénieur, docteur en médecine ou science vétérinaires, pharmacien	18	4-7	16-19	3	The number of years varies between 4 and 7, depending on the field of study.
5A	Long	2nd	Agrégation de l'enseignement secondaire supérieur (advanced university education)		22+	2	17		Programme to become an upper secondary teacher.
5A	Long	2nd	Programmes permettant l'accès à un diplôme complémentaire ou à une maîtrise (complementary university education)		22+	1	17		
5A	Long		Programme de recherche pouvant éventuellement préparer au doctorat (doctoral training)		22+	2+		5A (1st)	
6			Programmes de recherche tels que doctorats et agrégation de l'enseignement supérieur (doctorate)		22+	2+		5	

Canada

ISCED-97 level	Programme orientation	Cumulative duration at ISCED 5	Position in the national degree/qualification structure (Intermediate, First, Second, etc.)	Notes on programmes that span across ISCED levels or sub-categories	Descriptive name of the programme	Main diplomas, credentials or certifications	Typical starting ages	Theoretical length of the programme	Typical length of the programme	Cumulative years of education at the end of the programme	Minimum entrance requirement	Programme specifically designed for part-time attendance	Reported in the UOE	Enrolment 1996-97	Other relevant information
0					Preschool		5	0.5	0.5			Yes		89191	Half-day kindergarten for 5-year-olds in Quebec.
0					Kindergarten/Jr. K.		4-5	1	1					140466	Kindergarten for 4-year-olds in Ontario; kindergarten for 4- to 5-year-olds in New Brunswick, Manitoba, Saskatchewan.
0					Kindergarten		5-6	1	1					147568	
0					Pre-kindergarten/Nursery		2-5.5	3	3					22858	Pre-school or kindergarten programmes for children 2 to 5 years old. Only partially included in UOE.
1				Levels 0 and 1	Primary (3 years)		6	3	3	3	1		Yes	59000	Grades 1 to 3 in Province of Newfoundland.
1					Primary (Kinder to Gr. 3)		5-8	4.5	3.5	3.5					
1					Elementary (3 years)		9-9	3	3	6	1			25733	Grades 4 to 6 in Province of Newfoundland.
1					Grades 1 to 5		6-10	5	5	5				74592	Grades 1 to 5 in Saskatchewan.
1					Primary (6 years)		6	6	6	6				555417	Grade 1 to 6 in Province of Quebec.
1					Adult basic academic upgrading (< 1 year)	Certificate of achievement	18-70	0.83	0.83	9				1715	A typical participant dropped out of public school in grade 8. It takes about 1 year of studies to gain grade 6 equivalency in both maths and language. New Brunswick – Basic Upgrading – skills equivalent to grade 6 in public school system.
2				Levels 1 and 2	Elementary (8 years)		5-7	8	8	8				1474220	Grades 1 to 8 in Ontario and Manitoba.
2					Secondary – 1st stage/Jr. H.S.	Statement of marks	12-13	3	3	9	1			346934	Grades 7 to 9 in Quebec; Grades 7 to 9 in Newfoundland.
2				Levels 1 and 2	Grades 6 to 9		11-14	4	4	9	1			60383	Grades 6 to 9 in Saskatchewan.
3C				Levels 1, 2 and 3	Adult basic academic upgrading	High School Equivalency diploma, Transcripts Certificate	18-30	1-3	1-3	13				161046	These programmes are designed to give adults who have not completed high school a second chance to do so. Programmes are structured on a level basis and offer education ranging from basic skills to high school equivalency.
3A					Secondary 2nd stage	Secondary School Diploma, Dogwood Diploma, Statement of apprenticeship, Provincial school completion certificate	15-17	2	2	11	1, 2			452341	Grades 1-11 in Quebec.
3A					Independent study and mature student programme	Grade 12 diploma	14-20	2	2.5	12			Yes	5000	Correspondence elementary-secondary programme in Manitoba.
3A					Secondary – Sr. H.S.	General High School graduation diploma	15-16	3	3	12	3A			74725	Grades 1 to 12 in Newfoundland; Grades 1 to 12 in Saskatchewan.
3A				Levels 2 and 3	Secondary (4 years)	Grade 12 Diploma	13-15	4	4	12	1			65559	Grades 9 to 12 in Manitoba.
3A				Levels 2 and 3	Secondary (5 years)	Secondary School Diploma	13-14	5	5	12	1			712192	Grades 9 to 13 in Ontario.
3A				Levels 1, 2 and 3	Elementary/Secondary (12 years)		5-7	12	12	12				127259	Grades 1 to 12 in New Brunswick.
4C					Vocational training – other short AFP (1 year)	Attestation of vocational training	16	1	1	10	2			54155	Offered in Quebec as part of secondary school offerings. Requires completion of grade 9 for entry. Enrolment includes enrolment in vocational training (1.5 year).
4C					Vocational training (1.5 year)	Secondary school vocational diploma	16	1.5	1.5	12	2				Vocational secondary school offering in Quebec. Usual entry requirement is completion of grade 9 or 10.
4C					Vocational certificate programme (< 1 year)	Community college certificate, certificate of achievement, attestation of college studies, occupational specific certificate	17-40	0.75	1	13	2, 3A, 3B			106206	Entry-level training in designated trades or skills. May or may not require completion of high school for entry – many of these programmes require completion of grade 9, 10 or 11 for entry. Length of programmes varies from few weeks to months. Enrolment includes enrolment in the vocational training AVS (1 year), enrolment in trade/vocational certificate (1 year) and enrolment in the occupational/technology programme.
4C					Vocational training AVS (1 year)	Attestation of vocational specialisation	16	1	1	13	2				Vocational high school programme offered in Quebec. Students pursue this programme upon the attainment of a Secondary School Vocational Diploma. The programme is generally one year or less in duration.

Canada (continued)									
4C		Trade/vocational certificate (1 year)	Certificate, Applied Certificate, Advanced Certificate	17-65	1	1	13	3A	Usually involve one year of study at a community college or technical institute or other like institute.
4C		Occupational/technology programme	Certificate less than 2 years	18-35	2	2	14	3A, 3B	Mainly technology programmes offered by non-degree community colleges or technical institutes. Programmes that are less than 2 academic years will be allocated to 4C.
4C		Apprenticeship	Certificate of apprenticeship, Certificate of qualification, Journeyperson Certificate, Interprovincial Red Seal for most trades	16-30	1-5	4	16	2	89908 Usually industrial or trades oriented, offering training sufficient for graduates to be certified as apprentices by the provincial department responsible.
4A		University transfer/Quebec	Transcript	18-20	2	2	14		52786 A 2-year programme offered at CEGEPS in Quebec providing entrance to a bachelor degree programme.
5B	1st	Vocational Diploma (18 months)	Occupationally specific vocational diploma	18-30	1.5	1.5	14	3A	Involves two academic years of study in a career, technical, or academic programme.
5B	1st	College diploma programme (2-3 years)	Community college diploma, Diploma of college studies	15-34	2	2	14	3A, 3B	149048 Involves 2-3 years of study in a career, academic or technical programme. Offered in community college or technical institute system. Enrolment figure includes enrolment in Vocational Diploma (18 months), enrolment in occupational/technology programme and enrolment in Vocational Diploma (27 months).
5B	1st	Occupational/technology programme	Diploma – 2 years	18-35	2	2	14	3A, 3B	Mainly technology programmes offered by non-degree community colleges or technical institutes. Programmes that are the equivalent of 2 academic years will be allocated at 5B.
5B	1st	Vocational Diploma (27 months)	Occupationally specific vocational diploma	17-65	2.25	2.25	15	3A	Involves three years of study in a career, technical, or academic programme in a community college or technical institute.
5B	1st	College diploma programme (3-4 years)	Diploma	17-30	3	4	16	3A, 3B	149888 Involves three years of study in a career, technical or academic programme at a community college, or technical institute.
5A	Intermediate	Academic certificate programme (1-2 years)	Undergraduate diploma, C.C.S., C.E.S. in Ed., C.F.L.M., Associate of Arts, Science Degree	18-65	1-2	2	14	3A	Upon completion of these programmes, students can transfer their credits to a university's bachelor degree programmes.
5A	Intermediate	University transfer	Transcript	18-20	2	2	14		48794 University-level programme offered at colleges. Does not include 2-year university prerequisite programmes in Quebec. Normally covers the first two years of a Bachelor's Degree Programme – courses are accepted by universities as being equivalent to their own.
5A	Intermediate	University Diploma Programme	Diploma of Associate in Administration (D.A.A.)	18-40	2	3	14	3A	Non-degree programmes, designed to focus on topics of concern to people who are employed or will be employed in a related field. Cover material pertaining to 1st and 2nd years of a university undergraduate programme. Usually involve 2-3 years of study.
5A	Intermediate	University Certificate (1 year)	Certificate – First cycle	19-20	1	1	15	5B	53638 Upon completion of these programmes, students can transfer their credits to a university's bachelor degree programme. Enrolment figure includes enrolment in University Diploma Programme.
5A	Medium	Bachelor's degree (3-5)	B.A, B.Sc., B.Mus., B.Ed., B.Comm., B.A. (Honours), B. Sc. (Honours), B. Admin.	18-24	4	5	17	3A	640636 Enrolment figure includes enrolment in Academic certificate programme (1-2 years).
5A	1st	Post-graduate certificate programme (1 year)	Post-graduate Certificate, Certificate after Degree, Graduate Level Certificate	22-30	1	1	18	5A (1st, M)	5657 Involves one year of specialised study in a certain disciplines following completion of a Bachelor's degree. Enrolment figure includes enrolment in Post-graduate certificate programme (2 years).
5A	1st	Post-graduate certificate programme (2 years)	Diploma, Post-graduate Certificate, Teaching Certificate	22-30	2	2	19	5A (1st, M)	Involves one year of specialised study in a certain discipline following completion of a Bachelor's degree.
5A	Long 2nd	Master's (1-2 years)	Master's, M.A., M. Sc., LL. M., M. Acc.	21-35	1	2	18	5A (1st, M)	70161 Enrolment figure includes enrolment in Master's (2-3 years).
5A	Long 2nd	Master's (2-3 years)	Master's, M.A., M.Sc., MBA	21-35	2	3	19	5A (1st, M)	
5A	Long 1st	First Professional degree (1-2 years)	Bachelor's degree, B.Ed., B. Theo.	22-30	3	3	19	5A	11200
5A	Very long 1st	First Professional Degree (3-5 years)	M.D., D.D.S., O.D., D.VM., LLB.	21-30	4	5	20	5A	18435
6	Very long 3rd or +	Doctorate	Ph.D	24-40	5	7	22	5A (1st, M)	27582
NC		Intermediate (Gr. 4 to Gr. 10)		9-15	7	7	10		325000

* For ISCED 0,1,2 and 3, the enrolment for school year 1996-97 is estimated.

MANUAL FOR ISCED-97 IMPLEMENTATION IN OECD COUNTRIES – 1999 EDITION

Czech Republic

ISCED-97 level	Programme orientation	Cumulative duration at ISCED 5	Position in the national degree/qualification structure (intermediate, First, Second, etc.)	Notes on programmes that span across ISCED levels or sub-categories	Descriptive name of the programme	Main diplomas, credentials or certifications	Typical starting ages	Theoretical length of the programme	Typical length of the programme	Cumulative years of education at the end of the programme	Minimum entrance requirement	Programme specifically designed for part-time attendance	Reported in the UOE	Enrolment 1996-97	Other relevant information
0	G				Mateřská škola (kindergarten)	No	3	3	3					324316	The purpose of this programme is to develop speech and thinking, mostly through play. This programme is not compulsory, but 1 year of participation prior to entry into primary is recommended. This category includes special kindergartens (7, 157 children).
0	G				Přípravné třídy pro děti ze sociokulturně znevýhodněného prostředí (preparatory classes for socially disadvantaged children)	No	6	1	2.5					241	
0	G				Přípravný ročník na speciálních školách (preparatory year on special schools)	No	6	1	1					127	
0	G				Přípravný stupeň (auxiliary school – preparatory stage)	No	6	1	1					639	For (rather severely) mentally handicapped children.
1	G				Základní škola – 1. stupeň (basic school – 1st stage)	Certificate (vysvědčení)	6	5	5	5				636696	Designed to teach a core knowledge of general, polytechnical, physical, and aesthetic education; 1st stage of compulsory education.
1	G				Speciální základní škola – 1. stupeň (special basic school – 1st stage)	Certificate (vysvědčení)	6	5	5	5				6064	For physically handicapped children.
1	G				Zvláštní škola – 1. a 2. stupeň (remedial school – 1st and 2nd stages)	Certificate (vysvědčení)	6	5	5	5				19510	For children with learning difficulties (including those that are socially disadvantaged).
1	G				Pomocná škola – nižší, střední a vyšší stupeň (auxiliary school – lower, middle and upper stages)	Certificate (vysvědčení)	7							2436	For (rather severely) mentally handicapped children.
2C	G				Zvláštní škola – 3. stupeň (remedial school – 3rd stage)	Certificate (vysvědčení)	11	4	4	9				15836	For children with learning difficulties (including those that are socially disadvantaged).
2C	V				Učiliště – obory se zvláštní upravenými plány (vocational school – programmes with specially modified curriculum)	Certificate on final examination (vysvědčení o závěrečné zkoušce)	15	2	2	11	1			3673	Programme providing less general education and more practical vocational training – for those who left basic school prior to the last grade – organised by upper secondary schools.
2C	V				Odborné učiliště – obory se zvláští upravenými plány (special vocational school – programmes with modified curriculum)	Certificate on final examination (vysvědčení o závěrečné zkoušce) and certificate on apprenticeship (výuční list)	15	2	2	11	1			12493	For children who graduate from remedial schools.
2C	V				Praktická škola (special vocational school)	Certificate on final examination (vysvědčení o závěrečné zkoušce)	15	1-3	3	12	1			2557	Provides practical training for very simple activities; certificate on final examination for 3-year courses only (final certificate for shorter courses).
2C	V				Pracovní stupeň (auxiliary school – working stage)	Certificate (vysvědčení)		2			1			342	For (rather severely) mentally handicapped children.
2A	G				Základní škola – 2. stupeň (basic school – 2st stage)	Certificate (vysvědčení)	11	4	4	9	1			463110	End of compulsory education – further developing what was learned at 1st stage of basic school; for each subject there is a different teacher.
2A	G				Speciální základní škola – 2. stupeň (special basic school – 2st stage)	Certificate (vysvědčení)	11	4	4	9	1			4318	For physically handicapped children.
2A	G				Kursy pro doplnění základního vzdělání (courses for complementing of basic education)	Certificate (vysvědčení)					1	Yes			
2A	G				Kursy pro doplnění vzdělání na zvláštní škole (courses for complementing of education at schools for mentally handicapped)	Certificate (vysvědčení)					1	Yes			
3C	V				Střední odborná škola, studium bez maturity (secondary technical, courses school without maturita)	Certificate on final examination (vysvědčení o závěrečné zkoušce)	15	3	3	12	2			6811	Provides both general and technical education.
3C	V				Střední odborné učiliště, studium bez maturity (secondary vocational school, courses without maturita)	Certificate on final examination (vysvědčení o závěrečné zkoušce) and certificate on apprenticeship (výuční list)	15	3	3	12	2			126677	Provides both general education and practical vocational training.
3C	V				Rekvalifikační kursy (courses for retraining)	Certificate (vysvědčení)							No		
3A	G				Integrovaný 1. ročník (integrated 1st grade)	Certificate (vysvědčení)	15	1	1	10	2			48570	Common 1st year for secondary technical and vocational schools.
3A	G				4leté gymnázium (Gymnasium – 4 years)	Certificate on maturita examination (vysvědčení o maturitní zkoušce)	15	4	4	13	2			180259	Provides broad and thorough general education and prepares students specially for university studies.
3A	V				Střední odborná škola, studium s maturitou (secondary technical school, courses with maturita exam)	Certificate on maturita examination (vysvědčení o maturitní zkoušce)	15	4	4	13	2			180259	Provides both broad general and technical education.
3A	V				Střední odborné učiliště, studium s maturitou (secondary vocational school, courses with maturita)	Certificate on maturita examination (vysvědčení o maturitní zkoušce)	15	4	4	13	2			25048	Provides both broad general and technical education and vocational training.

78

Czech Republic (continued)

3A	G	First 2 years = 2A	Šesté gymnázium (Gymnasium – 6 years)	Certificate on maturita examination (vysvědčení o maturitní zkoušce)	13	6	6	13	1 (+following 2 years of basic school)		45057	Provides broad general education and prepares students mainly for university studies; usually bilingual.
3A	G	First 4 years = 2A	Šesté gymnázium (Gymnasium – 8 years)	Certificate on maturita examination (vysvědčení o maturitní zkoušce)	11	8	8	13	1		32728	Provides broad general education and prepares students mainly for university studies.
3A	G		Studium jednotlivých předmětů (study of selected subjects)	Certificate (vysvědčení)					2	Yes	13564	
4C	V		Nástavbové studium (follow-up courses)	Certificate on maturita examination (vysvědčení o maturitní zkoušce)	19	2	2	14	3C		8351	After completing a secondary technical school without maturita exam the students in this programme prepare for a broader technical qualification.
4C	V		Rekvalifikační kurzy (courses for retraining)	Certificate (osvědčení)					3C	No	70866	After completing a vocational school with a maturita exam the students prepare for a broader technical qualification.
4A	V		Nástavbové studium (follow-up courses)	Certificate on maturita examination (vysvědčení o maturitní zkoušce)	19	2	2	15	3C			
5B	Short	First 4 years = 2A, next 2 years = 3B	Konzervatoř, šesté studium (Conservatoire, 8 years)	Certificate on maturita examination (vysvědčení o maturitní zkoušce) and absolutorium	11	8	8	13	1		581	Prepares dancers.
5B	Short	First 4 years = 3B	Konzervatoř, šesté studium (Conservatoire, 6 years)	Certificate on maturita examination (vysvědčení o maturitní zkoušce) and absolutorium	15	6	6	15	2		2700	Prepares students for performing arts.
5B	Short		Vyšší odborná škola (higher technical school)	Absolutorium	19	2-2.5	2	15	3A, 4A		3028	Post-secondary non-university higher studies – technicians, hotel managers, bank clerks, nurses, etc. – developed from post-secondary studies at upper secondary, 2-2.5 years.
5B	Medium		Vyšší odborná škola (higher technical school)	Absolutorium	19	3-3.5	3	16	3A, 4A		23304	Post-secondary non-university higher studies – technicians, hotel managers, bank clerks, nurses, etc. – developed from post-secondary studies at upper secondary, 3-3.5 years.
5B	Medium		Bakalářské univerzitní studium (Bachelor university study)	Bc. – Bachelor (bakalář) BcA. – Bachelor of Arts (bakalář umění)	19	3	3	16	3A, 4A		Included in the next row	Ending qualification, not giving direct access to Master's studies.
5A	Medium	1st	Bakalářské studium (Bachelor university study)	Bc. – Bachelor (bakalář) BcA. – Bachelor of Arts (bakalář umění)	19	3-4	3	16	3A, 4A		36668	1st stage followed by Master's studies, state exam.
5A	Medium		Učitelství pro 1. stupeň základní školy (teacher training for primary)	Mgr. – Master (magistr)	19	4	4	17	3A, 4A		3953	Mainly teacher training for the primary level. Requires a state exam and defence of thesis.
5A	Long		Magisterské studium (Master university study)	Mgr. – Master (magistr) MgA. – Master of Arts (magistr umění) Ing. – Master (inženýr) Ing. arch. – Master (inženýr architekt)	19	5	5	18	3A, 4A		104525	1st stage of long university studies (without bachelor degree), state exam, defence of thesis.
5A	Long		Magisterské studium (Master university study)	MUDr. – Doctor of medicine (doktor medicíny) MVDr. – Doctor of veterinary medicine (doktor veterinární medicíny)	19	6	6	19	3A, 4A		10682	Medicine, dentistry, veterinary medicine and architecture. Requires a state exam and defence of thesis.
5A	Long		Další vzdělávání (further education)	Certificate (vysvědčení)					5A, Master		4195	Post-graduate studies to earn a pedagogical qualification.
5A	Long		Studium vybraných kurzů (study of selected courses)	Certificate (vysvědčení)						Yes	9776	Complementary courses for students who studied other fields; courses leading to re-qualification.
5A	Long	2nd	Magisterské studium (Master university study)	Mgr. – Master (magistr) MgA. – Master of Arts (magistr umění) Ing. – Master (inženýr) Ing. arch. – Master (inženýr architekt)	22	2-3	2	18	5A, Bachelor		Included in 104 525 Masters above	2nd stage after Bachelor (while it is the first stage in other universities, see above); requires a state exam and defence of thesis.
6	Long		Doktorské studium (doctoral university study)	Ph.D. – Doctor (doktor) Th.D. – Doctor of theology (doktor teologie)	24	3	3	21	5A, Master		10267	Research studies, Ph.D. Requires a state exam and defence of thesis.

Denmark

ISCED-97 level	Programme orientation	Cumulative duration at ISCED 5	Position in the national degree/qualification structure (First, Second, etc.)	Notes on programmes that span across ISCED levels or sub-categories	Descriptive name of the programme	Main diplomas, credentials or certifications	Typical starting ages	Theoretical length of the programme	Typical length of the programme	Cumulative years of education at the end of the programme	Minimum entrance requirement	Programme specifically designed for part-time attendance	Reported in the UOE	Enrolment 1996-97	Other relevant information
0	G				Børnehave (kindergarten)		2-5	4	3					158000	Age-integrated institutions included.
0	G				Børnehaveklasse (pre-school class in primary school)		5-6	1	1					63000	The pre-school class is voluntary for the children, but must be offered by municipalities. 97% accept this offer.
1	G				Grundskolen 1.-6. klasse (primary level 1st-6th grade)		6-7	6	6	6				346000	About 9-11% in government dependent school. A part of comprehensive basic school.
2A	G				Grundskolen 7.-10. Klasse (lower secondary level 7th-10th grade)	Folkeskolens afgangsprøver og udvidede afgangsprøver	12-13	3-4	4	9-10	1			201000	Continuation schools included. Part of comprehensive basic school; 13-15% in government dependent schools. 60% of students take the voluntary 10th grade.
2A	G				Almen voksenuddannelse (AVU) (general adult education 9th-10th grade)	Folkeskolens afgangsprøver, trin 1 og 2	18-50	0.2-1	0.2-1		2A	Yes	No	47000	Certificates correspond to certificates for single courses in grade 9 and 10 in basic school (included in FINANCE 1 and 2).
3C	V				EUD-enkeltfag (upper secondary, open vocational education)	EUD-enkeltfagsprøver, diploma	18-50	0.2-1	0.1		2A	Yes	No	19000	Certificates correspond to certificates for single courses in vocational upper secondary education for young people. Included in FINANCE 1 and 2.
3C	P	Pre-vocational and pre-technical			Erhvervsfaglig grunduddannelse (EGU) (basic vocational education)	EGU-afgangsbevis	16-20	2-3	2	12	2A		No	2000	Individual programme primarily aimed at personal development, although it provides a formal labour market relevant qualification. Not directed towards a specific trade or profession.
3C	V				Social- og sundhedsuddannelserne (SOSU) (social and health service assistant)	Social- og sundhedshjælper- og assistenteksamen	17-30	2-3.5	2	12-13	2A			12000	
3C	V				Eksamensuddannelser (Søfart, etc.) (upper secondary, vocational (maritime ed., etc.))	Afgangsbevis	16-20	3-4	3	13	2A			1000	
3C	V				Landbrugs-, gartner- og skovbrugsuddannelser (agriculture, horticulture, forestry)	Afgangsbevis	16-20	3-4	3	13	2A			2000	
3C	V				Erhvervsfaglige uddannelser (carpenter, blacksmith, electrician) (upper secondary, vocational education)	Afgangsbevis fra erhvervsskole, fagtalent	16-20	3-5	4	14	2A			114000	Primary vocational school. There are 86 different programmes in trade and technical fields. Most programmes between 3 and 4 years.
3C	V				Abejdsmarkedsuddannelserne (AMU) (adult vocational training)	AMU deltagerbevis	18-35	0.02	0.1		2A, 3C		No	176000	
3A	P	Pre-vocational and pre-technical			Håndarbejds- og husholdningsskoler (home economics and needlework)		16-20	0.5	0.5	11	2A	Yes		1000	
3A	G				Folke- og ungdoms Højskoler (folk-and youth high-school)		18-22	0.5	0.5				No	11000	
3A	G				HF-enkeltfag, studentereksamensfag (higher prepatory examination, single subject education)	HF-enkeltfagsprøve, studenterfagsprøve	18-55	0.5-2	1		2A	Yes	No	43000	
3A	G				Højere teknisk eksamen (HTX), Højere handelseksamen (HHX) (upper sec. higher technical ex. higher commercial ex.)	Htx-eksamen, hhx-eksamen	16-17	3	3	12-13	2A			34000	
3A	G				Højere Forberedelseseksamen (HF) (higher prepatory examination)	H-eksamen	170	2	2	12	2A			12000	
3A	G				Gymnasium (upper secondary school leaving examination)	Studentereksamen	16-17	3	3	12-13	2A			60000	
3	P	Pre-vocational and pre-technical			Fri ungdomsuddannelse (individual organised youth education)	Bevis	16-20	2-3	2	12	2A		No	4000	
4C	V				Korte videregående uddannelser af mindre end 2 års varighed, herunder teknikere (technician <2 years)	El-installatør, maskinstøk- niker, modeltekniker, fisken- teknolog, fiskeskipper m.fl.	20-35	1.5	1.5	14	3A, 3C			14000	
4A	P				TIF- kurser (værkstedskurser) (practical admittance courses for programmes at 5B)		18-25	0.5	0.5	12.5	3A, 3C	Yes	No	1000	
4A	G				Adgangskursus til ingeniøruddannelserne Gymnasiale suppleringskurser (admittance courses for programmes at 5A and 5B)		18-30	1	1	15	3C		No	1000	
5B	Short	1st			Tertiary ed. Open education (post-secondary, open education)	HD-eksamen, bachelor, åu-bevis for	18-50	0.5-4	3	13-15	3A	Yes	No	27000	
5B	Short	1st			Korte videregående uddannelser af mere end 2 års varighed, herunder teknikere (tertiary ed. short cycle, including technician >2 years)	Datamatiker, bygggetekniker, maskintekniker	18-30	2-3	2	14	3A, 3C			14000	
5B	Medium	1st			Mellemlange videregående uddannelser (tertiary ed. medium cycle)	Diplomingeniør, maskin- mester, sygeplejerske, folke- skolelærer m.fl.	18-30	3-5	4	16	3A			74000	
5A	Medium	1st			Bachelor	Bachelor B.A., B.Sc. ect.	18-30	3	3	15-16	3A			18000	A relatively new programme introduced in 1989. Relatively few students enter labour market with only a B.A., it is more commonly the first part of a course of studies leading to a M.A.
5A	Long	2nd			Lange videregående uddannelser (kandidatuddannelser) (tertiary ed., long cycle)	Cand. mag., cand. scient., cand. polyt., etc.	21-33	2	3-4	18-20	5A (1st)			40000	
5A	Long	2nd			Lange videregående uddannelser (tertiary ed., long cycle museum conservator, ex. from academi of music)	Konservator, konservatoriuddannelserne	18-30	5-7	6	18-20	3A			30000	The programmes are formally 1st degree, but because all other master degrees are 2nd, we also name these 2nd.
6		Very long	3rd or +		Doktorgrad (doctoral programmes)	Ph.D.	25-35	3	3	21-24	5A (2nd)			3000	
6		Very long			Doktorgrad (Doctorate)	Doktorgrad	30-40	5-10	4				No	100	Not a specific programme, but a degree to reach by several pathways, most often related to the job the person holds.

* The enrolments for school year 1996-97 are estimated.

Finland

ISCED-97 level	Programme orientation	Cumulative duration at ISCED 5	Position in the national degree/qualification structure (intermediate, First, Second, etc.)	Notes on programmes that span across ISCED levels or sub-categories	Descriptive name of the programme	Main diplomas, credentials or certifications	Typical starting ages	Theoretical length of the programme	Typical length of the programme	Cumulative years of education at the end of the programme	Minimum entrance requirement	Programme specifically designed for part-time attendance	Reported in the UOE	Enrolment 1997-98	Other relevant information
0					Esiopetus (preschool education including special education)		3-6	1-4						120000	Kindergartens (3 to 6 years old children) and pre-school classes attached to primary comprehensive schools.
1					Peruskoulun ala-aste (primary schools, including special education)		7	6	6	6				381000	Beginning of compulsory education. Comprehensive school grades 1-6.
2A	G				Peruskoulun ylä-aste (lower secondary schools, including special education)	Leaving certificate, completed the syllabus of the comprehensive school	13	3	3	9	1			205000	Comprehensive school grades 7-9. Compulsory education ends after 9th grade. Includes voluntary 10th grade.
3A	V				Ammatillinen koulu (upper secondary vocational programmes, including apprenticeship)	Leaving certificates, vocational qualifications	16-18	2-3	2-3	11-12	2			144000	Vocational programmes (2 to 3 years). Students must have completed comprehensive school (ISCED 2). Successful completion of vocational programme qualifies for higher studies in both 5A and 5B. Enrolment figure includes apprenticeships.
3A	G				Lukio, ylioppilastutkinto (upper secondary general schools)	The matriculation examination	16	3	3	12	2			126000	General programmes (3 years). Students must have completed comprehensive school (ISCED 2). Successful matriculation examination qualifies for higher studies in both 5A and 5B.
4C	V				Erikoisammattitutkinto (specialist vocational qualifications: a demonstration examination)	Specialist vocational qualifications					3A				A demonstration examination which is taken usually after some years of work experience (for example in crafts and technical skills). Participants must have completed ISCED 3 or have equivalent skills.
5B		Short			Ammatillinen opisto (vocational colleges)	e.g. Technician Engineers, Diploma in Business and Administration, Diploma in Nursing, etc.	19-22	2-3	2-3	14-15	3A			40000	Advanced vocational programmes (2 to 3 years).
5A		Medium	1st		Alemmat korkeakoulututkinnot, kandidaatin tutkinnot (lower university programmes)	Lower university degrees (Bachelors)	20-22	3	3-4	15-16	3A				Lower university programmes (3 years). Students must have completed ISCED 3. Enrolment included in higher university programmes.
5A		Medium	1st		Ammattikorkeakoulu (AMK) (the polytechnics)	Polytechnic degrees	20-22	3.5-4.5	3.5-4.5	15.5-16.5	3A			62000	Programmes (3,5 to 4,5 years) prepare for occupations with high skill requirements. Students must have completed ISCED 3 for entry.
5A		Long	2nd		Ylemmät korkeakoulututkinnot, maisterin tutkinnot (higher university programmes)	Higher university degrees (Master's)	20-22	5-6	6-8	17-19	3A			130000	Higher university programmes (5 to 6 years). Students must have completed ISCED 3 for entry. Graduates qualify for doctorate programmes. Enrolment figure includes both lower and higher university programmes, as well as specialist's degrees.
5A		Very long	3rd or +		Erikoislääkärit, erikoishammaslääkärit, erikoiseläinlääkärit (specialists in medicine, dentistry, veterinary)	Specialists' degree in medicine, dentistry, and veterinary medicine	35	6-8	6-8	24-26	5A (2nd)				Programmes (6 to 8 years) prepare for specialist medical occupations. Practical orientation.
6					Lisensiaatti (Doctorate programmes: licenciate)	Licentiate's degrees	29-35	2		19-20	5A (2nd)			18000	Doctorate studies programmes. Enrolment figure includes both licentiate's programmes and doctor's programmes.
6					Tohtori (Doctorate programmes: doctor)	Doctor's degree	29-35	4		21	5A (2nd)				Doctorate studies programmes. Enrolment included with licentiate's programmes.

France

ISCED-97 level	Programme orientation	Cumulative duration at ISCED 5	Position in the national degree/qualification structure (Intermediate, First, Second, etc.)	Notes on programmes that span across ISCED levels or sub-categories	Descriptive name of the programme	Main diplomas, credentials or certifications	Typical starting ages	Theoretical length of the programme	Typical length of the programme	Cumulative years of education at the end of the programme	Minimum entrance requirement	Programme specifically designed for part-time attendance	Reported in the UOE	Enrolment 1996-97	Other relevant information
0					Enseignement préélémentaire (pre-school education)		2-3	3-4	3					2450000	Pre-school classes are attached to primary comprehensive schools.
1					Enseignement primaire (primary education)		6	5	5	5				4000000	Compulsory for 6-year-olds.
2A	G			2A, 2B	Enseignement du premier cycle du second degré – Collège [secondary education (1st cycle)]	BREVET	11-12	4	4-5	9	1			3360000	Compulsory education, although all students do not complete this programme. It leads to general, vocational and technical education.
3C	V				Enseignement dans le cadre de contrat de qualification (niveau enseignement secondaire) (vocational training for young people without qualification)	CAP, BEP, Baccalauréat professionnel	16-25	1.5	1.5			Yes	No	100000	A work contract lasting between 6 and 24 months.
3C	V				Enseignement de second cycle professionnel du second degré (sous statut scolaire) [secondary education (2nd cycle), vocational training, first level]	Certificat d'aptitude professionnelle (CAP)	15-16	2	2-3	11	2			80000	Most students entering this programme have completed four years of secondary education (1st cycle), although students can prepare a CAP after having completed the two first years of the secondary education (1st cycle).
3C	V				Enseignement de second cycle professionnel du second degré (sous statut scolaire) [secondary education (2nd cycle), vocational training, first level]	Brevet d'études professionnelles (BEP)	15-17	2	2-3	11	2			510000	Typically, it is necessary to complete secondary education (1st cycle) in order to enrol in this programme. The BEP is classified at the same level as the CAP, but it opens more possibilities to continue studies (BP).
3C	V				Enseignement de second cycle professionnel du second degré (en apprentissage) [secondary education (2nd cycle), vocational training, second level]	Certificat d'aptitude professionnelle (CAP)	16-18	2-3	2-3	11	2			185000	The CAP earned through an apprenticeship is at the same level as the CAP earned in an educational institution.
3C	V				Enseignement de second cycle professionnel du second degré (en apprentissage) [secondary education (2nd cycle), vocational training, first level]	Brevet d'études professionnelles (BEP)	16-18	2	2-3	11	2			42000	The BEP prepared earned through apprenticeship is at the same level as the BEP earned in an educational institution.
3C	V				Enseignement de second cycle professionnel du second degré (sous statut scolaire) [secondary education (2nd cycle), vocational training, second level]	Mention complémentaire (MC)	18-19	1	1	12	3B			6000	Certificate prepared in an educational institution, 1 year after the completion of a vocational programme (BEP, CAP).
3C	V				Enseignement de second cycle professionnel du second degré (en apprentissage) [secondary education (2nd cycle), vocational training, second level]	Mention complémentaire (MC)	18-19		1	12				7000	Certificate earned through an apprenticeship, 1 year after the completion of a vocational programme (BEP, CAP).
3C	V				Enseignement des écoles sanitaires et sociales (specific schools)	Diplôme d'aide soignante, auxiliaire de puériculture, aide médico-pédagogique, aide à domicile	16-20	1-3	1-3	13	2		No	16000	Programmes offered in co-operation with the Ministry of Health.
3C	V				Enseignement de second cycle professionnel du second degré (en apprentissage) [secondary education (2nd cycle), vocational training, second level]	Brevet professionnel (BP)	18-22	2	2	14	3B			25000	In certain jobs the BP is necessary to become a craftsman. It is a programme undertaken through apprenticeship after the completion of a CAP.
3B	V				Enseignement de second cycle professionnel du second degré (sous statut scolaire) [secondary education (2nd cycle), vocational training, second level]	Baccalauréat professionnel	18-19	2	2	13	3B			150000	This programme allows for direct labour market entry. However, a minority of students who earn this baccalaureate continues their studies, primarily at enseignement des classes des sections de techniciens supérieurs (STS).
3B	V				Enseignement de second cycle professionnel du second degré (en apprentissage) [secondary education (2nd cycle), vocational training, second level]	Baccalauréat professionnel	18-20	2	2	13	3B			20000	This apprenticeship programme allows for direct labour market entry. However, a minority of students who earn this baccalaureate continues their studies, primarily at enseignement des classes des sections de techniciens supérieurs (STS).
3A	G				Enseignement de second cycle général du second degré [secondary education (2nd cycle), general]	Baccalauréat général	15-16	3	3-4	12	2			1100000	Almost all the persons with this diploma follow their studies in the higher educational system.
3A	G			3A, 3B	Enseignement de second cycle technologique du second degré [secondary education (2nd cycle), technology]	Baccalauréat technologique	16-17	3	3-4	12	2			480000	A major part of the students with this diploma follow their studies in the higher educational system, in general in a technical institute (IUT, STS).
4C	V				Enseignement des écoles sanitaires et sociales (specific schools)	Diplôme de moniteur éducateur, éducateur technique spécialisé	18-20	2-4		14				8000	Programmes offered in co-operation with the Ministry of Health.
4A	G				Enseignement pré-universitaire (pre-university education)	Diplôme de la capacité en droit, diplôme d'accès aux études universitaires	17-20	1-2		13				16000	Programmes allowing to access to the first cycle of university.

France (continued)										Yes	No	
5B	Short	1st	Enseignement dans le cadre de contrat de qualification (niveau enseignement supérieur) (vocational training for young people without qualification)	Brevet de technicien supérieur (BTS)	20-25	1.5	1.5	14			20000	Work contracts lasting between 6 and 24 months.
5B	Short	1st	Enseignement en institut universitaire de technologie (IUT) [specific vocational training (university)]	Diplôme universitaire de technologie DUT	18-20	2	2	14	3A, 3B		110000	This programme is at the same level as the BTS, although opens more possibilities to continue studies. The DUT is a technical programme, although most of the students enrolled in this section have a general baccalauréate.
5B	Short	1st	Enseignement d'écoles supérieures spécialisées (enseignement court, conduisant au niveau bac +2 ou bac +3) (specific schools)	Diplômes professionnels divers (éducateur spécialisé, laborantin, assistante sociale, etc.)	18-20	2-3	2-3	14	3A, 3B		70000	Short vocational training provided by specific schools. The majority of the training is in the paramedical and social sectors.
5B	Short	1st	Enseignement des classes des sections de techniciens supérieurs (sous statut scolaire) [specific vocational training (secondary schools)]	Brevet de technicien supérieur (BTS)	18-20	2	2	14	3A, 3B		235000	This programme has the same level as the DUT but it gives less possibility to continue the studies. The BTS is a more specialised programme than the DUT.
5B	Short	1st	Enseignement des classes des sections de techniciens supérieurs (en apprentissage) [specific vocational training (secondary schools)]	Brevet de technicien supérieur (BTS)	19-21	2	2	14	3B		20000	This programme has the same level as the DUT but it gives less possibility to continue studies. The BTS is a more specialised programme than the DUT.
5B	Short	Intermediate	Enseignement des classes préparatoires aux grandes écoles (CPGE) [specific general training (secondary schools)]	Concours d'entrée à une école d'ingénieur ou commerciale	17-19	2	2	14	3A, 3B		80000	The preparatory classes (CPGE), which generally recruit students that have earned the baccalauréat général, are 2- to 3-year programmes to prepare students to take the entrance examination for one of the grandes écoles, where the programmes typically last an additional 3 years.
5A	Short	Intermediate	Enseignement de premier cycle des études universitaires (university education, 1st cycle)	Diplôme d'études universitaires générales (DEUG)	18-20	2	2	14	3A, 3B		625000	The first two years of study in a 3-year programme leading to the first university diploma (licence).
5A	Medium	1st	Enseignement de deuxième cycle des études universitaires (university education, 2nd cycle, 1st year)	LICENCE	20-22	1	1	15			240000	The licence year follows the first two years of DEUG. Students coming from IUT or CPGE can also enter this university year (1st year, second cycle).
5A	Medium	1st	Enseignement des écoles d'ingénieur (higher engineering school)	Diplôme d'ingénieur	19-22	3-4	3-4	18			75000	There are several types of engineer schools (both private and public). They primarily select students coming from preparatory schools (CPGE) or who have performed well at university (after having earned the licence or maîtrise).
5A	Medium or long	1st	Enseignement des écoles de commerce (higher business school)	Diplôme d'ingénieur commercial	19-22	3	3-4	18			50000	There are several types of schools of commerce and management. They primarily select students coming from preparatory schools (CPGE) or who have performed well at university (after having earned the licence or maîtrise).
5A	Medium or long	2nd	Enseignement de deuxième cycle des études universitaires (university education, 2nd cycle, 2nd year)	MAITRISE	21-23	1	1	16	5A (1st, M)		200000	This programme follows the year of "licence". It is necessary to have a "maîtrise" to prepare a third cycle.
5A	Medium	1st	Diverses formations: architecture, études vétérinaires, art, etc... Écoles supérieures spécialisées (conduisant au niveau bac +4 ou bac +5) (specific schools)	Diplômes professionnels divers (notaire, architecte, vétérinaire, journaliste,...)	18-22	3-4	3-4	18	3A, 3B		30000	
5A	Long	2nd	Enseignement en institut universitaire de formation des maîtres (IUFM) (university departement)	Contest of recruitment of 1st and 2nd degree teachers, continuing education for teachers, CAPES, Professeur des écoles	21-30	2	2	17	5A (1st, M)		85000	Two year programme in pedagogy to prepare students to be teachers.
5A	Long	3rd or +	Enseignement de troisième cycle des études universitaires (university education, 3rd cycle)	Diplôme d'études supérieures spécialisées (DESS)	22-25	1	1	17	5A (2nd)		35000	This 1-year programme follows the maîtrise. The DESS is, in general, a terminal diploma.
5A	Very long	1st	Enseignement dans les universités qui comporte ces spécialités de formation (university education)	Diplôme de pharmacie, diplôme de dentiste	18-19	5	5	18	3A, 3B		35000	At the end of the first year of university studies, a limited number of students are selected to follow this programme in pharmacy or dentistry.
5A	Very long	1st	Enseignement dans les universités qui comporte cette spécialité de formation (university education)	Docteur en médecine	18-19	7	7	20	3A, 3B		115000	At the end of the first year of university studies, a limited number of students are selected to follow this programme in medicine.
5A	Very long	2nd	Enseignement de spécialisation des métiers de la santé (university education)	Diplôme d'études spécialisées	23-26	3	3	22	5A (1st, L)		30000	Studies leading to a specialisation in medicine.
6	Long	1st	Enseignement de troisième cycle des études universitaires (university education, 3rd cycle)	Diplôme d'études approfondies (DEA)	22-25	1	1	17	5A (2nd)		35000	This 1-year programme follows the maîtrise. The DEA is a necessary diploma to in order to earn a Doctorate.
6	Very long	2nd	Enseignement de troisième cycle des études universitaires (Doctorate)	Diplôme de docteur	23-26	3	3-4	20	5A (2nd)		65000	Three years of research following the DEA year.

MANUAL FOR ISCED-97 IMPLEMENTATION IN OECD COUNTRIES – 1999 EDITION

Germany

ISCED-97 level	Programme orientation	Descriptive name of the programme	Main diplomas, credentials or certifications	Typical starting ages	Theoretical length of the programme	Typical length of the programme	Cumulative years of education at the end of the programme	Minimum entrance requirement	Enrolment 1996-97	Other relevant information
0		01 Kindergarten (kindergartens)		3	3	3			2261100	Centre-based institutions for children aged 3 to less than 6. The programme includes educational activities. As a rule, the staff have special educational qualifications, which are officially recognised.
0		02 Schulkindergarten (school kindergartens)		6	1	1			42995	School-based programme for children of at least compulsory school age (6 years) who are not yet ready to attend primary school. They prepare for entry into primary school. As a rule, staff have teaching qualifications. Most are attached to primary schools
0		03 Vorklassen (pre-school classes)		5	1	1			39425	School-based programme designed for children from the age of 5 to under 6 who are capable to attend school but who have not yet reached compulsory school age (6 years). As a rule, staff have teaching qualifications. Mostly attached to primary schools.
1		04 Primary schools		6	4	4	4		3859490	Programme is marked by the beginning of systematic studies characteristic for primary education. Start of compulsory education (first four years of schooling) at age 6. Prepares children for secondary schools.
2A	G	05 Lower secondary schools, no access to general	Hauptschul-/Realschulabschluß	10	6	6	10	1	3292501	Programme (grades 5 to 9 or 10) following 4 years of primary school, which is marked by the beginning of subject presentation and enables students to enter education in the Dual System (17) or to attend different programmes at vocational schools.
2A	G	06 Lower secondary schools, access to general	Realschulabschluß (Gymnasium, Integrierte Gesamtschule, Freie Waldorfschule)	18-35	6	6	10	1	2033063	Programme (grades 5 to 10) following 4 years of primary school which is marked by the beginning of subject presentation. Successful graduates are entitled to enter studies at upper secondary general schools (22) which qualify for ISCED 5A programmes.
2A	G	07 Kollegschulen, die einen mittleren Bildungsabschluß vermitteln (Kollegschulen: intermediate school certificate)	Realschulabschluß or equivalent	17-18	1	1	11		1032	General programme attended by students after completion of compulsory full-time schooling. Awards a certificate equivalent to the intermediate school certificate. Graduates qualify for ISCED 3A or 3B.
2A	G	08 Lower secondary schools evening schools	Hauptschul-/Realschulabschluß	18-35	2	2	12	1	14566	Programme (of 1-2 years of duration) especially intended for adults with no or lower graduation (e.g. Hauptschulabschluß) who want to obtain a higher qualification at lower secondary education (mostly Realschulabschluß).
2A	G	09 Berufsaufbauschulen (vocational extension schools)	Realschulabschluß/Fachschulreife	18-22	1	1	14	2	2851	Gen. programme (1 to 2 years) designed for students with Hauptschulabschluß only who want to obtain an intermediate school certificate. Students undergo at the same time vocational training or pursue an occupation. Graduates qualify for ISCED 3A or 3B.
2A	P	10 Berufsvorbereitungsjahr (pre-vocational training year)	Abschlußzeugnis Berufsvorbereitungsjahr	16-18	1	1	11		65198	1-year pre-vocational programme designed for students with 9 or 10 years of general education who did not obtain a contract in the Dual System. It prepares students for vocational training (ISCED 3B).
3B	V	11 Berufsschulen, die einen mittleren Bildungsabschluß vermitteln (specialised vocational schools: intermediate school certificate)	Realschulabschluß or equivalent	16-17	1	2	11	2	121467	Vocational programme attended by students after completion of compulsory full-time schooling. Awards a certificate equivalent to the intermediate school certificate. Successful completion may lead to a reduction of the duration of training in the Dual System (ISCED 3B).
3B	V	12 Berufsgrundbildungsjahr (basic vocational training year)	Abschlußzeugnis Berufsgrundbildungsjahr	16-18	1	1	11	2	39966	1-year vocational programme with both general and occupational field-related basic education. This programme substitutes the first year of the Dual System (ISCED 3B). Students must have successfully completed ISCED 2.
3B	V	13 Berufsfachschulen, die berufliche Grundkenntnisse vermitteln (specialised vocational schools: basic vocational knowledge)	Abschlußzeugnis Berufsfachschule (Berufliche Grundkenntnisse)	16-17	1	1	11	2	55733	Voc. programme which includes both general and occupational field-related basic education. Attended by students with intermediate school certificate (Realschulabschluß). Successful completion may lead to a reduction of the duration of training in the Dual System.
3B	V	14 Schulen des Gesundheitswesens, 1 jährig (health sector schools, 1 year)	Abschlußzeugnis Schulen für medizinische Hilfsberufe	19-20	1	1	14	2	4955	School-based vocational education (1 year) for auxiliary medical occupations. Often these schools are associated with hospitals where training is provided in theory and practice. Students must have completed ISCED 2. Designed for direct labour market entry.
3B	V	15 Kollegschulen, die einen Berufsabschluß vermitteln (Kollegschulen: occupational qualification)	Beruflicher Abschluß	17-18	2	3	12	2	62878	School-based vocational programme for special occupations which awards a qualification equivalent to the Dual System. Students must have completed ISCED 2. Graduates qualify for Fachoberschulen (ISCED 4A). Fachschulen (ISCED 5B) and for entry into the labour market.
3B	V	16 Berufsfachschulen, die einen Berufsabschluß vermitteln (specialised vocational schools: occupational qualification)	Beruflicher Abschluß	16-17	3	3	13	2	90655	School-based vocational programme for special occupations which awards a qualification equivalent to the Dual System. Students must have completed ISCED 5B) and for entry into the labour market.
3B	V	17 Berufsschulen (Duales System) (Dual System)	Lehrabschluß	16-18	3	3	13	2	1247465	Special form of apprenticeship which comprises education and training both at a vocational school and in an enterprise. Students must have completed ISCED 2. Graduates qualify for Fachoberschulen (4A), Fachschulen (5B) or for entry into the labour market.
3A	G	18 Fachoberschulen, 2 jährig (specialised vocational high schools, 2 years)	Fachhochschulreife	16-18	2	2	12	2	73376	Upper secondary general programme (2 years). Students must have the intermediate school certificate. Graduates have equivalent qualification as in programme 24, i.e. they are entitled to start studies at Fachhochschulen (ISCED 5A).
3A	G	19 Berufsschulen, die eine Studienberechtigung vermitteln (specialised vocational schools: qualification for ISCED 5A)	Fachhochschulreife/Hochschulreife	16-17	2	3	12	2	39893	Upper secondary general programme (2 or 3 years). Students must have an intermediate school certificate or equivalent. Graduates are entitled to start studies at ISCED 5A (equivalent to programmes 20 and 21).
3A	G	20 Kollegschulen, die eine Studienberechtigung für ISCED 5A, also in some cases occupational qualification)	Fachhochschulreife/Hochschulreife and Beruflicher Abschluß (in some cases)	17-18	2	3	12	2	17493	Upper secondary general programme (2 or 3 years). Students must have an intermediate school certificate or equivalent. Graduates are entitled to start studies at ISCED 5A. In some cases students also obtain additional qualifications equivalent to the Dual System (ISCED 3B).
3A	G	21 Fachgymnasien (Fachgymnasien)	Hochschulreife	16-17	3	3	13	2	90179	Upper secondary general programme (3 years) with a large part of vocational courses. Students must have an intermediate school certificate or equivalent. Graduates are entitled to start studies at ISCED 5A.
3A	G	22 Upper secondary schools (general)	Abitur (Hochschulreife)	16-17	3	3	13	2	691124	3-year upper secondary general programme comprising grades 11 to 13. It is attended by students who have successfully completed programme 06. Successful graduates of this programme are entitled to enter ISCED 5A programmes.

84

Germany (continued)

4B	V		23 Berufsschulen (Duales System) (Dual System)	Lehrabschluß	19-21	3	3	16	3B		18506	Special form of apprenticeship (second cycle) which comprises education and training both at a vocational school and in an enterprise. Students must have completed ISCED 3B. Graduates qualify for Fachoberschulen (4A), Fachschulen (5B) or for entry into the labour market.
4A	G		24 Fachoberschulen, 1 jährig (specialised vocational high schools, 1 year)	Fachhochschulreife	19-20	1	1	14	2, 3B		7903	Second cycle general programme (1 year). Both the intermediate school certificate and the successful completion of education in the Dual System are entrance requirements. Graduates are entitled to start studies at Fachhochschulen (ISCED 5A).
4A	G		25 Berufsoberschulen/Technische Oberschulen	Hochschulreife	19-20	2	2	15	2, 3B		3743	Second cycle general programme (2 years). Both the intermediate school certificate and the successful completion of vocational education (ISCED 3B) are required by students in this programme. Graduates are entitled to start studies at ISCED 5A.
4A	V		26 Berufsfachschulen, die einen Berufsabschluß vermitteln (specialised vocational schools: occupational qualification)	Beruflicher Abschluß	19-20	3	3	16	3A		22072	School-based vocational programme (second cycle) for special occupations which awards a qualification according to the Dual System. Students must have completed ISCED 3A. Graduates qualify for Fachschulen (ISCED 5B) and for entry into the labour market.
4A	V		27 Berufsschulen (Duales System) (Dual System)	Lehrabschluß	19-21	3	3	16	3A		192897	Special form of apprenticeship (second cycle) which comprises education and training both at a vocational school and in an enterprise. Students must have completed ISCED 3A. Additionally graduates qualify for Fachs. (5B) or for entry into the labour market.
4A	G		28 Upper secondary evening schools	Abitur (Hochschulreife)	19-35	3	3	16	2, 3B		30496	3-year general upper secondary programme for adult students. Admission requirements include: minimum age of 19, completion of vocational training or at least 3 years work experience. Successful graduates of this programme are entitled to enter ISCED 5A programmes.
5B		Short or medium	29 Fachakademien (Bavaria) (specialised academies)	Abschluß der Fachakademie/ Fachhochschulreife (in some cases)	19-20	2	2	15	2, 3B		7919	Tertiary dual programme which prepares for entry into a advanced vocational career. Requires both the intermediate school certificate and completion of the Dual System or practical experience which served the occupation. Designed for direct labour market entry.
5B		Short	30 Schulen des Gesundheitswesens, 2 jährig (health sector schools, 2 years)	Abschlußzeugnis für medizinische Assistenten	19-20	2	2	15	2		17807	School-based vocational education (2 years) for medical assistants. Often these schools are associated with hospitals where training is provided in theory and practice. Designed for direct labour market entry.
5B		Short	31 F412, 2 jährig (trade and technical schools, 2 years)	Fachschulabschluß, Meister/Techniker, Erzieher	21-23	2	2	15	2, 3B		75923	Advanced vocational programme (2 years). Attended after completion of the Dual System and several years of work experience to obtain master's/technician's qualifications or to qualify for occupations in the social sector. Aims at direct labour market entry.
5B		Medium	32 Fachschulen, 3 jährig (trade and technical schools, 3 years)	Fachschulabschluß, Meister/Techniker, Erzieher	21-23	3	3	16	2, 3B	Yes	53421	Advanced vocational programme (3 years), mainly part-time. Attended after compl. of the Dual System and several years of work exp. to obtain a master's/technician's qualif. or to qualify for occupations in the social sector. Aims at direct labour market entry.
5B		Medium	33 Fachschulen, 4 jährig (trade and technical schools, 4 years)	Fachschulabschluß, Meister/Techniker	21-24	4	4	17	2, 3B	Yes	21856	Advanced part-time vocational programme (4 years). Attended after successful completion of the Dual System and several years of work experience to obtain a master's/technician's qualification. Aims at direct labour market entry.
5B		Medium	34 Schulen des Gesundheitswesens, 3 jährig (health sector schools, 3 years)	Abschlußzeugnis für Krankenschwestern/-pfleger	19-20	3	3	16	2		11927	School-based vocational education (3 years) for nurses, midwives, etc. Often these schools are associated with hospitals where training is provided in theory and practice. Designed for direct labour market entry.
5B		Medium	35 Berufsakademien (Schleswig-Holstein) (vocational academies)	Abschluß der Berufsakademie	20-22	3	3	16	3A		m	Tertiary dual vocational programme (at academies and in enterprises) which prepares for higher-level positions in business. Students must already hold a qualification for ISCED 5A programmes. Designed for direct labour market entry.
5B		Medium	36 Berufsakademien (Baden-Württemberg) (vocational academies)	Diplom (BA)	19-20	3	3	16	3A	No	9850	Tertiary dual programme (2 to 3 years) which comprises both science-oriented and practice-related vocational education at academies and training enterprises. Students must already hold a qualification allowing entry to an ISCED 5A programme. Designed for direct labour market entry.
5B		Medium	37 Verwaltungsfachhochschulen (colleges of public administration)	Diplom (FH)	19-20	3	3	16	3A		42603	Special type of "Fachhochschulen" run by the public administration to provide training for the medium-level non-technical career within the public sector. Students must already hold a qualification allowing entry to an ISCED 5A programme. Designed for direct entry into civil service.
5A		Medium or long	38 Fachhochschulen	Diplom (FH)	19-24	4	5	17	3A		397192	Programme (4 or 5 years) at the university level which prepares for occupations which require the application of scientific findings and methods. Students must at least have completed Fachoberschule (18, 24) or equivalent. First degree.
5A		Long or very long	39 Universitäten (university studies)	Diplom oder Staatsprüfung	19-24	5	6.5	18	3A		1398304	Programme of universities (i.e. in academic disciplines) of 5 to 7 years which prepare for occupations which require the application of scientific knowledge and methods. Students must have completed ISCED 3A. First degree. Graduates may enter ISCED 6.
6		Short, medium or long	40 Promotionsstudium (doctoral studies)	Promotion	25-29	2	4	20	5A (1st, L)	No	m	Doctoral studies programme (2 to 5 years). In most cases students must have successfully completed programmes at universities. A doctoral degree is awarded to successful graduates.

Greece

ISCED-97 level	Programme orientation	Cumulative duration at ISCED 5	Position in the national degree/qualification structure (intermediate, First, Second, etc.)	Notes on programmes that span across ISCED levels or sub-categories	Descriptive name of the programme	Main diplomas, credentials or certifications	Typical starting ages	Theoretical length of the programme	Typical length of the programme	Cumulative years of education at the end of the programme	Minimum entrance requirement	Programme specifically designed for part-time attendance	Reported in the UOE	Enrolment 1995-96	Other relevant information
0					Nepiagogeion (kindergarten)		4	1-2	1-2					133000	The aim of kindergarten is to help children's physical, emotional, social and mental development, within the framework of the broader aims of the primary and secondary education.
1A	G				Dimotikon (elementary school)	Titlos spoydon	6	6	6	6				724000	The aim of the elementary school is the physical and mental development of the students within the framework of the general aims and objectives of primary and secondary education.
2A	G				Gymnasion (Gymnasium: lower secondary education)	Apolytirio	12	3	3	9				439000	Attendance at a Gymnasium is compulsory. The purpose of the Gymnasium is to promote the pupils' all-round development in relation to the abilities which they have at this age, and the corresponding demands of life.
3C	V				Technika kai Epagelmatika Ekpaideftiria (technical-vocational training institutes: TEE, from 1998)	Ptychio	15	2-3	2-3	11-12				22000	According to a recent law some changes applied to the Greek educational system. This new type of institutes, which will replace the Technical Vocational Schools (TES) will include two areas of studies for a total duration of three years.
3A	G				Eniaio Lykeio (comprehensive Lyceum)	Ethniko apolytirio	15	3	3	12				391814	
4C	V				Instituto Epagelmatikis Katartisis (institute of vocational training (upper secondary education) – IEK)	Certification of vocational training	18	0.5-2	0.5-2	13-14				26000	New reforms in the Greek education system regarding primary and secondary education were made during the period 1992-93, including the creation of a National System for Vocational Education and Training, which comprises a number of public and private institutions.
5B		Medium	1st		Technologika Ekpaideftika Idrimata (technological education institutions: non-university type institutions – TEI)	Ptychio	18	3-4	3-4	15.5				64000	Non-university studies lasting 3 years, in general, although some majors (fields of study) call for an additional 6-month on-the-job practical training.
5A		Medium	1st		Programmata Spoudon Epilogis (extended university programmes)	Ptychio	18	4	4	16					
5A		Medium	1st		Anotata Ekpaideftika Idrimata – Panepsistimo (universities and university type institutions (AEI))	Ptychio	18	4-6	4-6	16-18				111000	Universities and Polytechnic Schools (AEI) offer the highest level of education and related degrees and diplomas. Under the 1992 law, studies leading to a first degree last at least 4 years for the majority of disciplines, 5 years for engineering studies.
5A		Long	1st		Anoikto Panepsistimio (Greek Open University)	Ptychio	25+	8	20						
5A		Long	2nd		Metaptychiako (post-graduate studies, Master)	Metaptychiako diploma spoydon	22	1-2	1-2	17-18				352	
6					Didactoriko (post-graduate studies, Doctorate)	Didactoriko diploma	23	2-4	2-4	19-21				669	The Ph.D. degree typically requires the submission of a thesis or dissertation of publishable quality which is the product of original research and represents a significant contribution to knowledge.

MANUAL FOR ISCED-97 IMPLEMENTATION IN OECD COUNTRIES – 1999 EDITION

Hungary

ISCED-97 level	Programme orientation	Cumulative duration at ISCED 5	Position in the national degree/qualification structure (Intermediate, First, Second, etc.)	Notes on programmes that span across ISCED levels or sub-categories	Descriptive name of the programme	Main diplomas, credentials or certifications	Typical starting ages	Theoretical length of the programme	Typical length of the programme	Cumulative years of education at the end of the programme	Minimum entrance requirement	Programme specifically designed for part-time attendance	Reported in the UOE	Enrolment 1997-98	Other relevant information
0	G				01 Óvoda (kindergarten, of which one-year compulsory pre-school education)	Iskolaérettségi bizonyítvány (school maturity report)	3	3	3-4					383486	School-based programme for children aged 3-7. Includes basic skills development, pre-reading, drawing, singing and school preparation. Kindergarten are sometimes (but not often) attached to primary schools.
0	G				02 Gyógypedagógiai óvoda (kindergarten, special education)	Iskolaérettségi bizonyítvány (school maturity report)	3	3	4					1183	School-based programme for children of age 3-7. Basic skills development programmes with special corrective skills development. Special education kindergartens are usually attached to special education primary schools.
1A	G				03 Általános iskola 1-4. (general school primary level, Grades 1-4)	Certificate	6-7	4	4	4				483998	Primary education, including classroom teaching, basic reading, maths, science and social studies, singing, sports, arts education, etc. (National Core Curriculum, Key Stage Grade 4).
1A	G				04 Gyógypedagógiai általános iskola előkészítő és 1-4. évfolyam (general school primary level, Grades preparatory and 1-4, special education)	Certificate	7	4	5	4				19904	Primary education with special corrective skills development (National Core Curriculum, Key Stage Grade 4 with allowances by type of handicap).
1A	G				05 Dolgozók általános iskolája 1-4. évfolyam (adult literacy courses)	Certificate	25+	1-2	1	4		Yes		154	Adult literacy course for illiterates and early dropouts.
2A	G				06 Általános iskola 5-8, 6 és 8. évfolyamos gimnázium 7-8., ill. 5-8. (general school upper level, Grades 5-8, and Grades 5-8 and 7-8 of the eight-year and six-year general secondary programmes, respectively)	Certificate	10-11	4	4	8	1			479553	Lower secondary education (National Core Curriculum Key Stage Grade 8).
2A	G				07 Gyógypedagógiai általános iskola 5-8. (general school upper level, special education)	Certificate	11-12	4	5	8	1			22465	Lower secondary education, with compensatory skills development (National Core Curriculum Key Stage Grade 8).
2A	P				08 Művészeti általános iskola (basic – lower secondary – education with art/music pre-vocational programmes)	Certificate	10-11	4	4	8	1				Lower secondary education with additional music, dance, or sports teaching in preparation for higher studies in these areas (National Core Curriculum Key Stage Grade 8). Enrolment is included in 06.
2A	G				09 Felnőttek általános iskolája 5-8. évfolyam (est, levelező, távoktatás) (general school upper level part-time)	Certificate	16-40	4	2	8	1	Yes		3011	Lower secondary education. Target group: youth and adult drop-outs and late maturers, re-entrants.
2B	G				10 Felzárkóztató általános iskola programok (second chance programmes for late maturers preparing for Level 3 education)	Certificate	14-20	1-2	2	8	1		No		Remedial programme for drop-outs and poor learners that provides a second chance for further education. Typically attended by late maturers and low achievers.
2C	V			Vocational or technical	11 Szakiskola alapfokú iskola végzettség nélkül számukra (vocational programmes requiring less than 10 years of completed general education)	Vocational certificate	16-24	2	2	10	1		No		NVQL (National Vocational Qualification List) training in programmes that do not require the completion of basic education for entry.
2C	P				12 Speciális gyógypedagógiai szakiskola (értelmi fogyatékosok részére) (vocational education for special education children)	School progress report	16-18	4	5	12	1			5260	Basic skills and labour market oriented development programme for special education children.
3C	G				19 Általános iskola, szakiskola általánosan képző 9-10. évfolyamai (basic education programme of the vocational school)	Certificate	14-15	2	2	10	2			10289	Grades 9-10 – general subject courses preparing pupils for entering into to NVQL programmes that require 10 years of general education.
3C	P			Vocational or technical (disappears by 2000)	20 Szakmunkásképző iskola 1985. Törvény szerint (vocational school-3 according to the Education Act of 1985)	Vocational certificate	14-15	2-3	3	10-11	2			132637	Three-year general/vocational programme, starting after grade 8 of the general school. 1997/98 is the last year of new enrolments, because the new law does not allow dual-system vocational education before age 16.
3C	V			Vocational or technical	21 Szakiskolai szakképző évfolyamok és programok (vocational programmes preparing for NVQL examinations)	NVQL vocational certificate	16-17	1-2	1	11-12	3CG			985	NVQL training in programmes where the entry requirement is the completion of basic education (entry requirement the completion of Grade 10).
3C	V			Vocational or technical	22 Szakiskolai szakképző évfolyamok és programok (est, levelező képzés) (vocational programmes preparing for NVQL examinations, part-time)	NVQL vocational certificate	18-40	1-2	2	11-12	3CG	Yes			NVQL training in programmes where the entry requirement is the completion of basic education (Grade 10) (part-time and distance learning programmes).
3B	P				18 Felnőttek szakközépiskolája 9-12. évfolyam (upper vocational secondary part-time programmes, pre-matura course)	Érettségi bizonyítvány (certificate of the Maturity Examination)	17-40	4	4	12	2	Yes		13368	Upper level part-time secondary education preparing pupils for the Maturity Examination with pre-vocational programme elements.
3A	G				13 Gimnázium 9-12. évfolyam (grammar school)	Érettségi bizonyítvány (certificate of the Maturity Examination)	14-15	4	4	12	2			136260	Upper level general secondary education preparing pupils for the Maturity Examination.
3A	G				14 Kéttannyelvű gimnázium/szakközépiskola 9-13. évfolyam (bilingual upper secondary school)	Érettségi bizonyítvány (certificate of the Maturity Examination)	14-15	5	5	13	2			8006	Upper level bilingual secondary education preparing pupils for the Maturity Examination.

87

Hungary (continued)

ISCED-97 level	Programme orientation	Cumulative duration at ISCED 5	Position in the national degree/qualification structure (Intermediate, First, Second, etc.)	Notes on programmes that span across ISCED levels or sub-categories	#	Descriptive name of the programme	Main diplomas, credentials or certifications	Typical starting ages	Theoretical length of the programme	Typical length of the programme	Cumulative years of education at the end of the programme	Minimum entrance requirement	Programme specifically designed for part-time attendance	Reported in the UOE	Enrolment 1997-98	Other relevant information
3A	P				15	Szakközépiskola nappali képzés 9-12. évfolyam (secondary vocational school – pre-matura stage)	Érettségi bizonyítvány (certificate of the Maturity Examination)	14-15	4	4	12	2			181216	Upper level secondary education preparing pupils for the Maturity Examination with pre-vocational programme elements.
3A	P			Continuation of the Level 2 equivalent (08)	16	Művészeti szakközépiskola 9-13. évfolyam (upper secondary education with art/music pre-vocational programmes)	Érettségi bizonyítvány (certificate of the Maturity Examination)	14-15	5	5	13	2AP			3765	Upper level general secondary education preparing pupils for the Maturity Examination with parallel art/music pre-vocational and vocation training.
3A	G				17	Felnőttek gimnáziuma 9-12. évfolyam (upper secondary part-time programmes)	Érettségi bizonyítvány (certificate of the Maturity Examination)	17-40	4	3	12	2	Yes		25734	Upper level part-time secondary education preparing pupils for the Maturity Examination.
4C	V			Vocational or technical	23	Szakképző évfolyamok és programok érettségire épülő OKJ szakmákban (post-secondary vocational programmes)	NVQL vocational certificate (post-secondary)	18-19	1-2	1	13-14	3A			39398	NVQL training in programmes where the entry requirement is the completion of secondary education (Maturity Examination).
4C	V			Vocational or technical	24	Szakképző évfolyamok és programok érettségire épülő OKJ szakmákban (esti-levelező) (post-secondary vocational programmes, part-time)	NVQL vocational certificate (post-secondary)	18-40	1-2	2	13-14	3A	Yes		6308	NVQL vocational training with the Maturity Examination as an entry requirement (part-time and distance education programmes).
4A	G				25	Szakmunkások érettségire felkészítő középiskolája (general secondary programme for vocational school graduates)	Érettségi bizonyítvány (certificate of the Maturity Examination)	17-18	2-3	2-3	13-14	3CV			32882	General secondary programme preparing for the Maturity Examination for graduates of 3C vocational programmes.
5B					26	Akkreditált iskolai rendszerű, felsőfokú szakképzés (post-secondary vocational programmes accredited by the Hungarian Higher Education Accreditation Committee)	NVQL vocational certificate (post-secondary)	18-20	1-2	1-2	13-14	3A		No		Programmes leading to "non-graduate" vocational qualifications with credit courses acknowledged in higher education.
5A		Medium	1st		28	6 és 7 féléves főiskolai szintű első alapképzések (college first programmes – 3 years)	College diploma in (+ fields of study)	18-20	3	4	15	3A			14928	Business school, kindergarten teacher training, engineering.
5A		Medium	1st		29	8 féléves főiskolai szintű első alapképzések (college graduate education – 4 years)	College diploma in (+ fields of study)	18-20	4	4	16	3A			54135	Teacher training, sports, healthcare, art and music higher education, etc.
5A		Medium	1st		30	8 és 9 féléves egyetemi szintű első alapképzések (university first programmes – 4 years)	University diploma in (+ fields of study)	18-20	4-5	4	16	3A				Languages and social studies.
5A		Long	1st		31	10 féléves egyetemi szintű első alapképzés (university first programmes – 5 years)	University diploma in (+ fields of study)	18-20	5	5	17	3A			75314	University diploma (engineering, business and economy, sciences, arts and languages, education, law, agriculture, veterinary, dentistry).
5A		Long	1st		32	11 és 12 féléves egyetemi szintű első alapképzés (university first programmes – 6 years)	University diploma in (+ fields of study)	18-20	6	6	18	3A			8512	University of medicine.
5A		Long	2nd		27	Szakképzés felsőfokú végzettséggel igénylő OKJ szakmákra (vocational programmes with an entrance requirement of Level 5 qualification)	NVQL vocational qualification	23-62	2	2	19	5A (1st, M)	*	No		NVQL vocational programmes in areas like auditing, etc.
5A		Long	2nd		33	Főiskolai szakirányú továbbképzés (college post-graduate specialisation programme)	Diploma (+ field of specialisation)	30-55	1-2	1-2	17	5A (1st, M)				Specialisation programmes for college graduates. Enrolment is included in Egyetemi szakirányú továbbképzés (university post-graduate specialisation programme).
5A		Long	2nd		34	Kiegészítő egyetemi képzés főiskolai végzettek számára (mérnök, közgazdász, agrármérnök, nyelvtanár) (university supplementary programme)	University diploma in (+ field of study)	22-29	2	2	18-19	5A (1st, M)				Master programmes for college graduates. Enrolment is included in Műszaki tanárképzés műszaki főiskolát végzetteknek (supplementary teacher training programme for engineers).
5A		Long	2nd		35	Műszaki tanárképzés műszaki főiskolát végzetteknek (supplementary teacher training programme for engineers)	Teacher diploma in (+ field of engineering studies)	22-29	2	2	17	5A (1st, M)			3055	Teacher training for engineers.
5A		Very long	2nd		36	Egyetemi szakirányú továbbképzés (university post-graduate specialisation programme)	Diploma (+ field of specialisation)	30-55	2	2	19	5A (1st, L)			17031	Specialisation programmes for university graduates.
5A					37	DLA (művészképzésben megfelel a Ph.D.-nek) (doctoral degree in liberal arts)	Doctoral degree in liberal arts (DLA)	27-50	3	3	20	5A (1st, L)			35	Studies for a higher degree in art and music.
6					38	Ph.D. (doctoral programme)	Doctoral (Ph. D.) degree	27-50	3	3	20	5A (1st, L)			3970	Ph.D. courses, research work, and dissertation.

Iceland

ISCED-97 level	Programme orientation	Cumulative duration at ISCED 5	Position in the national degree/qualification structure (Intermediate, First, Second, etc.)	Notes on programmes that span across ISCED levels or sub-categories	Descriptive name of the programme	Main diplomas, credentials or certifications	Typical starting ages	Theoretical length of the programme	Typical length of the programme	Cumulative years of education at the end of the programme	Minimum entrance requirement	Programme specifically designed for part-time attendance	Reported in the UOE	Enrolment 1996-97	Other relevant information
0					Leikskóli (pre-primary schools)	None	3-5	3	1-3					14600	
1					Grunnskóli I (primary schools 1st section)	None	6	7	7	7				29300	The Icelandic grunnskóli is a comprehensive single structure, compulsory with 10 grades for children age 6-15. Grades 1-7 (first section) have been allocated to ISCED 1. There is no certificate given at the completion of each grade except the last one, the tenth.
2B	P				Sérdeildir fatlaðra (special education programmes for the mentally handicapped)	Certificate on leaving school	16	1-2	1.5	11-12				80	Special education programme.
2A	G				Grunnskóli II (primary school 2nd section)	Primary level certificate	13	3	3	10	1			12800	The Icelandic grunnskóli is a comprehensive single structure with 10 grades, compulsory for children age 6-15. Grades 8-10 have been allocated to ISCED 2. Upon completion of grunnskóli the pupil has general access to programmes in schools at Level ISCED 3
2A	G				Fornám í framhaldsskóla (preparatory programmes at the upper secondary level)	Certificate on leaving school	16	1	1	11				300	This is a programme for students who need additional instruction in the grunnskóli teaching material to be prepared for upper secondary education.
3C	V				Vélstjórn 1. stig (marine engineering programmes, 1st grade)	Marine engineer certificate 1st grade	16-18	0.5	0.5	10.5	2			80	Each level of study in the marine engineer's programme gives the right to work with larger engines.
3C	V				1 s árs verknámsbraut framhaldsskólastigs (1-year upper secondary level vocational programmes)	Upper secondary level vocational 1-year certificate	16	1	1	11	2			100	
3C	V				Búfræði á framhaldsskólastigi (agricultural programmes, 1-year programme at upper secondary level)	Certificate in agriculture at second level upper stage	17-21	1-2	1-2	11-12	2			80	
3C	V				Skipstjórn 1. stig (marine captain programmes, 1st grade)	Marine captain's 1st grade certificate	18-26	1	1	11-12	2			70	Each level of study in the marine captain's programme gives the right to work with larger vessels.
3C	V				Skipstjórn 2. stig (marine captain programmes, 2nd grade)	Marine captain's 2nd grade certificate	23-31	1	1	12-13	3C			40	Each level of study in the marine captain's programme gives the right to work with larger vessels.
3C	V				Vélstjórn 2. stig (marine engineering programmes, 2nd grade)	Marine engineer certificate 2nd grade	17-19	1.5	1.5	12	3C			100	Each level of study in the marine engineer's programme gives the right to work with larger engines.
3C	V				Löggilt iðngrein 2ja ára (certified indentured trades, 2 years contract time)	School certificate	16-17	2.5	2.5	12-13	2			20	Those who acquire the school certificate after having completed the programmes in school and fulfilled the apprenticeship contract with a trade master, proceed to journeyman's examination.
3C	V				2ja ára verknámsbrautir framhaldsskólastigs (upper secondary level vocational 2-year programmes)	Upper secondary level vocational 2-year certificate	16-17	2	2	12	2			1000	
3C	V				Sveinspróf í löggiltri iðngrein (exam for a journeyman's qualification in a certified indentured trade)	Journeyman's certificate	20-24	0-0	0-0	13-14	3C			800	The journeyman's qualification is acquired after completing school education in a certified trade and fulfilment of contract time between the apprentice and master. Only after completing the journeyman's exam can the journeyman practice his trade.

Iceland (continued)

ISCED-97 level	Programme orientation	Cumulative duration at ISCED 5	Position in the national degree/qualification structure (intermediate, First, Second, etc.)	Notes on programmes that span across ISCED levels or sub-categories	Descriptive name of the programme	Main diplomas, credentials or certifications	Typical starting ages	Theoretical length of the programme	Typical length of the programme	Cumulative years of education at the end of the programme	Minimum entrance requirement	Programme specifically designed for part-time attendance	Reported in the UOE	Enrolment 1996-97	Other relevant information
3C	V				Skipstjórn 3. stig (marine captain programmes, 3rd grade)	Marine captain's 3rd grade certificate	24-32	1	1	13-14	3C			0	Each level of study in the marine captain's programme gives the right to work with larger vessels.
3C	V				Garðyrkja á framhaldsskólastigi (horticulture 2-3 years programmes at upper secondary level)	Examination in horticulture	21-26	2-3	2-3	13-15	3A			25	
3C	V				Heilbrigðisgreinar 3ja ára á framhaldsskólastigi (health related auxiliary 3-year programmes at upper secondary level)	Health related auxiliary 3-year certificate	16-17	3	3	13	2			300	
3C	V				3ja ára verknámsbraut framhaldsskólastigs (upper secondary level vocational 3-year programmes)	Upper secondary level vocational 3-year certificate	16	3	3	13	2			450	
3C	V				Löggilt iðngrein 3ja ára (certified indentured trades, 3-year contract time)	School certificate	17-25	3	3	13	2			200	Those who acquire the school certificate after having completed the programmes in school and fulfilled the apprenticeship contract with a trade master, proceed to journeyman's examination.
3C	V				Vélsjórn 3. stig (marine engineering programmes, 3rd grade)	Marine engineer certificate 3rd grade	18-20	1.5	1.5	13.5	3C			100	Each level of study in the marine engineer's programme gives the right to work with larger engines.
3C	V				Fiskvinnsla á framhaldsskólastigi (fish processing programmes at upper secondary level)	Fish processing certificate	17-18	2	2	14	3A			50	
3C	V				Löggilt iðngrein 4ra ára (certified indentured trades, 4-year contract time)	School certificate	16-25	4	4	14	2			2600	Those who acquire the school certificate after having completed the programmes in school and fulfilled the apprenticeship contract with a trade master, proceed to journeyman's examination.
3C	V				Heilbrigðisgreinar 4ra ára á framhaldsskólastigi (health related auxiliary 4-year programmes at upper secondary level)	Health related auxiliary 4-year certificate	17-19	4	4	14	2			60	
3C	V				Heilbrigðisgreinar 5 ára á framhaldsskólastigi (health related auxiliary 5-year programmes at upper secondary level)	Health related auxiliary examination	16-17	5	5	15	2			50	
3B	P				Listnám á framhaldsskólastigi (fine and applied arts at upper secondary level)	Fine arts examination	16-20	4	4	14	2			200	Sometimes these programmes are attended part-time alongside of other more general studies.
3A	G				2ja ára bóknámsbraut framhaldsskólastigs (upper secondary level general 2-year programmes)	Upper secondary level general 2-year certificate	16-17	2	2	12	2			300	
3A	G				Frumgreinadeild Samvinnuháskóla, eins árs (preparatory courses to commercial college, 1 year)	Qualification to further studies	25	1	1	14	3C			20	This is a preparatory course to a specified private commercial college; all the students have considerable work experience and previous studies at second level, general or vocational.
3A	G				Bóknámsbraut til stúdentsprófs, 4ra ára (general programmes leading to matriculation examination at upper secondary level, 4 years)	Stúdentspróf. Matriculation examination certificate (granting access to university studies)	16	4	4	14	2			11300	
3A	G				Tækninbraut til stúdentsprófs (technical course to matriculation examination at upper secondary level)	Matriculation examination	19-22	2	2	15-16	3C			50	A course for students who have completed another vocational programme at the upper secondary level, giving access to the tertiary level.
3A	G				Frumgreinadeild Tækniskóla 2 ár (preparatory courses to technical college, 2 years)	Qualification to further studies	22-26	2	2	15-16	3C			130	This is a preparatory course to a specified technical college; all the students have considerable work experience and previous vocational studies at second level.
4C	V				Skipstjórn 4. stig (marine captain programmes at post-secondary level, 4th grade)	Marine captain certificate, 4th grade	21-35	1	1	14-15	3C			0	Each level of study in the marine captain's programme gives the right to work with larger vessels.

Iceland (continued)									Yes	No	
4C	V		Meistaranám í lögiltri iðngrein (trade master's programmes at post-secondary level in a certified indentured trade)	Trade master's certificate	23-30	1	1	14-15	3C			130	Trade master's certificate is a precondition for the trade master to practice his trade as an employer.
4C	V		Vélstjórn 4. stig (marine engineering programmes at post-secondary level, 4th grade)	Marine engineer certificate, 4th grade	20-24	1.5	1.5	15	3C			50	Each level of study in the marine engineer's programme gives the right to work with larger engines.
4C	V		Heilbrigðisgreinar 1,5 ár á millinámsstigi (health related auxiliary 1.5-year programmes at post-secondary level)	Health related auxiliary intermediate level certificate without university degree	21	1.5	1.5	15-16	3A			10	
4C	V		Löfntræði í tækniskóla, 1,5 ár (short technical programmes at post-secondary level, 1.5 years)	Technician's certificate	23-25	1.5	1.5	15-16	3A			20	These are programmes to a technician's certificate; all the students have considerable work experience and previous vocational studies at second level plus at least 1-year general studies, i.e. the first year of the preparatory courses to the technical college.
5B	Short		Æðra nám í 2 ár í háskóladgráðu (tertiary programmes 2 years not leading to a university degree)	Tertiary diploma without university degree	21-25	2	2	16	3A			500	
5B	Medium		Æðra nám í 3 ár í háskóladgráðu (tertiary programmes 3 years not leading to a university degree)	Tertiary diploma without university degree	21-23	3	3	17	3A			400	
5B	Medium		Listnám í æðri skóla, 3ja ára (fine and applied arts at tertiary level, 3 years)	Fine arts certificate without university degree	21-25	3	3	17	3A, 3B			200	
5B	Medium		Listnám í æðri skóla, 4ra ára (fine and applied arts at tertiary level, 4 years)	Fine arts certificate without university degree	19-23	4	4	18	3A, 3B			25	
5B	Medium	1st	Háskólanám tækniffræði 3,5 ára til fyrstu gráðu (tertiary technical programmes 3.5 years, first university degree)	B.Sc. in technical college	22-25	3.5	3.5	20	3A			160	The participants in these programmes usually have a trades certificate (4 years study duration) and 2-year general preparatory courses, and after that they go over to the technical studies to acquire a B.Sc. degree in engineering.
5A	Medium	1st	Háskólanám 3ja ára til fyrstu gráðu (tertiary programmes 3 years, first university degree)	B.A. or B.Sc. or B.Ed	20-24	3	3-4	17-18 del	3A			3500	
5A	Medium	1st	Háskólanám 4ra ára til fyrstu gráðu (tertiary programmes 4 years, first university degree)	B.Sc., Cand. (name of field)	20-22	4	4-5	18	3A			1400	
5A	Medium		Háskólanám, 1 viðbótarár ofan á 3 ár, ekki viðbótargráða (tertiary programmes, 1 year in addition to 3-year studies, not leading to a second degree)	Credentials without degree-awarding	33-37	1	1	18	5A			200	This is a one-year programme that provides a diploma or a certificate, but does not give a second tertiary degree at a higher level.
5A	Long		Háskólanám, 1 viðbótarár ofan á 4 ár, ekki viðbótargráða (Tertiary programmes 1 year in addition to 4 years studies, not leading to a second degree)	Credentials without degree-awarding	29-31	2	2	19	5A			50	This is a one-year programme that provides a diploma or a certificate, but does not give a second tertiary degree at a higher level.
5A	Long	1st	Háskólanám 5 ára til fyrstu gráðu (tertiary programmes, 5 years, first university degree)	Cand. (name of field)	20-22	5	5-6	19	3A			600	
5A	Long	1st	Háskólanám 6 ára til fyrstu gráðu (tertiary programmes, 6 years, first university degree)	Cand. (name of field)	20-21	6	6-7	20	3A			400	
5A	Long	2nd	Háskólanám, 2 viðbótarár ofan á 3 ár, leiðir viðbótargráða (tertiary programmes, 2 years in addition to 3-year studies, leading to a second degree)	M.A. or M.Sc. or M.Ed.	23-27	2	2	19	5A			200	
6			Doktorsnám (Ph.D.)	Ph.D.	26-36	4		23	5A			10	The Ph.D. programme is a recent programme at the University of Iceland. Thus, we do not have information on the typical length of the programme.

Manual for ISCED-97 Implementation in OECD Countries – 1999 Edition

ISCED-97 level	Programme orientation	Cumulative duration at ISCED 5	Position in the national degree/qualification structure (intermediate, First, Second, etc.)	Notes on programmes that span across ISCED levels or sub-categories	Descriptive name of the programme	Main diplomas, credentials or certifications	Typical starting ages	Theoretical length of the programme	Typical length of the programme	Cumulative years of education at the end of the programme	Minimum entrance requirement	Programme specifically designed for part-time attendance	Reported in the UOE	Enrolment 1996-97	Other relevant information
Ireland															
0					Pre-primary education (early start + private)	None	3-4	1	1				No	3987	Only a very small number is reported in the UOE. Most of these pupils are missing from the data collection
1					Primary education	None	4-5	8	8	8				474213	Programme is divided into two ISCED levels in the UOE data collection, ISCED 0 and ISCED 1. For UOE reporting, ISCED Level 0 comprises the first two years of this programme.
2C	P				Youth Reach (Youth Reach II)	Basic Skills Training Certificate	15	2	1	10-11			No	1770	For young persons who have dropped out of lower secondary education. About 30 per cent of participants complete the 2-year programme.
2A	G				Junior Certificate (and JCEP)	Junior Certificate	12-13	3	3	11	1			199571	
3C	P				Core VTOS	Junior Cert., Leaving Cert., NCVA Foundation Level, NCVA Level 1 and NCVA Level 2	21+	2	1.5	11	1		No	2300	Provides second chance education to long-term unemployed adults.
3C	G				Transition year programme	None	15-16	1	1	12	2			24300	
3C	P				Leaving Certificate Applied	Leaving Certificate Applied	15-16	2	2	13-14	2			3595	The Leaving Certificate Applied is intended to meet the needs of those students who are not adequately catered for by other Leaving Certificate programmes or who chose not to opt for such programmes.
3A	P				Leaving Certificate Vocational Programme	Leaving Certificate Vocational	15-16	2	2	13-14	2			16511	
3A	G				Leaving Certificate (established)	Leaving Certificate	15-16	2	2	13-14	2			109320	
4C	V				Diploma in Horticulture (Teagasc)	Diploma in Horticulture (Teagasc)	18-19	1	1	13-14	2			400	
4C	V				Apprenticeship	National Craft Certificate	17-18	4	4	13-15	2			4100	Usually industrial or trades oriented.
4C	V				Vocational preparation and training II (PLC) Yr. 1 and 2	NCVA Level 2 Award	17-19	1-3	1	14-15	3			18720	
4C	V				Secretarial/Technical Training Programme	Certificate	17-18	1	1	14	2			2750	
4C	V				Certificate in Farming (Teagasc)	Certificate in Farming (Teagasc)	18-19	3	3	14-16	2			1165	
5B		Short	1st		Cadetship (Army, Air Corps and Naval Service Training)	Diploma in Military Studies	18-19	1.75	1.75	15	3A			7	21 months of full-time study (3 500 hours).
5B		Short	1st		Certificate (NCEA, IoT)	Certificate (NCEA, IoT)	17-19	2	2	15-16	3A, 4	Some		28500	
5B		Short	1st		National Diploma in Police Studies	National Diploma in Police Studies	21-24	2	2	15-16	3			685	
5B		Medium	2nd		Diploma (NCEA, IoT)	Diploma (NCEA, IoT)	17-20	3	3	16-17	3A, 4, 5B	Some		15300	
5A		Medium	1st		Primary Degree Level	Bachelor of Arts, Bachelor of Business Studies, Bachelor of Commerce, Bachelor of Design, Bachelor of Law, Bachelor of Radiography, Bachelor of Social Science, Bachelor of Physiotherapy, Bachelor of Engineering, Bachelor of Science, Bachelor of Education	17-19	3-4	4	17	3A	Some		66200	Estimated FTE enrolment includes enrolment in the Primary Degree Level and enrolment in Post-graduate Diploma.
5A		Long	1st		Primary Degree Level	Medical Degree (M.B., B.Ch., B.A.O.), Degree in Veterinary Medicine (M.V.B.), Bachelor of Dental Science, Bachelor of Architecture	17-19	5-6		19	3A				
5A		Medium	2nd		Post-graduate Diploma	Graduate Diploma, Higher Diploma, Diploma	21-23	1	1	18	5A (1st, M), 5A (1st, L)				
5A		Medium	2nd		Master Degree (taught)	Master of Arts, Master of Science, Master of Commerce, Master of Literature, Master of Philosophy, Master of Architecture, Master of Agricultural Science, Master of Medicine, Master of Dentistry	21-23	1	1	18	5A (1st, M), 5A (1st, L)	Some		10100	Estimated FTE enrolment includes enrolment in the Master Degree by Research and enrolment in doctoral programmes.
5A		Long	2nd		Master Degree by Research	Master of Arts, Master of Science, Master of Commerce, Master of Literature, Master of Philosophy, Master of Architecture, Master of Agricultural Science, Master of Medicine, Master of Dentistry	21-23	2	2	19	5A (1st, M), 5A (1st, L)				
6		Very long			Doctorate (Ph.D.)	Doctor of Philosophy, Doctor of Laws, Doctor of Literature, Doctor of Science, Doctor of Music	22-26	3	3	21	5A (2nd)				

92

Italy

ISCED-97 level	Programme orientation	Cumulative duration at ISCED 5	Position in the national degree/qualification structure (Intermediate, First, Second, etc.)	Notes on programmes that span across ISCED levels or sub-categories	Descriptive name of the programme	Main diplomas, credentials or certifications	Typical starting ages	Theoretical length of the programme	Typical length of the programme	Cumulative years of education at the end of the programme	Minimum entrance requirement	Programme specifically designed for part-time attendance	Reported in the UOE	Enrolment 1996-97	Other relevant information
0					Scuola Materna (pre-school education)		3	3	3					1594283	
1					Scuola Elementare (primary school)	Licenza elementare	6	5	5	5				2810158	
1					Corsi per soggetti analfabeti e analfabeti di ritorno (ciclo elementare) (adult literacy school (1st cycle))	Licenza elementare				5				7000	
1					Scuola elementare speciale per disabili (special education school elementary education)	Licenza elementare	6	5	5	5					
2A	G				Scuola Media (lower secondary education)	Licenza media	11	3	3	8	1			1851225	
2A	G				Corsi sperimentali di scuola media per lavoratori (adult literacy school, 2nd cycle)	Licenza media				8	1			58947	Enrolment data is for the scholar year 1995/96.
2A	G				Scuola media speciale per disabili (special education school lower secondary education)	Licenza media	11	3	3	8	1				
3C	V				Conservatorio musicale (3-5 anni) (music conservatory, 3-5 years)	Diploma di conservatorio musicale	11-13	3-5	3-5	8-11				23245	
3C	V				Formazione professionale regionale (post-obbligo) (regional vocational education)	Qualifica professionale regionale di I livello	14-18	2	2	10	2			102483	
3C	V				Istituto professionale, Istituto d'Arte, (I ciclo) (vocational institute, art institute, 1st cycle)	Qualifica di istituto professionale e licenza di maestro d'arte	14	3	3	11	2			401502	
3C	V				Accademia di danza (dance studies)	Diploma di maestro di danza, Diploma di composizione di danza	19	8	8	13	1		No		
3C	V				Conservatorio musicale (9-10 anni) (music conservatory, 9-10 years)	Diploma di conservatorio musicale	11-14	9-10	9-10	14-15				4058	
3B	P				Liceo artistico (I ciclo) (art high school, 1st cycle)	Maturità artistica	14	4	4	12	2			31874	Provides direct access to architectural studies (only) at university or access the Accademia di belle arti (fine-arts academy, classified at ISCED 5B).
3A	G				Liceo (classico, scientifico, linguistico), istituto e scuola magistrale (dall'anno scolastico 1998-99) (secondary general education)	Maturità classica e scientifica, licenza linguistica, Maturità magistrale, licenza di assistente di comunità infantile	14	5	5	13	2			918048	Up until 1997-98, "magistrali" schools (scuola) were considered at the same level as istituto professionale (vocational institutes – ISCED 3C vocational) and "magistrali" institutes (instituto) were considered at the same level as Liceo artistico (the first 4 years at ISCED 3B prevocational and the last year at ISCED 3A).
3A	G				Liceo artistico (II ciclo) (art high school, 2nd cycle)	Attestato di idoneità	18	1	1	13	3B			1582	Provides direct access to university (all fields of study).
3A	V				Istituto tecnico (technical institute)	Maturità tecnica	14	5	5	13	2			1079431	
3A	V				Corsi sperimentali tecnico-professionali (vocational and technical experimental courses)	Maturità sperimentale tecnico-professionale-artistico	14	5	5	13	2				
3A	V				Istituto professionale, Istituto d'Arte (II ciclo) (vocational institute, art institute, 2nd cycle)	Maturità professionale e d'arte applicata	17	2	2	13	3C			216098	
4C	V				Formazione professionale (post-maturità) regionale o scolastica (regional vocational education)	Qualifica professionale regionale di II livello	19-21	0.5	0.5	14	3A, 3B		No	39563	
5B		Medium	1st		Istituto Superiore di Educazione Fisica (sport studies)	Diploma di Educazione fisica	19	3	3	16	3A, 3B			17026	
5B		Medium	1st		Accademia di belle arti (fine-arts academy)	Diploma di accademia di belle arti	19	4	4	17	3A, 3B			14751	
5B		Medium	1st		Accademia di arte drammatica e Istituto Superiore Industrie Artistiche (dramatic art and higher artistic studies)	Diploma di regista, Diploma di Istituto Superiore Industrie artistiche	19	4	4	17	3A, 3B		No		
5B		Short	2nd		Conservatorio musicale (specializzazione di 2 anni) (music conservatory, 2-year specialisation)	Diploma di conservatorio musicale (specializzazione)	14	2	2	10-17	3C			6316	
5A		Medium	1st		Corsi di Diploma universitario e Scuole dirette a fini speciali (university education, special courses)	Diploma universitario (Laurea breve)	19	3	3	16	3A, 3B			62227	
5A		Medium	1st	Medium or long	Corsi di Laurea (university education)	Diploma di laurea	19	4-6	4-6	17-19	3A, 3B			1694433	
5A		Very long	2nd		Specializzazione post-laurea e Corsi di perfezionamento (doctoral training)	Diploma di specializzazione, attestato di partecipazione al corso di perfezionamento	24-26	2-5	2-5	19-24	5A			52173	
6		Very long	2nd		Dottorati di ricerca (doctorate)	Titolo di Dottore di ricerca	24-26	3-5	3-5	20-24	5A			12369	

93

ISCED-97 level	Programme orientation	Cumulative duration at ISCED 5	Position in the national degree/qualification structure (Intermediate, First, Second, etc.)	Notes on programmes that span across ISCED levels or sub-categories	Descriptive name of the programme	Main diplomas, credentials or certifications	Typical starting ages	Theoretical length of the programme	Typical length of the programme	Cumulative years of education at the end of the programme	Minimum entrance requirement	Programme specifically designed for part-time attendance	Reported in the UOE	Enrolment 1996-97	Other relevant information
0					Hoikusho (day nursery)		3-5	1-3						1628	Hoikusho is within the jurisdiction of the Ministry of Health and Welfare.
0					Tokushu-kyoiku-gakko Yochi-bu (special education school, kindergarten department)		3-5	1-3							
0					Yochien (kindergarten)		3-5	1-3						1798051	
0					Tokushu-kyoiku-gakko Shogaku-bu (special education school, elementary department)		6	6	6	6				26830	
1					Shogakko (elementary school)		6	6	6	6				8105629	
2A	G				Tokushu-kyoiku-gakko Chugaku-bu (special education school, lower secondary department)	Certificate of graduation	12	3	3	9	1			20508	
2A	G				Chugakko (lower secondary school)	Certificate of graduation	12	3	3	9	1			4527400	
3C	V				Senshugakko Koto kate (specialised training college, upper secondary course)	Certificate of graduation and various vocational qualifications	15	1+		10	2			87895	
3C	V				Koto gakko Teijisei Honka Senmon (upper secondary school, day/evening specialised course)	Certificate of graduation	15	3+		12	2			35245	
3C	V				Koto gakko Teijisei Bekka Senmon (upper secondary school, day/evening short-term general course)	Certificate of completion	15	1+			2				
3C	V				Koto gakko Tsushinsei Senmon (upper secondary school, correspondence specialised course)	Certificate of completion	15	3+		12	2	Yes		15676	
3C	V				Koto gakko Zennichisei Honka Senmon (upper secondary school, full day specialised course)	Certificate of completion	15	3	3	12	2			1133457	
3C	V				Koto gakko Zennichisei Bekka Senmon (upper secondary school, full day short-term specialised course)	Certificate of completion	15	1+			2				
3A	G				Koto gakko Teijisei Honka Futsu (upper secondary school, day/evening general course)	Certificate of graduation	15	3+		12	2			70137	
3C	V				Koto gakko Teijisei Bekka Futsu (upper secondary school, day/evening short-term general course)	Certificate of completion	15	1+			2				
3A	G				Koto gakko Tsushinsei Futsu (upper secondary school, correspondence general course)	Certificate of graduation	15	3+		12	2	Yes		138939	
3A	G				Koto gakko Zennichisei Honka Futsu (upper secondary school, full day general course)	Certificate of completion	15	3	3	12	2			3286706	
3C	V				Koto gakko Zennichisei Bekka Futsu (upper secondary school, full day short-term general course)	Certificate of completion	15	1+			2				
3A	G				Koto gakko Teijisei Honka Sogo (upper secondary school, day/evening general course)	Certificate of graduation	15	3	3	12	2			13948	
3C	V				Koto gakko Teijisei Bekka Sogo (upper secondary school, full day integrated course (general)]	Certificate of completion	15	1+			2				
3A	G				Koto gakko Tsushinsei Bekka Sogo (upper secondary school, full day short-term integrated course (general)]	Certificate of graduation	15	3+		12	2			199	
3C	V				Koto gakko Teijisei Bekka Sogo (upper secondary school, day/evening short-term integrated course)	Certificate of completion	15	1+			2				
3A	G				Tokushu-kyoiku-gakko Koto-bu Zennichisei Honka Futsu (special education school, upper secondary department, full day general course)	Certificate of graduation	15	3	3	12	2				
3C	V				Tokushu-kyoiku-gakko Koto-bu Zennichisei Bekka Futsu (special education school, upper secondary department, full day short-term general course)	Certificate of completion	15	1+			2				
3A	G				Tokushu-kyoiku-gakko Koto-bu Zennichisei Honka Senmon (special education school, upper secondary department, full day specialised course)	Certificate of graduation	15	3	3	12	2				
3C	V				Tokushu-kyoiku-gakko Koto-bu Zennichisei Bekka Senmon (special education school, upper secondary department, full day short-term specialised course)	Certificate of completion	15	1+			2				
3A	G				Tokushu-kyoiku-gakko Koto-bu Zennichisei Honka Sogo (special education school, upper secondary department, full day integrated course (general)]	Certificate of graduation	15	3	3	12	2				
3C	V				Tokushu-kyoiku-gakko Koto-bu Zennichisei Bekka Sogo (special education school, upper secondary department, full day short-term integrated course)	Certificate of completion	15	1+			2				
3A	G				Tokushu-kyoiku-gakko Koto-bu Teijisei Honka Futsu (special education school, upper secondary department, day/evening general course)	Certificate of graduation	15	3	3	12	2				
3C	V				Tokushu-kyoiku-gakko Koto-bu Teijisei Bekka Futsu (special education school, upper secondary department, day/evening specialised course)	Certificate of graduation	15	3+		12	2				
3A	G				Tokushu-kyoiku-gakko Koto-bu Teijisei Honka Senmon (special education school, upper secondary department, day/evening specialised course)	Certificate of graduation	15	3+		12	2				
3C	V				Tokushu-kyoiku-gakko Koto-bu Teijisei Bekka Senmon (special education school, upper secondary department, day/evening short-term specialised course)	Certificate of completion	15	1+			2				

Japan (continued)										
3A	G		Tokushu-kyoiku-gakko Koto-bu Teijisei Honka Sogo (special education school, upper secondary department, day/evening integrated course (general))	Certificate of graduation	15	3+	3	12	2	
3C	V		Tokushu-kyoiku-gakko Koto-bu Teijisei Bekka Sogo (special education school, upper secondary department, day/evening short-term integrated course)	Certificate of completion	15	1+			2	
4			Koto gakko Zenmichisei Senkoka Futsu (upper secondary school, full day advanced general course)	Certificate of completion	18	1+			3	
4			Koto gakko Teijisei Senkoka Futsu (upper secondary school, day/evening advanced general course)	Certificate of completion	18	1+			3	
4			Koto gakko Zenmichisei Senkoka Senmon (upper secondary school, full day advanced specialised course)	Certificate of completion	18	1+			3	
4			Koto gakko Teijisei Senkoka Senmon (upper secondary school, day/evening advanced specialised course)	Certificate of completion	18	1+			3	
4			Koto gakko Zenmichisei Senkoka Sogo (upper secondary school, full day advanced integrated course)	Certificate of completion	18	1+			3	
4			Koto gakko Teijisei Senkoka Sogo (upper secondary school, day/evening advanced integrated course)	Certificate of completion	18	1+			3	
4			Tokushu-kyoiku-gakko Koto-bu Zenmichisei Senkoka Futsu (special education school, upper secondary department, full day advanced general course)	Certificate of completion	18	1+			3	
4			Tokushu-kyoiku-gakko Koto-bu Teijisei Senkoka Futsu (special education school, upper secondary department, day/evening advanced general course)	Certificate of completion	18	1+			3	
4			Tokushu-kyoiku-gakko Koto-bu Zenmichisei Senkoka Senmon (special education school, upper secondary department, full day advanced specialised course)	Certificate of completion	18	1+			3	
4			Tokushu-kyoiku-gakko Koto-bu Teijisei Senkoka Senmon (special education school, upper secondary department, day/evening advanced specialised course)	Certificate of completion	18	1+			3	
4			Tokushu-kyoiku-gakko Koto-bu Zenmichisei Senkoka Sogo (special education school, upper secondary department, full day advanced integrated course)	Certificate of completion	18	1+			3	
4			Tokushu-kyoiku-gakko Koto-bu Teijisei Senkoka Sogo (special education school, upper secondary department, day/evening advanced integrated course)	Certificate of completion	18	1+			3	
4			Tanki-daigaku Bekka (university, short-term course)	Certificate of completion	18	1+			3	
4			Daigaku Gakubu Bekka (university, short-term course)	Certificate of completion	18	1+	2		3	
5B			Senshugakko Senmon katei (specialised training college, post-secondary course)	Senmonshi (technical associate)	18	2		14	3A, 3B, 3C	659057
5B	Short	Intermediate	Tanki-daigaku Tsushinsei (junior college, correspondence course)	Jungakushi (associate)	18	2-3		14	3A, 3B, 3C	40431 Cumulative duration at tertiary: 2 years.
5B	Short	Intermediate	Tanki-daigaku Hon-ka (junior college, regular course)	Jungakushi (associate)	18	2-3		14-15	3A, 3B, 3C	463948
5B			Tanki-daigaku Senkoka (junior college, advanced course)	Certificate of completion	20	1+			5B	
5B	Short	Intermediate Three first years = 3B	Koto senmongakko Honka (college of technology, regular course)	Jungakushi (associate)	15	5	5	14	2	56396
5B			Koto senmongakko Senkoka (college of technology, advanced course)	Certificate of completion	20	1+			5B	
5A	Medium	1st	Daigaku Gakubu (university, undergraduate)	Gakushi (Bachelor's degree)	18	4		16	3A, 3B, 3C	2368992
5A			Daigaku Senkoka (university, advanced course)	Certificate of completion	22	1+			5A	
5A	Medium	1st	Daigaku Tsushinsei katei (university, undergraduate, correspondence course)	Gakushi (Bachelor's degree)	18	4+		16	3A, 3B, 3C	149124 Cumulative duration: 4 Yes
5A	Long	1st	Daigaku Ishigaku Jyugaku-bu (university, undergraduate of medicine, dentistry and veterinary medicine)	Gakushi (Bachelor's degree)	18	6		18	3A, 3B, 3C	71613
5A	Long	2nd	Daigakuin Shushi katei (university, graduate school, Master's course)	Shushi (Master's degree)	22	2		18	5A (1st, L)	115902
6			Daigakuin Hakushi Ishiji-gaku (university, graduate school, Doctor's course of medicine, dentistry and veterinary medicine)	Hakushi (Doctor's degree)	24	4		22	5A (1st, L)	13397
6			Daigakuin Hakushi katei (university, graduate school, Doctor's course)	Hakushi (Doctor's degree)	22	5		21	5A (1st, L)	48448
NC			Kakushugakko (miscellaneous schools)	Certificate of graduation and various vocational qualifications		1				
NC			Senshugakko Ippan katei (specialised training college, general course)	Certificate of graduation and various vocational qualifications		1+				

Korea

ISCED-97 level	Programme orientation	Cumulative duration at ISCED 5	Position in the national degree/qualification structure (intermediate, First, Second, etc.)	Notes on programmes that span across ISCED levels or sub-categories	Descriptive name of the programme	Main diplomas, credentials or certifications	Typical starting ages	Theoretical length of the programme	Typical length of the programme	Cumulative years of education at the end of the programme	Minimum entrance requirement	Programme specifically designed for part-time attendance	Reported in the UOE	Enrolment 1997-98	Other relevant information
0					Yuchiwon (kindergarten)	Certification	4-5	1	1					568096	Kindergarten is not yet covered by the public system of education, although the educational objectives have been proclaimed by the state.
0					Teuksu-hakgyo(yuchiwon kwajong) (special school, kindergarten course)	Certification	4+	1	1					1071	
1					Kongmin-hakgyo (civic school)	Certification	5-6	3	3	3				195	
1					Chodeung-hakgyo (primary school)	Certification	6+	6	6	6				3783996	By new law in effect from 1996, theoretical starting age has changed from 6 years to 5 years.
1					Teuksu-hakgyo(chodeung-hakgyo kwajong) (special school, primary school course)	Certification	6+	6	6	6				10266	
2A	G				Kakjong-hakgyo(jung-hakgyo kwajong) (miscellaneous school, middle school course)	Certification	11-12	3	3	9	1			5926	
2A	G				Kodeung kongmin hakgyo (civic high school)	Certification	11-12	3	3	9	1			418	
2A	G				Jung-hakgyo (middle school)	Certification	11-12	3	3	9	1			2180283	
2A	G				Sanupche-busol junghakgyo (middle school attached to industrial firms)	Certification	11-12	3	3	9	1			12	
2A	G				Teulbul hakgyo(junghakgyo) (special evening classes for working youths, middle school)	Certification	11-12	3	3	9	1			17	No
2A	G				Teuksu-hakgyo (jung-hakgyo kwajong) (special school, middle school course)	Certification	12+	3	3	9	1			5758	
3C	V				Kodeung kisul-hakgyo (trade high school)	Certification	14-15	3	3	12	2			9365	
3C	V				Silupgye kodeung-hakgyo (vocational high school)	Certification	14-15	3	3	12	2			960037	A 2-year schooling and one-year on-the-job training system is being introduced.
3C	V				Teulbul hakgyo (silupgye kogyo) (special evening classes for working youths, vocational high school)	Certification	14-15	3	3	12	2			13034	
3C	V				Sawhakgyoyuksised hakgyo (accredited non-formal education facilities schools)	Certification	14-15	3	3	12	2			25043	
3A	G				Kakjong-hakgyo(kodeung-hakgyo kwajong) (miscellaneous school, high school course)	Certification	14-15	3	3	12	2			825	
3A	G				Ilbangye kodeung-hakgyo (general high school)	Certification	14-15	3	3	12	2			1376688	
3A	G				Sanupche-busol kodeung-hakgyo (high school attached to industrial firms)	Certification	14-15	3	3	12	2			7956	Private enterprises run these schools for their employees.
3A	G				Bangsonglongsin kodeung-hakgyo (air and correspondence high school)	Certification	14-15	3	3	12	2			14624	No
3A	G				Teulbul hakgyo(ilbangye kogyo) (special evening classes for working youths, general high school)	Certification	14-15	3	3	12	2			1783	No
3A	G				Teuksu-hakgyo(kodeung-hakgyo kwajong) (special school, high school course)	Certification	15+	3	3	12	2			5474	
5B		Short	Intermediate		Jeonmun daehak (junior college)	Certification	17-18	2-3	2-3	14-15	3A	Yes		724741	
5B		Short	Intermediate		Kinung daehak (polytechnic college)	Certification	17-18	2	2	14	3A		No		
5B		Short	Intermediate		Kakjong-hakgyo (jeonmun daehak kwajong) (miscellaneous school, junior college course)	Certification: some schools cannot confer certification	17-18	2	2	14	3A			3652	
5B		Short	Intermediate		Kisul daehak (technical college)	Certification	17-18	2-4	2-4	14-16			No		This programme does yet exist, although it will most likely be included in the new system.

(Korea (continued)										
5B	Medium	1st	Yukkun samsakwan hakgyo (third military academy)	Bachelor's degree	19-20	2	2	16	5B (SM)	No	
5B	Medium	1st	Semu daehak (national college of taxation)	Bachelor's degree	17-18	4	4	16	3A	No	This is a programme for training revenue officers.
5B	Medium	1st	Kakjong-hakgyo (daehak kwajong) (miscellaneous school, undergraduate course)	Certification; some schools cannot confer certification	17-18	4	4	16	3A		9596 Two kinds of school; the first is authorised to confer publicly recognised certificates, the is not authorised to do so.
5B	Medium	1st	Sanup daehak (gaebang daehak) (open university, polytechnic university)	Certification, Bachelor's degree	17-18	4	4	16	3A	Yes	141099 The open university provides employed youths and adults with an alternative approach to higher education. This system commends itself for its positive impact on the job-performance of student workers.
5B	Medium	1st	Yukkun sakwan hakgyo (military academy)	Bachelor's degree	17-18	4	4	16	3A	No	This is a programme for training commissioned officers (military, naval, air-force).
5B	Medium	1st	Geongchal daehak (national college of police)	Bachelor's degree credential for civil servant of police	17-18	4	4	16	3A	No	This is a programme for training the managing staff of the police.
5B	Medium	1st	Gyoyuk daehak (university of education)	Bachelor's degree	17-18	4	4	16	3A	No	20948
5B	Medium	1st	Kukkunganho sakwan hakgyo (nursing academy)	Bachelor's degree	17-18	4	4	16	3A	No	
5B	Medium	1st	Haekun sakwan hakgyo (naval academy)	Bachelor's degree	17-18	4	4	16	3A	No	
5B	Medium	1st	Konggun sakwan hakgyo (air force academy)	Bachelor's degree	17-18	4	4	16	3A	No	
5B	Long	2nd	Kukbang daehakwon (school of national securities)	Master	21+	2	2	18	5A (1st)	No	
5B	Long	2nd	Teuksu daehakwon (graduate school, special)	Master	21+	2-3	2-3	18-19	5A (1st)		67463
5B	Long	2nd	Jeonmun daehakwon (graduate school, professional)	Master	21+	2.5	3	18.5	5A (1st)		
5A	Short	1st	Bangsongtongsin daehak (air and correspondence university (open university)]	Certification, Bachelor's degree	17-18	2-4	2-4	14-16	3A, 3C	Yes	370879
5A	Medium	1st	Daehak(gyo) (university)	Bachelor's degree	17-18	4	4	16	3A	Yes	1338493
5A	Medium	1st	Hankuk kwahak kisulwon (Korea advanced institute of science and technology)	Bachelor's degree	17-18	4	4	16	3A	No	
5A	Medium	1st	Hankuk yeosuljonghap hakgyo (yeosulsa kwajong) (the Korean National University of Arts)	Bachelor's degree	17-18	4	4	16	3A	No	
5A	Long	1st	Wolkwa deahak,chikwa daehak (university, medical-dentistry)	Bachelor's degree	17-18	6	6	18	3A		29968
5A	Long	2nd	Hankuk jeongsin munwha yeonku won (seoksa kwajong) (the Academy of Korean Studies, MA course	Master	21+	2-3	2-3	18-19	5A (1st)	No	
5A	Long	2nd	Ilbandaehakwon(seoksa kwajong) (graduate school, Master's degree programme, short)	Master	21+	2	3	18	5A (1st)		60634
5A	Long	2nd	Hankuk kwahak kisulwon (seoksa kwajong) (Korea Advanced Institute of Science and Technology, MA course	Master	21+	2	2	18	5A (1st)	No	
5A	Long	2nd	Daehakwon daehak (seoksa kwajong) (university of graduate school)	Master	21+	2	3	18	5A (1st)	No	
5A	Long	2nd	Hankuk yeosuljonghap hakgyo (jeonmun yeosulsa kwajong) (the Korean National University of Arts, MA course)	Master	21+	2	2	18	5A (1st)	No	
6	Very long	1st	Hankuk kwahak kisulwon(baksa kwajong) (Korea Advanced Institute of Science and Technology)	Doctor	23+	3	5	21	5A (2nd)	No	
6	Very long	1st	Hankuk jeongsin munwha yeonku won (baksa kwajong) (Academy of Korean Studies, Ph.D.)	Doctor	23+	3	5	21	5A (2nd)	No	
6	Very long	1st	Ilban daehakwon (baksa kwajong) (graduate school, Doctorate programme)	Doctor	23+	3	5	21	5A (2nd)		23261 Length of attendance vary from 2 years to 8 years upon fields of study or students' backgrounds.
6	Very long	1st	Daehakwon daehak(baksa kwajong) (university of graduate school)	Doctor	23+	3	5	21	5A (2nd)	No	

Manual for ISCED-97 Implementation in OECD Countries – 1999 Edition

Luxembourg

ISCED-97 level	Programme orientation	Cumulative duration at ISCED 5	Position in the national degree/qualification structure (Intermediate, First, Second, etc.)	Notes on programmes that span across ISCED levels or sub-categories	Descriptive name of the programme	Main diplomas, credentials or certifications	Typical starting ages	Theoretical length of the programme	Typical length of the programme	Cumulative years of education at the end of the programme	Minimum entrance requirement	Programme specifically designed for part-time attendance	Reported in the UOE	Enrolment 1995-96	Other relevant information
0					01 Enseignement préscolaire (pre-primary education)		4-5	2	2					9882	
1					02 Enseignement primaire (primary education)		6-7	6	6	6				27640	
2					03 Régime préparatoire de l'EST (preparatory regime of the technical secondary education)		12-13	1-3	1-3	7-9	1			2388	
2A	G				04 Cycle inférieur de l'EST (lower technical secondary education)		12-13	3	3	9				7278	
2A	G				05 Cycle inférieur de l'EST (lower general secondary education)		12-13	3	3	9				4782	
3C	V				07 Apprentissage à deux degrés (cdp) (apprenticeship at two degrees: cdp/certificate of technical and professional initiation)	cdp (certificate of technical and professional initiation)	15-16	2-4	2-4	11-13	2			192	
3C	V				06 Régime professionnel com (professional regime com: certificate of manual capacities)	com (certificate of manual capacities)	15-16	3	3	12				414	
3C	V				09 Régime professionnel concomitant (professional regime with part-time school)	catp (certificate of technical and professional proficiency)	15-16	3	3	12	2			1402	This enrolment figure includes the students enrolled in programme 10 (régime professionnel filière mixte).
3C	V				10 Régime professionnel filière mixte (professional mixed regime)	catp (certificate of technical and professional proficiency)	15-16	3	3	12	2				The number of students enrolled in this programme are included in programme No. 9 (régime professionnel concomitant).
3C	V				08 Régime professionnel plein temps (professional regime with full-time school)	catp (certificate of technical and professional proficiency)	15-16	3	3	12	2			1318	
3B	V				11 Régime de la formation de technicien (technical training regime)	Diplôme de technicien	15-16	4	4	13	2			1871	
3B	V				14 Formation d'éducateurs (plein temps) (training of educators, full-time)	Diplôme d'éducateur	17-18	3	3	14				227	
3B	V				15 Formation d'éducateurs (en cours d'emploi) (training of educators, while working)	Diplôme d'éducateur	17-18	6	6	17		Yes		m	This programme lasts 3 years (full-time).
3A	V				12 Régime technique (technical regime)	Diplôme de fin d'études secondaires techniques	15-16	4	4	13	2			3266	
3A	G				13 Cycles moyen et supérieur de l'enseignement secondaire général (middle and upper general secondary education)	Diplôme de fin d'études secondaires	15-16	4	4	13	2			4571	
4B	V				18 Brevet de maîtrise (Master craftsman's diploma)	Brevet de maîtrise	20-21	3	3	15	3C			836	
5B		Short			16 Brevet de technicien supérieur (bts) (higher technician certificate)	Brevet de technicien supérieur	19-20	2	2	15	3A, 3B	Yes		224	
5B		Short			17 Cycle court d'études supérieures en gestion (short-term course in higher studies of administration)	Diplôme d'études supérieures de gestion	19-20	2	2	15	3A, 3B			244	
5B		Medium			22 Formation des ingénieurs-techniciens (training of technical engineers)	Technical engineers diploma	19-20	3	3	16	3A, 3B			296	
5B		Medium			21 Formation des instituteurs (initial training of primary and pre-primary teachers)	Certificate of educational proficiency (either for pre-school or for primary school)	19-20	3	3	16	3A, 3B			274	
5B		Medium			19 Formation d'éducateurs gradués (plein temps) (training of graduated educators, full-time)	Diplôme d'éducateur gradué	19-20	3	3	16	3A, 3B			153	
5B		Medium			20 Formation d'éducateurs gradués (en cours d'emploi) (training of graduated educators, while working)	Diplôme d'éducateur gradué	19-20	6	6	19	3A, 3B	Yes			This programme lasts 3 years (full-time).
5A		Very short			23 Cours universitaires (university courses)	No diploma: in Luxembourg, students can only attend a first year of university classes. They have to continue their studies at a foreign university.	19-20	1	1	14	3A, 3B			473	After this year of study, students can continue university courses in a foreign country.

Mexico

ISCED-97 level	Programme orientation	Cumulative duration at ISCED 5	Position in the national degree/qualification structure (intermediate, First, Second, etc.)	Notes on programmes that span across ISCED levels or sub-categories	Descriptive name of the programme	Main diplomas, credentials or certifications	Typical starting ages	Theoretical length of the programme	Typical length of the programme	Cumulative years of education at the end of the programme	Minimum entrance requirement	Programme specifically designed for part-time attendance	Reported in the UOE	Enrolment 1996-97	Other relevant information
0					Educación preescolar (pre-primary education)		3-5	1-3	1-3					3238337	In this programme, 51 868 students (headcount) are age 2, referred to as initial education students. This programme is also known as pre-school education.
1					Educación primaria (primary education)	Diploma: Primary Certificate	6-8	6	6	6				14650521	
2C	V				Capacitación para el trabajo [lower secondary (job training)]	Diploma: Job Training Certificate	12	4	3	10	1			498800	Job Training programmes are designed to help students to get jobs quickly. The typical duration of these programmes is 4 years, although there are also shorter programmes. Students in this programme are commonly adults.
2A	G				Educación secundaria (lower secondary education)	Diploma: Secondary Certificate	12-13	3	3	9	1			4809266	It is obligatory to attend this programme (compulsory according to the Mexican Constitution).
3C	V				Profesional medio [upper secondary (vocational or technical programme)]	Diploma: High School Equivalency Certificate	15	4	3	12	2			383760	These programmes are designed to help students get jobs quickly. Graduates of these programmes are considered technicians.
3A	G				Bachillerato general, Bachillerato por cooperación, Bachillerato pedagógico, Bachillerato de arte (upper secondary (high school programme)]	Diploma: High School Certificate	14-16	2-3	2-3	12	2			1507028	The duration of some programmes in this level is less than 3 years – sometimes 2 years. It is also known as Bachillerato.
3A	G				Bachillerato tecnológico [upper secondary (combined general and technical programmes)]	Diploma: High School Certificate	15	3	3	12	2			715311	This programme is considered as general, although more specialisation may be included to assist students in acquiring practical skills that prepare people to the labour market.
5B		Short			Licenciatura tecnológica [technological universities programmes (vocational associate's degree programmes)]	Diploma: Vocational Associate Degree	18	2	2	14	3B			8561	This programme was included as part of ISCED Level 6 in 1998 UOE data collection. Graduates from this programme are considered as technicians.
5A		Medium	1st		Educación normal licenciatura [teacher training school programmes (Bachelor's degree programme)]	Diploma: Bachelor's degree	18	4	4	16	3A			185533	Teacher Training School was included as part of non-university education in the 1998 UOE data collection (ISCED 5).
5A		Medium	1st		Licenciatura universitaria [university degree programmes (Bachelor's degree programme)]	Diploma: Bachelor's degree	18	4-5	4-5	16-17	3A			1321107	The typical duration of these programmes is between 4 and 5 years, although there are few programmes longer than 5 years (e.g. Concert Performer, Medicine – 6 years).
5A		Medium	1st		Programas de institutos tecnológicos [technological institutes programmes (Bachelor's degree programme)]	Diploma: Bachelor's degree	18	4-5	4-5	16-17	3A				The typical duration of this programme is between 4 and 5 years.
5A		Long	2nd		Programa de especialización (specialisation degree programme (Master's degree programme) (short)]	Diploma: Master's degree	23	0.5-1	0.5-1	17-18	5A (1st, L)	Yes		22044	This programme was classified as ISCED 7 under ISCED-76. The typical duration of this tertiary programme is 1 year, although medical specialisation takes longer (4 or 5 years).
5A		Very long	2nd		Programa de maestría [Master's degree programme (long)]	Diploma: Master's degree	23	2	2	18-19	5A (1st, L)			66095	The Master's degree is not a necessary entrance requirement for some Ph.D. programmes. This programme was classified at ISCED 7 under ISCED-76.
6		Very long			Programa de doctorado [Doctoral programme – Doctorate (Ph.D. Research)]	Diploma: Doctorate (Ph.D.) degree	26	3		20-21	5A (1st, L), 5A (2nd)			6158	Some programmes in this level do not require the Master's degree for entry. This programme was classified at ISCED 7 under ISCED-76. This level prepares students to earn an advanced research qualification.
NC					Educación inicial (initial education programmes)								No	357325	Non-formal education. This is an education programme designed to increase the physical, cognitive and social aspects of the population.
NC					Educación especial (special education programmes)								No	287295	This programme provides educational services to mentally, physically, or emotionally disadvantaged students and other groups with special learning needs.
NC					Educación para adultos (adult education programmes)								No	2499617	The objective of this programme is to teach literacy skills to adults (15 years and over), especially in compulsory education (primary and lower secondary).

Netherlands

ISCED-97 level	Programme orientation	Cumulative duration at ISCED 5	Position in the national degree/qualification structure (First, Second, etc.)	Notes on programmes that span across ISCED levels or sub-categories	Descriptive name of the programme	Main diplomas, credentials or certifications	Typical starting ages	Theoretical length of the programme	Typical length of the programme	Cumulative years of education at the end of the programme	Minimum entrance requirement	Programme specifically designed for part-time attendance	Reported in the UOE	Enrolment 1996-97	Other relevant information
0	G				Groep 1 en 2 basisonderwijs en speciaal onderwijs (group 1 and 2 of primary education and of special education)		4	2	2					394000	
1	G				Groep 3-8 basisonderwijs (group 3-8 of primary education and of special education)		6	6	6	6				1231000	
2C	V				WEB-assistentenopleiding (training to assistant level; level 1)	Vocational qualification level 1	16	0.5-1		10	About 2 years at 2B				WEB = Wet Educatie en Beroepsonderwijs = adult and vocational education act. The assistant training programme has been designed for drop-outs from other schools at level 2. Provides access to WEB level 2 programmes in the same field.
2B	G				Middelbaar algemeen voortgezet onderwijs (MAVO) (MAVO = junior general secondary education)	Mavo-diploma	12	4	4-5	10	1			514000	
2B	P				Voorbereidend beroepsonderwijs (VBO) (pre-vocational education)	Vbo-diploma	12	4	4-5	10	1			134000	Of which 5 000 part-time. Enrolment in class 3-4.
2A	G				Klas 1-3 hoger algemeen vormend onderwijs (HAVO) (HAVO = senior general secondary education)		12	3	3-4	9	1			31000	Enrolment in class 3.
2A	G				Klas 1-3 voorbereidend wetenschappelijk onderwijs (VWO) (VWO = pre-university education)		12	3	3-4	9	1			32000	Enrolment in class 3.
2A	G			2ABC, 3ABC	Voortgezet speciaal onderwijs (VSO) (secondary special education)		11-14	4-6	4-6	10				39000	This is a very heterogeneous group of schools.
3	V			2C, 3AC, 4C	Middelbaar beroepsonderwijs (mbo) (different types of vocational training, including apprenticeships, which are phasing out and are replaced by WEB-programmes		16	1-4						449000	Of which 36 000 part-time.
3C	V				WEB-basisberoepsopleiding (basic vocational training; level 2)	Vocational qualification level 2	16	2-3		12					Provides access to WEB level 3 programmes in the same field.
3C	V				WEB-vakopleiding (professional training; level 3)	Vocational qualification level 3	16	2-4	3-4	13	2				Provides access to WEB level 4 programmes in the same field.
3A	V				WEB-middenkaderopleiding (middle-management training; level 4)	Vocational qualification level 4	16	3-4	3-4	13.5	2				Access to all HBO-programmes in the same field.
3A	G				Klas 4-5 hoger algemeen vormend onderwijs (HAVO) (HAVO = senior general secondary education)	Havo-diploma	15	2	2-3	11	2			105000	Of which 11 000 part-time. Access to HBO-programmes, dependent of the examined subjects at HAVO.
3A	G				Klas 4-6 voorbereidend wetenschappelijk onderwijs (VWO) (VWO = pre-university education)	Vwo-diploma	15	3	3-4	12	2			110000	Of which 10 000 part-time. Access to university programmes, dependent of the examined subject at VWO.
4C	V				WEB-specialistenopleiding (specialist training; level 4)	Vocational qualification level 4	19	1-2		16	WEB level 3				Limited access to HBO.
4C	V				Hoger beroepsonderwijs (HBO) (higher professional education) 1-year programmes		17	1	1	12	3A				Enrolment included in HBO >1- and <4-year programmes. Programmes provided by private education institutes.
4A	G				Voorbereidend hoger beroepsonderwijs (VHBO) (VHBO = pre-higher professional education)			3		16					Education to fill gaps in previous education in order to have access to HBO.
5B	Short				Hoger beroepsonderwijs HBO) (higher professional education) >1-,<4-year programmes		17	2-3	4-5	17	3A			16000	
5A	Medium	1st			Hoger beroepsonderwijs (HBO) (higher professional education) 4-year programmes	Ingenieur (Ing), baccalaureus (Bc)	17	4	5-6	15	3A			270000	Of which 43 000 part-time. Internationally, HBO (4-year programme) graduates may adopt the Bachelor's title (B.).
5A	Medium	1st			Universitair onderwijs (WO) (university education)	Doctorandus (Drs), meester (Mr)	18	4	5-6	16	3A			145000	Of which 12 000 part-time. Internationally, university graduates may adopt the Master's title.
5A	Long	1st			Universitair onderwijs (WO) (university education)	Ingenieur (Ir), doctorandus (Drs)	18	5	7-8	17	3A			16000	Mainly full-time. Primarily programmes in the exact sciences. Internationally, university graduates may adopt the Master's title.
5A	Long	2nd			Hoger beroepsonderwijs (HBO) tweede fase (higher professional training second stage)		21	1.5-4		17	HBO 4 years			6500	Mainly part-time enrolment. Programmes for first degree holders: teachers, architecture, advanced music.
5A	Long	2nd			Universitair onderwijs (wo) tweede fase (university education second stage)		22	1-2		18	5A (1st)			5000	Mainly full-time. Programmes for medical doctors and teachers who have a first degree.
6		1st			AIO's en OIO's (research assistants)	Doctor (Dr)= Ph.D.	22	3	3	19	5A (1st)			7000	

MANUAL FOR ISCED-97 IMPLEMENTATION IN OECD COUNTRIES – 1999 EDITION

ISCED-97 level	Programme orientation	Cumulative duration at ISCED 5	Position in the national degree/qualification structure (Intermediate, First, Second, etc.)	Notes on programmes that span across ISCED levels or sub-categories	Descriptive name of the programme	Main diplomas, credentials or certifications	Typical starting ages	Theoretical length of the programme	Typical length of the programme	Cumulative years of education at the end of the programme	Minimum entrance requirement	Programme specifically designed for part-time attendance	Reported in the UOE	Enrolment 1996-97 *	Other relevant information
New Zealand															
0					Early childhood education	None	0.5-3.5	2	2	2		Yes		102969	Children aged 3 and over at licensed centres with qualified teachers.
1					Primary	None	5	6	6	6				357568	Students in Year 1 to Year 6 of schooling.
2	G				Secondary (Year 7 to Year 10)	None	11-12	4	4	10	1			221976	Students in Year 7 to Year 10 of schooling.
3C	V				Certificate	Certificate, National Certificate (Levels 1, 2)	17-20	<1	<1	12	2			36664	Pre-employment. National Certificate Levels 1-2.
3B	P				Certificate	Certificate, National Certificate (Levels 1, 2)	17-20	<1	<1	12	2			43648	Bridging type programmes. National Certificate Levels 1-2.
3A	G				Upper Secondary (Year 11 to Year 13)	Y11=School Cert.; Y12 = 6th form Cert.; Y13= Bursary	15-16	3	2	13	2			132731	Students in Year 11 to Year 13 of schooling. Graduates from this level include only those who leave school with 6th form Certificate.
4C					Certificate	Certificate, National Certificate (Levels 3-5)	17-20	1	1	13	3			2552	
4B					Certificate	Certificate, National Certificate (Levels 3-5)	17-20	1	1	13	3			6134	
5B	Medium		1st		Diploma	Diploma, National Diplomas (Levels 5, 6)	18-19	3	3	16	3A or 3B			43498	Vocationally-oriented programme of 2-3 years cumulative duration.
5A	Medium		1st	5A, 5B	Bachelor's degree	Bachelor's degree, National Diploma (Level 7)	18-19	3	3	16	3A			93407	Majority are 3-year programmes.
5A	Medium		2nd		Post-graduate	Bachelor's Honours, Post-graduate Certificates, Post-graduate Diplomas, Masters	21-24	1-2	1-2	18	5A (1st)			19649	Can be done as 1 year in addition to the Bachelor's degree or for capable students as a 4-year, first degree.
6		Very long			Doctorate, Higher Doctorates	Ph.D.	24-25	3-5	3-5	21-23	5A (1st)			2744	
NC					Community/Continuing education	None	17-60	0.2	0.2	13		Yes	No		Hobby classes, therefore excluded from the UOE data collection.

* The enrolments for school year 1996-97 are estimated.

101

Norway

ISCED-97 level	Programme orientation	Cumulative duration at ISCED 5	Position in the national degree/qualification structure (intermediate, First, Second, etc.)	Notes on programmes that span across ISCED levels or sub-categories	Descriptive name of the programme	Main diplomas, credentials or certifications	Typical starting ages	Theoretical length of the programme	Typical length of the programme	Cumulative years of education at the end of the programme	Minimum entrance requirement	Programme specifically designed for part-time attendance	Reported in the UOE	Enrolment 1996-97	Other relevant information
0					Barnehage (kindergarten) og Førskole (pre-school)		3	3	3					183500	Centre-based institutions for children aged 3 to less than 6. As a rule, the staff have special educational qualifications, which are officially recognised.
1					Grunnskole 1.-7. klasse (primary school)		6	7	7	7				330600	Start of compulsory education at age 6. Grades 1-7.
2A	G				Ungdomsskole 8.-10. klasse (lower secondary)	Grunnskolens avgangsvitnemål	13	3	3	10				155600	Part two of compulsory education. Grades 8-10.
3C	V				Videregående opplæring, yrkesfag (upper secondary vocational)	Vitnemål, fagbrev	15-17	1-3	1-3	13	2			107000	3-year vocational programme with mainly occupational basic education. Includes apprenticeships.
3A	G				Videregående opplæring, Allmennfag (upper secondary, giving access to further education, general)	Vitnemål	15-16	3	3	13	2			100000	3-year upper secondary, general programme. Successful graduates of this programme are entitled to enter ISCED 5A programmes.
4C	V				Teknisk fagskole (specialist vocational education)	Vitnemål	17-40	2	2	15	3C			3700	2-year vocational programme which requires completion of the first year (grunnkurs) of vocational upper secondary school, or relevant vocational practice.
4C	V				Arbeidsmarkedsopplæring (AMO) (labour market courses)		20-60	0.5-3	1		2			19300	This programme comprises a whole range of different courses offered to the unemployed, both long and short, vocational and general.
4A	G				Forberedende prøver (preparatory courses)		18-23	1	1	14	3A			11700	This programme comprises several preparatory courses for entry to higher (tertiary) education.
5A		Short			Høgre utd., <3 år, lavere grad (tertiary education, <3 years, 1st degree)	Høgskolekandidat, reseptar, dørvetolk, tamptøer, audiograf	19	1-2.5	1-2.5	14-16	3A			approx. 12000	These are short tertiary programmes, duration: 1-2.5 years. Generally vocationally oriented, but can also be included in a longer programme.
5A		Medium			Høgre utd., lavere grad (tertiary education, 3 years)	Sykepleier, fysioterapi, ergoterapi, bioing., radiograf, vernepleier, sosionom, ortopedi, barnevernsped, førskolelærer, faglærer, bibliotekut, ingeniør, maritim utd.	19	3-5	1-3	14-16				approx. 32600	These are short tertiary programmes, duration: 3 years. Generally vocationally oriented, but can also be included as part of a longer general programme.
5A		Medium			Høgre utd., 4 år, lavere grad (tertiary education, 4 years, 1st degree)	Cand.mag., allmennlærer, siviløkonom	19	4	4	17	3A			approx. 60000	These are medium length programmes, which could be the first part of a longer programme, or a more vocational aimed independent education. The cand. mag is a modular programme where the students can combine a variety of different subjects and courses.
5A		Long			Høgre utdanning, langtprofesjonsutdanninger (tertiary education long/professional education, 1st degree)	Cand. pharm., cand.jur., cand.med., cand.psychol., cand.theol., cand.odont., cand.sosion., siving., fiskerikandidat, arkitekt	19	5-6.5	5-6.5	17-20	3A			approx. 24000	These are long programmes, 5-6 years of duration, primarily aimed at professional education.
5A		Long			Hovedfag/mag.art (tertiary education, second degree)	Cand.polit., cand.philol., cand.scient., mag.art	23	6-7	5.5-7.5	18.5-20	3A, 5A (1st, M)			approx. 20000	This programme is a long programme. The students have to attain a cand. mag degree to continue the second part of the programme.
6					Doktorgrad (Doctorate)	Dr.philos., dr.philol., dr.scient., dring., dr.jur., dr.art, dr.theol., dr.polit., dr.techn., dr.med., dr.odont.	25	4		23	5A (2nd, VL)			3072	Advanced research programme.

Poland

ISCED-97 level	Programme orientation	Cumulative duration at ISCED 5	Position in the national degree/qualification structure (intermediate, First, Second, etc.)	Notes on programmes that span across ISCED levels or sub-categories	Descriptive name of the programme	Main diplomas, credentials or certifications	Typical starting ages	Theoretical length of the programme	Typical length of the programme	Cumulative years of education at the end of the programme	Minimum entrance requirement	Programme specifically designed for part-time attendance	Reported in the UOE	Enrolment 1996-97	Other relevant information
0					Wychowanie przedszkolne (pre-school education)		3	1-4	4						Holistic approach is taken for the individual development of children and for their school preparation. Pre-school studies are not compulsory. Programme duration is 1 to 4 years and entry to the compulsory education is preceded by one-year long pre-school preparation.
2A	G		ISCED 1 and 2	Levels 1 and 2A	Szkoła podstawowa (primary school)	Primary school leaving certificate entitles its holder to apply for education at the secondary level	7	8	8	8					
3C				General and vocational	Szkoła zasadnicza (basic vocational school)	Basic vocational school leaving certificate; qualified worker or worker with equivalent qualification	15	3	3	11					
3A				General and vocational	Liceum zawodowe (secondary school of vocational education)	"Matura" certificate (entitles to apply for higher education institutions), secondary school of vocational education certificate (without taking examination "matura", qualified worker certificate)	15	4	4	12					
3A				General and vocational	Technikum (secondary technical school)	"Matura" certificate (as above), secondary technical school certificate (as above), technician diploma	15	4-5	5	12-13					This programme can be done after basic vocational school, and in this case it lasts 2.5 to 3 years (entrance age 18) and the entrance qualification is the basic vocational school leaving certificate in the discipline to be continued at the higher level.
3A				General and vocational	Liceum techniczne (technical secondary liceum)	"Matura" certificate (as above), technical secondary liceum certificate (as above)	15	4	4	12					
3A	G				Liceum ogólnokształcące (secondary school of general education)	"Matura" certificate (as above), secondary general school certificate (as above)	15	4-5	4	12-13					
4B	V				Szkoła policealna (post-secondary school)	Post-secondary school certificate, technician or other equivalent diploma or certificate, qualified worker or worker with equivalent qualification diploma or certificate	19	1-2.5	2	13-15.5	3A				
5B		Medium			Kolegium nauczycielskie (teacher training college)	Teacher training college graduation diploma, teacher's qualification to perform at pre-school institutions, primary school and other educational institutions	19-20	3	3	13-16	3A				As to the typical entry qualification, candidates must go through the enrolment procedure established by the school.
5B		Medium			Nauczycielskie kolegium języków obcych (foreign language teacher training college)	Foreign language teacher certificate training college graduation diploma, teacher's qualification to teach West European languages	19-20	3	3	13-16	3A				
5A		Medium	1st		Wyższe studia zawodowe (higher education professional studies)	Professional degree: "licencjat" (licentiate), "inżynier" (engineer) diploma or equivalent certificate	19-20	3-4	3-4	15-17	3A				Licentiate courses last 3 years, engineer courses last 3.5 to 4 years.
5A		Long	2nd		Studia magisterskie (university studies)	"Magister" (Master) degree, "magister inżynier" (master-engineer)	19-20	5-5.5	5	17-18.5	3A				Person eligible for study at any age.
5A		Long	2nd		Studia medyczne (university medical studies)	Lekarz (physician)	19-20	6	6	17-19	3A				Person eligible for study at any age.
5A		Long	2nd		Post-graduate courses	Post-graduate courses graduation certificate	24	0.5-2	1.5-2	16-17	5A (1st, M)				Person eligible for study at any age.
5A		Long	2nd	Long or very long	Studia uzupełniające magisterskie (post-licentiate master diploma studies)	"Magister" (master) degree, "magister inżynier" degree	22-23	1.5-2	2	17	5A (1st, L), 5A (2nd)				
6		Very long	3rd or +		Studia doktoranckie (doctoral studies)	Scientific degree of Doctor (it can be compared to Ph.D.)	24-30	4	4	21	5A (1st, M)				Lasts no longer than 4 years and most programmes last 4 years.

103

Portugal

ISCED-97 level	Programme orientation	Cumulative duration at ISCED 5	Position in the national degree/qualification structure (Intermediate, First, Second, etc.)	Notes on programmes that span across ISCED levels or sub-categories	Descriptive name of the programme	Main diplomas, credentials or certifications	Typical starting ages	Theoretical length of the programme	Typical length of the programme	Cumulative years of education at the end of the programme	Minimum entrance requirement	Programme specifically designed for part-time attendance	Reported in the UOE	Enrolment 1995-96	Other relevant information
0					Educação Pré-Escolar (pre-school education)		3-5	3	3					190870	
1					Formação Profissional – Pré-Aprendizagem (vocational training – level I)	Diploma de Nível I	14-15	1 500 hours	1 500 hours	6	1				
1					Educação Extra-Escolar – Actualização (adult education – primary education)	Certificado	15-70	Variable	Variable			Yes	No	372	
1					Educação Extra-Escolar Sócio-Profissionais (adult education – primary education)	Certificado	15-70	Variable	Variable			Yes	No	5374	
1					Educação Extra-Escolar: Sócio- Educativos (adult education – primary education)	Certificado	15-70	Variable	Variable			Yes	No	5997	
1					C. Form. Prof. Extra-Escolar (vocational training – level I)	Certificado	15-70	Variable	Variable			Yes	No		
1					Educação Extra-Escolar – Alfabetização (adult education – literacy programmes)	Certificado	15-70	Variable	Variable			Yes	No	741	
1					C.T.P. da Casa Pia – Nível I (vocational training – level I)	Certificado de Nível I e Equivalência ao 6º ano	13-16	2	2	6	1				
1					Ensino Básico 1º e 2º Ciclos (primary education)		6-15	6	6	6				807882	
1					Ensino Recorrente (1º e 2º Ciclos) (adult education – primary education)		15-65	6	6	6		Yes	No	20134	
1					Curso Básico de Música (music studies – elemental level)	Certificado	6-14	5	5	9	1			2496	
2C	V				C.F.Prof. Regime Aprendizagem (vocational training – level II)	Diploma de Nível II e Equivalência ao 9º ano de Escolaridade	14-15	3	3	9	1		No		
2C	V				Form.Profissional nas Empresas (vocational training – level II)	Diploma de Nível II e Equivalência ao 9º ano de Escolaridade	14-15	3	3	9	1	Yes	No		
2B	P				Escolas Profissionais Nível II (vocational training – level II)	Diploma de Nível II e Equivalência ao 9º ano de Escolaridade	11-16	3	3	9	1			1393	
2B	P				Cursos Gerais Técnicos (vocational training – level II)	Diploma	14-18	3	3	9	1	Yes	No	2935	
2B	P				C.T.P. da Casa Pia Nível II (vocational training – level II)	Diploma de Nível II e Equivalência ao 9º ano de Escolaridade	15-18	3	3	9	1				
2B	P				Curso Geral de Dança (dance studies – elemental level)	Certificado	9-14	5	5	9	1			74	
2A	G				Ensino Básico 3º Ciclo (lower secondary education)	Diploma do Ensino Básico	11-15	3	3	9	1			429278	
2A	G				Ens. Recorrente (3º Ciclo) (adult education – lower secondary education)	Diploma do Ensino Básico e Certificado	15-70	3	3	9	1	Yes		38181	
2A	G				Curso Geral Liceal (old educational system programmes)	Diploma	15-18	3	3	9	1	Yes	No		
3C	G				Cur. Complementar Liceal (upper secondary education – general education)	Diploma	15	2	2	11	2	Yes		46025	
3C	V				Cur. Complementares Técnicos (upper secondary education – vocational education)	Diploma	15	2	2	11	2	Yes		10407	
3C	V				Escolas Profissionais Nível III (vocational training – level III)	Diploma de Nível III e Equivalência ao 12º ano de Escolaridade	15-17	3	3	12	2			25114	Enrolment data for all Escolas Profissionais, level III.
3C	V				C.T.P. da Casa Pia – Nível III (vocational training – level III)	Certificado de Nível III e Equivalência ao 12º ano de Escolaridade	15-18	3	3	12	2		No		

Portugal (continued)										
3C	V		Form. Prof. em Estab. Militares (vocational training – level III in military schools)	Diploma de Nível III e Equivalência ao 12º ano de Escolaridade	18-21	3	3	12	2		No
3C	V		Instituto Form. Bancária (vocational training – level III – banking)	Diploma de Nível III e Equivalência ao 12º ano de Escolaridade	18-65	3	3	12	2	Yes	No
3C	V		C. de Educador Social (vocational training – level III – social worker)	Diploma de Nível III e Equivalência ao 12º ano de Escolaridade	15-65	3 195 hours	3 195 hours	12	2		No
3C	V		Escolas Profissionais Nível III (Pós laboral) (vocational training – level III)	Diploma de Nível III e Equivalência ao 12º ano de Escolaridade	15-65	3 600 hours	3 600 hours	12	2	Yes	
3C	V		C. Téc. Prof. (Pós Laborais) (vocational training – level III)	Diploma de especialização e Equivalência ao 12º ano	16-65	5	5	14	2	Yes	1585
3B	P		Curso Complementar de Música (music studies – intermediate level)	Diploma de Nível III e Equivalência ao 12º ano de Escolaridade	15	3	3	12	2		13367 Enrolment data for ISCED 2 and 3.
3B	P		Curso Complementar de Dança (dance studies – intermediate level)	Diploma e Equivalência ao 12º ano de Escolaridade	14-21	3	3	12	2		52
3B	V		Artes Visuais – Secundário (fine arts – intermediate level)	Diploma de Nível III e Equivalência ao 12º ano de Escolaridade	15-21	3	3	12	2		1717
3B	V		Ens. Sec. Cursos Tecnológicos (upper secondary education – vocational education)	Diploma de Nível III e Equivalência ao 12º ano de Escolaridade	15-18	3	3	12	2		84292
3B	V		Ensino Recorrente (Secundário) Cursos Técnicos (adult education – upper secondary education – vocational training)	Diploma de Nível III e Equivalência ao 12º ano de Escolaridade	18-65	3	3	12	2	Yes	
3A	G		12º ano – Via de Ensino (upper secondary education – general education)	Certificado	16-18	1	1	12	2	Yes	66887
3A	G		Ensino Secundário Cursos Gerais (upper secondary education – general education)	Diploma do Ensino Secundário	14-18	3	3	12	2		227197
3A	G		Ensino Recorrente (Secundário) Curso Geral (adult education – upper secondary education – general education)	Diploma do Ensino Secundário	18-65	3	3	12	2	Yes	12064 Data for all Recorrente Secundário.
5B		Medium	Ensino Superior – Bacharelato (higher education – first degree)	Diploma de Bacharel	18-20	3-4	3-4	15	3A, 3B		70299
5A		Medium	Ensino Superior – Licenciatura (university education)	Diploma de Licenciatura	18-23	4	4	16	3A, 3B		223739 Data for all Licenciatura.
5A		Long	Ensino Superior – Licenciatura (university education)	Diploma de Licenciatura	18-23	5	5	17	3A, 3B		
5A		Very long	Ensino Superior – Licenciatura (university education)	Diploma de Licenciatura	18-23	6	6	18	3A, 3B		
5A		Long	Ensino Superior – Licenciatura Terminal	Diploma de Licenciatura	22-24	1-2	1-2	16-17	5A (1st, M), 5A (1st, L)		
5A		Long	Ensino Superior – Pós-Licenciatura (university education)	Diploma de Pós-Licenciatura	23-25	1	1	17-19	5A (1st)		1749 Data for all Pós-Licenciatura.
5A		Long	Ensino Superior – DESE (higher education – second degree)	Diploma de DESE	21	2	2	17	5B (1st, M)		13494
5A		Very long	Ensino Superior – Pós-Licenciatura (university education)	Diploma de Pós-Licenciatura	24-26	2	1	18-20	5A (1st)		
6		1st	Ensino Superior – Mestrado (university education)	Diploma de Mestre	23-25	2	2	18-20	5A (1st, M), 5A (1st, L)		10244
6		2nd	Ensino Superior – Doutoramento (university education – doctorate)	Diploma de Doutor	25	4-5	4-5	22-25	6 (1st)		No
NC			Cur. Línguas – Extra-Escolar (1) (languages studies)	Certificado	15-70					Yes	No

ISCED-97 level	Programme orientation	Cumulative duration at ISCED 5	Position in the national degree/qualification structure (Intermediate, First, Second, etc.)	Notes on programmes that span across ISCED levels or sub-categories	Descriptive name of the programme	Main diplomas, credentials or certifications	Typical starting ages	Theoretical length of the programme	Typical length of the programme	Cumulative years of education at the end of the programme	Minimum entrance requirement	Programme specifically designed for part-time attendance	Reported in the UOE	Enrolment 1996-97	Other relevant information
Spain															
0					Educación Infantil (pre-school education)		2-4		3					1115244	This programme was introduced by the 1990 General Arrangement of Education System Act (L.O.G.S.E.).
1					Educación Primaria (primary education)		6	6	6	6				2682730	This programme was introduced by L.O.G.S.E. and completely replaced the old system in the school year 1995-96.
1					Enseñanzas Iniciales de Educación Básica para personas en edad adulta (adult education – primary level)		18-65			6		Yes	No	58621	
2C	V				F.P. Aprendizaje de Tareas (vocational training – special education)	School's certification	16-18	0.25-1	3	12-13				6929	If the main criteria were to be the "age of participants", this programme might be classified at Level 3, Technical/vocational
2C	V			2C, 3C	Formación ocupacional (occupational training)	Certificado de profesionalidad	16-55	0.25-1	0.25-1		2		No	247063	There are programmes with different entry requirements (from Level 2 to Level 5A), so the cumulative years of schooling change with the programmes.
2B	P				E. de la Danza-Grado Elemental (dance studies – elementary level)	Certificado elemental	8-12		4			Yes	No	5095	
2B	P				E. de la Música-Grado Elemental (music studies – elementary level)	Certificado elemental	8-12		4			Yes	No	70018	
2A	G				E. General Básica (Ciclo Superior) [general basic education (upper cycle)]	Graduado Escolar	11-13	3	3	8	1			454384	Programme left over from the old educational system: since school year 1994-95, the upper level of General Basic Education (E.G.B.) has been the only cycle with students still enrolled. Initial and Medium had been replaced by Educación Primaria. EGB-Ciclo Superior disappeared in 1996/97.
2A	G				Enseñanzas de adultos conducentes al Certificado de Escolaridad y al Graduado Escolar (adult education)	Certificado de Escolaridad, Graduado Escolar	18-65			8	1	Yes	No	138483	
2A	G				Educación Secundaria para Adultos (adult secondary education)	Graduado en Educación Secundaria	18-65	2	2	10	1	Yes	No	11291	
2A	G				Educación Secundaria Obligatoria (compulsory secondary education)	Graduado en Educación Secundaria	12-13	4	4	10	1			1181466	This programme belongs to the new education system (L.O.G.S.E.) and it will completely replace the programmes at this level belonging to the old system in 1999/2000.
3C	P				Escuelas Oficiales de Idiomas (languages studies at the official school languages)	Certificado de aptitud	14-30	2	5	10-12	2	Yes		271289	Only the second stage of this programme is included in the UOE data collection.
3C	V				Formación Profesional I (vocational training – first tier)	Técnico Auxiliar (equivalent to Técnico)	14-20	2	2	10	2			232113	This programme belongs to the old education system and it is being replaced by the new system. It will disappear in 1999/2000.
3C	V				F.P. I para Adultos (vocational training – first tier – adult education)	Técnico Auxiliar (equivalent to Técnico)	18-65			10	2	Yes		44797	
3C	V			Levels 3/4/5, vocational and technical	Casas de oficio (craft trades)	Certification	16-25	1	1	<=11	2			11680	There are programmes with different entry requirements (from Level 2 to Level 5A), so the cumulative years of schooling change with the programmes.
3C	V				Capacitación agrícola (agricultural qualification)	Capataz agrícola	16-30	2	2	10	2			1119	
3C	V				Programas de Garantía Social (vocational training for young people without qualifications)	School's certification	16-20	1-2	1-2	11-12	2			15713	This programme belongs to the new system (L.O.G.S.E.) and at the moment is still in an experimental stage.
3C	V				Artes Aplicadas y Oficios Artísticos – Cursos comunes (applied arts and artistic crafts – common grades)		14-30	3	3	11	2			16214	
3C	V				Ciclos Formativos de Formación Profesional de Grado Medio (specific vocational training – intermediate level)	Técnico	16-20	1.5-2	1.5-2	11.5	2			48609	This programme belongs to the new system (L.O.G.S.E.).
3C	V				C.Format. G°Medio (Distancia)	Técnico	18-30	1.5-2	1.5-2	11.5	2	Yes		203	This programme belongs to the new system (L.O.G.S.E.).
3C	V				Ciclos Formativos de Artes Plásticas y Diseño de Grado Medio (specific vocational training of plastic arts and design – intermediate level)	Técnico	16-20	1.5-2	2	12	2			1249	
3C	V				E. de la Danza-Grado Medio (dance studies – intermediate level)	Título Profesional	12-16	2	6	12		Yes		73	
3C	V				E. de la Música-Grado Medio (music studies – intermediate level)	Título Profesional	12-16	2	6	12		Yes		41896	
3C	V			Levels 3/4/5, vocational and technical	Escuelas taller (workshop training)	Certification	16-25	2	2	12	2	Yes		44510	There are programmes with different entry requirements (from Level 2 to Level 5A), so the cumulative years of schooling change with the programmes.
3B	V				Escala básica guardia civil (civil guard basic school)	Guardia civil, cabo de la guardia civil	16	3	3	13	2		No	745017	This programme belongs to the old education system. It is being replaced in advance by Bachillerato L.O.G.S.E. and will disappear in 2000/01.
3A	G			3B, 3C	B.U.P. (unified polyvalent general upper secondary education)	Bachiller	14-16	3	3	11	2			36333	This programme will disappear in 2001/02.
3A	G				B.U.P. (Distancia) [unified polyvalent general upper secondary education (distance)]	Bachiller	18-30	3	3	11	2	Yes			
3A	G				C.O.U. (university guidance course)	It does not award any diploma or certification, but it is necessary to pass it in order to apply for the access to the university. It belongs to the old education system; will disappear in 2001/02.	17-22	1	1	12	3A			335767	This programme is a preparatory course for entry into university, so it has been included in Level 3A. It is part of the old education system and will disappear in 2001/02.

MANUAL FOR ISCED-97 IMPLEMENTATION IN OECD COUNTRIES – 1999 EDITION

Spain (continued)

3A G			C.O.U. (Distancia) [university guidance course (distance)]	It does not award any diploma or certification, but it is necessary to pass it in order to apply for the access to the university. It belongs to the old education system; will disappear in 2001/02.	18-30	1	1	12	3A	Yes	12131 This programme is a preparatory course for entry into university, so it has been included in Level 3A. It is part of the old education system and will disappear in 2001/02.
3A G			Bachillerato L.O.G.S.E. [general upper secondary education (new educational system)]	Bachiller	16-18	2	2	12	2		153836 This programme belongs to the new system (L.O.G.S.E.) and it will completely replace B.U.P./C.O.U. 2001/02.
4B V			Artes Aplicadas y Oficios Artísticos - Especialidad (applied arts and artistic crafts – speciality)	Graduado en Artes Aplicadas y Oficios Artísticos	17-30	2	2	13	2		9250
4A V		Level 3, P	Formación Profesional II (vocational training – second tier)	Técnico Especialista (equivalent to Técnico Superior)	16-30	3	3	13	3A, 3C		369369 This programme belongs to the old education system. It was included in the 1998 UOE data collection at ISCED 3, 2nd programmes. It will disappear in 2002/03.
5B	1st		Formacion militar grado básico (military programme, basic grade)	Militar de carrera de la escala básica (equivalent to Técnico Superior)	18-25	2	2	14	3A		1939
5B	1st		Ciclos Formativos de Artes Plásticas y Diseño de Grado Superior (specific vocational training of plastic arts and design – advanced level)	Técnico Superior	18-25	2	2	14	3A, 4B		2877
5B	1st		Título de piloto comercial de avión	Piloto comercial de avión	18	2	2	14	3A		385
5B	1st		Ciclos Formativos de Formación Profesional de Grado Superior (specific vocational training – advanced level)	Técnico Superior	18-30	2	2	14	3A, 4A		54465 This programme belongs to the new system (L.O.G.S.E.).
5A	Short	Intermediate	Estudios Universitarios Primer Ciclo (university education – first cycle)	Certification of the university	18-20	2-3		14-15	3A, 5B		Enrolment included in Licenciatura universitaria.
5A	Medium	1st	Estudios de Turismo (tourism studies)	Técnico de Empresas y Actividades Turísticas (equivalent to Diplomado Universitario)	18	3	3	15	3A		18651
5A	Medium	1st	Diplomatura Universitaria (university education – first degree)	Diplomado Universitario, Arquitecto Técnico e Ingeniero Técnico	18-20	3	3-4	15	3A, 4A, 5B		532069
5A	Medium	1st	Formación superior militar grado medio (military programme, medium grade)	Militar de carrera de la escala media (equivalent to Diplomado Universitario)	18-22	3	3	15	3A		659
5A	Medium	1st	Conservación y Restauración de Bienes Culturales (conservation and restoration of cultural assets)	Conservación y Restauración de Bienes Culturales (this diploma is equivalent to "Diplomado Universitario")	18-30	3	3	15	3A		389
5A	Medium	2nd	Título de piloto transporte de líneas aéreas	Piloto de transporte de línea aérea	21	2	2	15-16	3A, 5B		112
5A	Medium	2nd	Militar grado medio postgrado (post-first degree military programmes)	Militar de carrera de la escala media especialista	21-31	1	1	16-	5A (1st, M)	No	53
5A	Medium	2nd	E. de la Danza-Grado Superior (dance studies – advanced level)	Titulación Superior por especialidad (equivalent to Licenciado universitario)	18-30	4	4	16	3A		New: no enrolment yet.
5A	Medium	2nd	E. de la Música-Grado Superior (E. Musicales-Grado Superior)	Titulación Superior por especialidad musical (equivalent to Licenciado universitario)	18-30	4	4	16	3A		5310
5A	Medium	2nd	Estudios Superiores de Arte Dramático (higher dramatic art studies)	Título Superior de Arte Dramático (equivalent to Licenciado universitario)	18-30	4	4	16	3A		1084
5A	Long	2nd	Estudios Universitarios de Segundo Ciclo-Licenciatura universitaria (university education – second cycle)	Licenciado e Ingeniero	21-22	2	3	17-18	5A (1st, M)		Enrolment included in Licenciatura universitaria.
5A	Long	2nd	Licenciatura universitaria	Licenciado, Arquitecto e Ingeniero	18-20	4-6	4-6	17	3A		1004167 Enrolment includes "Estudios Universitarios de primer ciclo" and "Estudios universitarios de segundo ciclo".
5A	Long	2nd	Formación militar grado superior (military programme, higher grade)	Militar de carrera de la escala superior (equivalent to Licenciado universitario)	18-22	5	5	17	3A, 5B, 5A (1st)		1213
5A	Long	3rd or +	Militar superior postgrado (post-second degree military programmes)	Militar de carrera de la escala superior especialista	23-31	1	1	18	5A (2nd, L)	No	108
5A	Long	3rd or +	Máster y Estudios Postgrado de las Universidades (post-degree studies of universities)	Certificación de cada Universidad	22-26	1-2	1-2	18-20	5A (2nd)		
5A	Very long	3rd or +	Especialidades Sanitarias	Título Oficial de Postgrado de la Especialidad Profesional	24-	3-5	3-5	21-23	5A (1st, 2nd)	No	15000
6			Doctorado (university education – Doctorate)	Doctor	23-27	4-6	4-6	21-22	5A (2nd)		60833

107

MANUAL FOR ISCED-97 IMPLEMENTATION IN OECD COUNTRIES – 1999 EDITION

Sweden

ISCED-97 level	Programme orientation	Cumulative duration at ISCED 5	Position in the national degree/qualification structure (Intermediate, First, Second, etc.)	Notes on programmes that span across ISCED levels or sub-categories	Descriptive name of the programme	Main diplomas, credentials or certifications	Typical starting ages	Theoretical length of the programme	Typical length of the programme	Cumulative years of education at the end of the programme	Minimum entrance requirement	Programme specifically designed for part-time attendance	Reported in the UOE	Enrolment 1996-97	Other relevant information
0					Daghem (day care centres)		2-6	2.5	5			Yes		270400	Day care centres deliver a combination of day care and pre-primary education, with the education component estimated to be 50%.
0					Förskolan (preschool)		5-6	0.5	1			Yes		73900	Pre-primary school will most likely disappear in the future as more 6-year-olds enter primary school.
1C	G			Levels 1 and 2	Grundläggande vuxenutbildning (municipal basic adult education)	Slutbetyg från grundläggande vuxenutbildning	20-55	2	3	9		Yes		36000	This programme is compulsory school and comprises both ISCED 1 and 2.
1A	G			Levels 1 and 2	Grundskolan (compulsory basic school)	Slutbetyg från grundskolan	6-7	9	9	9				959000	This programme is compulsory school and comprises both ISCED 1 and 2.
1B	G			Levels 1 and 2	Obligatoriska särskolan (compulsory basic school for mentally handicapped)	Slutbetyg från grundsärskolan	6-8	10	10	10				9900	This programme is special education for young persons with special needs.
1A	G			Levels 1 and 2	Specialskolan (special school for those with impaired sight/hearing and speech)	Slutbetyg från specialskolan	6-8	10	10	10				800	This programme is special education for young persons with a double handicap.
1				Levels 1 to 3	Särskolan för vuxna (adult education for the mentally handicapped)		17-55	12	12	12				3900	This programme is special education for adults with special needs.
1					Svenska för vuxna invandrare (Swedish for immigrants)	Betyg, SFI	20-55	1		7-20			No	41100	This programme is education in Swedish for adult immigrants.
2A	G			Divided into 2A/G and 3C/V	Gymnasieskolan IV (upper secondary school, individual programmes)		16	3	1	10-12				16000	The programme is individually designed to meet the needs of each student. Eventually the student will transfer to another programme at the same level of education after one year.
3C	V			Levels 3 to 5	Arbetsmarknadsutb (labour market training)		17-55	1		10			No		Labour market relevant education.
3C	V			Levels 3 to 5	Folkhögskolan yrkes (folk high school, vocational)	Professional certificates	17-55	3	3	12	2		No	2500	Professional certificates.
3C	V			Divided into 2A/G and 3C/V	Gymnasiesärskolan (upper secondary education for the mentally handicapped)	Slutbetyg från gymnasiesärskolan	16	4	4	14	2			4050	This programme is special education for young persons with special needs.
3	V			Levels 3 or 4	Komvux yrkes (municipal adult education, vocational)	Slutbetyg från gymnasial vuxenutbildning eller påbyggnadsutbildning	20-55	3	3	12	2				Adult education on Level 4: vocational education is classified in 4C, general education is classified in 4A.
3A	V				Gymnasieskolan övriga (upper secondary school, other programmes)	Slutbetyg från gymnasieskolan	16	3	3	12	2			154700	
3A	V				Gymnasieskolan NV SP (upper secondary school, science programmes + International Baccalaureate – IB)	Slutbetyg från gymnasieskolan	16	3	3	12	2			135400	
3A	G			3A, 3B	Folkhögskolan allmän inr (folk high school, general)	Studentexamen	17-55	3	3	12	2		No	11000	
3	G			Levels 3 or 4	Komvux allmän (municipal adult education, general)	Slutbetyg från gymnasial vuxenutbildning	20-55	3	3	12	2			132000	The enrolment figure comprises both komvux allmän and komvux yrkes. Adult education on Level 4: vocational formation is classified in 4C, general formation is classified in 4A.
3	G			Levels 3 or 4, general and vocational	Staters skolor för vuxna (national school for adults)	Studentexamen	20-55	3	3	12	2			25200	
5B		Short	1st		Higher education < 3 years	Högskoleexamen/Yrkesexamen < 120 poäng, Kvalificerad yrkesutbildning	19	2-3	2-3	13.5-14.5	3A, 3C			260000	This group of programmes includes different types of teacher education, vocational education and engineering as well as specialisation in one subject which might lead on to post-graduate education. The enrolment figure includes "higher education >4 years"
5A		Medium	1st		Higher education 3-4 years	Bachelor of .../University diploma in... (Kandidatexamen i.../Yrkesexamen i...)	19	3-4		15-16	3A, 3C				Some typical fields are education of agronomists, civil engineers, medical doctors, dentists, veterinarians, pharmacists.
5A		Medium	1st		Higher education >4 years	Master of .../University diploma in... (Magisterexamen i.../Yrkesexamen i...)	19	4.5-5.5		16-17.5	3A, 3C				When the students graduate it is possible to determine the relative size of this programme (843 in 1996/97).
6					Post-graduate education shorter	Licentiate examination	22	2-2.5		17-17.5	5A (1st, M) 5A (1st, L)				
6					Post-graduate education longer	Doctor's degree	22	4		19	5A (1st, M) 5A (1st, L)			16000	Enrolment number includes "post-graduate education shorter".

Switzerland

ISCED-97 level	Programme orientation	Cumulative duration at ISCED 5	Position in the national degree/qualification structure (Intermediate, First, Second, etc.)	Notes on programmes that span across ISCED levels or sub-categories	Descriptive name of the programme	Main diplomas, credentials or certifications	Typical starting ages	Theoretical length of the programme	Typical length of the programme	Cumulative years of education at the end of the programme	Minimum entrance requirement	Programme specifically designed for part-time attendance	Reported in the UOE	Enrolment 1997-98	Other relevant information
0					Vorschule, préscolarité, prescolarità (kindergarten)		4-6	2	2					160000	The programmes in Switzerland last for one or two years (the length offered being the choice of the canton or the commune within the canton).
1					Primarschule, école primaire, scuola elementare (primary school)		6-7	6	6	6				493000	The entry age to primary education is either 6 years (4 cantons), 6 1/2 years (2 cantons) or 7 years (17 cantons). One canton leaves the decision whether to start school within 6 or 7 years to the communes.
1					Besondere Lehrplan, programme d'enseignement spécial, programma scolastico speciale (special education programmes)		5-6	6	6	6				29000	Programmes for students with special education needs that are similar in content to primary education.
1					Programmes for adults in basic literacy skills							Yes	No		No data available.
2A	G				Sekundarschule, Realschule, Oberschule, (Pro-) Gymnasium, Cycle d'orientation, Scuola media (secondary education, first stage)		11-12	3	3	9	1			245000	Together with primary education, these education programmes make up the 9 years of compulsory schooling. The programmes therefore actually last between three and five years, and are reported as three years for international comparison.
2A	G				10. Schuljahr, Vorkurs, préapprentissage, corsi preparatori (preparatory course for vocational education, 1 year)		15-17	1	1	10	2			14000	The programmes last one year, are general in content and prepare the students mainly for vocational education in the dual system (by "upgrading" the skills of students coming from lower secondary programmes with basic demands, for instance).
2A	G				Besondere Lehrplan, programme d'enseignement spécial, programma scolastico speciale (special education programmes)		5-6	3	3	9	1			16000	Programmes for students with special education needs that are similar in content to secondary education, first stage.
2A	G				Programmes for adults to prepare for exams of secondary education, first stage							Yes	No		No data available.
3C	G				Allgemeinbildende Schule, école de culture générale, 2 Jahre/années (general education programmes, 2 years)		15-17	2	2	11			No	5000	
3C	V				Anlehre, formation professionnelle élémentaire (basic vocational education, dual system)	Fähigkeitsausweis – certificate of basic vocational education	15-17	2	2	11	2		No	3200	Vocational education organised as an apprenticeship in the dual system for the less gifted students. The educational content is individually adapted to the ability of the student.
3C	V				Berufslehre, Berufsbildung, apprentissage, formation professionnelle, 1 und/et 2 Jahre/années (vocational education, in school or in the dual system, 1 and 2 years)	Fähigkeitsausweis – certificate of vocational education	15-17	2	2	11	2			20000	Vocational education either organised as an apprenticeship in the dual system or as a full-time school lasting one or two years and following directly after compulsory school.
3B	G				Diplommittelschule, école de degré intermédiaire, 3 Jahre/années (intermediate diploma school – 3 years)	Diplom – Intermediate Diploma	15-17	3	3	12	2			6000	General education programmes of three years duration preparing students for vocational education on ISCED Level 3B, 4B or 5B. The majority of the students will enter programmes at ISCED Level 4B.
3B	V				Berufslehre, Berufsbildung, apprentissage, formation professionnelle, 3 und/et 4 Jahre/années (vocational education, in school and in the dual system, 3 and 4 years)	Fähigkeitsausweis – Certificate of vocational education	15-17	3-4	3-4	12-13	2			149000	Vocational education either organised as an apprenticeship in the dual system or as a full-time programme at school lasting three or four years. Apprenticeships and full-time schools lead to the same type of diploma and are considered to be equivalent.
3B	V				For adults: preparation for the vocational education exam (Art. 41)	Fähigkeitsausweis – Certificate of vocational education						Yes		400	No data available.
3A	G			Combined – general and vocational education	Berufsmaturität, maturité professionnelle, maturità professionale, 3 und/et 4 Jahre/années (vocational baccalaureat, dual system, 3 and 4 years)	Berufsmaturität – vocational baccalaureat	15-17	3-4	3-4	12-13	2			13000	The programme combines an apprenticeship of 3 or 4 years duration with additional schooling in general subjects. It gives unconditional access to the newly created "Fachhochschulen". This type of programme has been in place since 1993.
3A	G				Primarlehrerseminar I (teacher training I)	Primarlehrerpatent, 1. Phase – teacher's certificate (primary), first stage	15-17	3	3	12	2			6000	The first three years of the traditional form of teacher's education, beginning after compulsory school and lasting 5 years. These programmes are generally devoted to general education equivalent to the "maturité gymnasiale".
3A	G				Gymnasiale Maturität, maturité gymnasiale, maturità (school preparing for the university entrance certificate)	Matura – university entrance certificate	15-17	3.5	3.5	12.5	2			60000	The programme preparing students for the school leaving certificate lasts for a total of 12 1/2 or 13 years after the beginning of primary school. Programmes that commence after the completion of primary school last 6 1/2 years.
4B	V				Berufliche Zweitausbildung auf Sekundarstufe II – second vocational programmes at upper secondary level (1 year)	Fähigkeitsausweis – Certificate of vocational education	18-20	1	1	13-14	3		No	6000	

Manual for ISCED-97 Implementation in OECD Countries – 1999 Edition

Switzerland

ISCED-97 level	Programme orientation	Cumulative duration at ISCED 5	Position in the national degree/qualification structure (Intermediate, First, Second, etc.)	Notes on programmes that span across ISCED levels or sub-categories	Descriptive name of the programme	Main diplomas, credentials or certifications	Typical starting ages	Theoretical length of the programme	Typical length of the programme	Cumulative years of education at the end of the programme	Minimum entrance requirement	Programme specifically designed for part-time attendance	Reported in the UOE	Enrolment 1997-98	Other relevant information
4B	V				Ausbildung für Krankenpflege, formation pour les professions de la santé, 3 Jahre/années (vocational education for health professions, 3 years)	Fähigkeitsausweis – Certificate of vocational education	18-20	3	3	15	3			8000	
4A	G				Berufsmaturität nach der Lehre, maturité professionnelle après l'apprentissage, 1 Jahr/année (vocational baccalaureate after obtention of the certificate of vocational education, 1 year)	Berufsmaturität – vocational baccalaureat	18-20	1	1	13-14	3B			1500	
4A	G				Gymnasiale Maturität für Erwachsene, maturité gymnasiale – programmes pour adultes (school preparing for the university entrance certificate for adults)	Matura – university entrance certificate	20-30	3	3	15.5	3B			2400	Programmes preparing adult student for the "maturité gymnasiale" lasting generally three years. The public programmes require a completed education at ISCED Level 3 for entrance.
5B		Short	1st		Berufsprüfung, examen professionnel (higher vocational education, stage I)	Diploma of higher vocational education	20-25	1-2	1-2	13-14	3B, 4B	Yes		9500	
5B		Short	1st		Höhere Fach- und Berufsschule, école technique (technical school)	Diploma of technical school	18-20	2	2	14	3B, 4B			7500	
5B		Short	1st		Primarlehrerseminar II (teacher training II)	Primarlehrerpatent, Fachlehrerpatent – teacher's certificate	18-20	3	3	16	3A, 3B			3000	The last two years of the traditional form of teacher's education beginning after compulsory school and lasting 5 years. These programmes are devoted to the teaching of specific professional skills.
5B		Medium	1st		Höhere Fachschule, école professionnelle supérieure, scuola professionale superiore, full-time (higher vocational college)	Diploma of polytechnical school	20-30	3	3	15-17	3B, 4B			3000	Programmes lasting at least three years of full-time school. The typical prerequisite is a vocational education of at least three years or an equivalent general education at ISCED Level 3.
5B		Medium	1st		Höhere Fachschule, école professionnelle supérieure, scuola professionale superiore, part-time (higher vocational college)	Diploma of polytechnical school	20-30	3	3	15-17	3B, 4B	Yes			Programmes lasting at least three years of full-time school. The typical prerequisite is a vocational education of at least three years or an equivalent general education at ISCED Level 3.
5B		Medium	2nd		Höhere Fachprüfung, examen professionnel supérieur (higher vocational education, stage II)	Master's diploma or equivalent	23-26	1-2	1-2	15-16	5B	Yes		12000	
5A		Medium	1st		Pädagogische Hochschule, haute école spécialisée pédagogique (pedagogical university)	Teacher's certificate	19-23	3	3	16	3A, 3A			4000	This type of programme has not yet been officially inaugurated. The programmes will demand a "Berufsmaturität/maturité professionnelle" (vocational education of three or four years' duration with a substantially enlarged general education part) or a "matura".
5A		Medium	1st		Fachhochschule, haute école spécialisée ("Fachhochschule" university of applied science)	Fachhochschuldiplom – Fachhochschul diploma	20-23	3	3	15-17	3A, 4A			17000	This type of programme will officially be inaugurated in 1998. The programmes will demand a "Berufsmaturität/maturité professionnelle" (vocational education of three or four years' duration with a substantially enlarged general education part).
5A		Long	1st		Hochschulen, hautes écoles, Lizentiat, licence, Diplom (university diploma)	Lizentiat, Diplom, Staatsexamen – university diploma	19-23	4	5.5	18	3A, 4A			76000	The first stage of university education lasts at least 4 years, the mean duration is 5.5 years.
5A		Medium	2nd		Fachhochschule Nachdiplom, haute école spécialisée diplôme postgrade (Fachhochschule, post-graduate)	Fachhochschul Nachdiplom – "Fachhochschul" post-graduate degree	23-26	1	1	16-18	5A	Yes		1000	The "Fachhochschulen" offer programmes for specialisation after the first degree. They typically last one year. Examples include business administration for engineers or specialisation in environmental aspects for chemical engineers.
5A		Very long	2nd		Universität Nachdiplom, troisième cycle, diplôme postgrade (university post-graduate)	Nachdiplom – post-graduate diploma	24-28	1	4	19	5A			5000	After the first degree, universities offer specialisation programmes not leading to a research degree. They generally last one or two years. Some examples are specialisation in urban planning, in health care management or in environmental studies.
6					Doktorat, doctorat (university Doctorate)	Doktorat – Ph.D.	24-28	2	5	20	5A			12000	
NC					Programmes not allocated to a level									7000	"Foreign" programmes.

Turkey

ISCED-97 level	Programme orientation	Cumulative duration at ISCED 5	Position in the national degree/qualification structure (intermediate, First, Second, etc.)	Notes on programmes that span across ISCED levels or sub-categories	Descriptive name of the programme	Main diplomas, credentials or certifications	Typical starting ages	Theoretical length of the programme	Typical length of the programme	Cumulative years of education at the end of the programme	Minimum entrance requirement	Programme specifically designed for part-time attendance	Reported in the UOE	Enrolment 1996-97	Other relevant information
0					Okul Öncesi Eğitim – Uygulamalı Anasınıfı (pre-school education - practising nursery classes within vocational high schools for girls)		3	3	3						Optional
0					Okul Öncesi Eğitim – Anasınıfı (pre-school education – nursery class)		3	3	3						Optional
0					Okul Öncesi Eğitim – Anaokulu (pre-school education – kindergarten)		3	3	3						Optional
1				Levels 1 and 2	İlköğretim (primary education)	İlköğretim Diploması (primary education diploma)	6	8	8	8					Start of systematic studies, including a Foreign Language Programme, Citizenship and Human Rights courses, Environment and Traffic Lessons. Also called basic education. It is recommended that years 6-8 be classified as ISCED level 2.
3C	V				Çıraklık Eğitimi – Aday Çırak (apprenticeship training – candidate of apprenticeship)		14	3-4	3-4	11-12	1				
3C	V				Çıraklık Eğitimi – Çırak (apprenticeship training – apprenticeship education)		14	3-4	3-4	11-12	1				In apprenticeship training, adults younger than 18-year-old can attend.
3C	V				Çıraklık Eğitimi – Kalfa (apprenticeship training – journeymanship)	Kalfalık Belgesi (certificate of journeymanship)	14	3-4	3-4	11-12	1				
3C	V				Çıraklık Eğitimi – Usta (apprenticeship training – mastership)	Ustalık Belgesi (certificate of Master)	14	3-4	3-4	11-12	1				
3A	G				General high schools	General high schools diploma	14	3	3	11	1				Entrance Exam.
3A	G				Anatolia high schools	Anatolia high schools diploma	14	4	4	12	1				Entrance Exam. There is a year of preparation for a foreign language in Anatolia schools.
3A	V				Vocational high schools	Vocational high schools diploma	14	4	4	12	1				Entrance Exam.
3A	V				Anatolia vocational high schools	Anatolia vocational high schools diploma	14	5	5	13	1				Entrance Exam. There is a year of preparation for a foreign language in Anatolia schools.
3A	V				Technical high schools	Technical high schools diploma	14	4	4	12	1				Entrance Exam.
3A	V				Anatolia technical high schools	Anatolia technical high schools diploma	14	5	5	13	1				Entrance Exam. There is a year of preparation for a foreign language in Anatolia schools.
3A	V				Imam and Preacher high schools	Imam and Preacher high schools diploma	14	4	4	12	1				
3A	V				Anatolia Imam and Preacher high schools	Anatolia Imam and Preacher high schools diploma	14	5	5	13	1				Entrance Exam. There is a year of preparation for a foreign language in Anatolia schools.
5B		Medium			Meslek Yüksek Okulları (vocational training schools)	Ön-Lisans derecesi (associate degree)	17	2	2	13	3A				Entrance Exam after high schools. Orientation to a vocation.
5B		Medium			Meslek Yüksek Okulları (vocational training schools)	Lisans Diploması (Bachelor's degree)	17	4	4	15	3A				Entrance Exam after high schools. Vocationally oriented.
5A		Long	1st		Üniversiteler (universities)	Lisans Diploması (Bachelor's degree)	17	4-6	4-6	15	3A				Entrance Exam after high schools.
5A		Long	2nd		Master	Master derecesi (Master's degree)	21	2	2	17	5A (1st, M)				
5A		Very long	2nd		Tıpta Uzmanlık (speciality in medicine)		24	4	4	21					Specialist training exam in the various branches of medicine.
6					Doktora (Ph.D.)		23	3	3	20	5A (2nd)				Entrance Exam after Master.

United Kingdom

ISCED-97 level	Programme orientation	Cumulative duration at ISCED 5	Position in the national degree/qualification structure (Intermediate, First, Second, etc.)	Notes on programmes that span across ISCED levels or sub-categories	Descriptive name of the programme	Main diplomas, credentials or certifications	Typical starting ages	Theoretical length of the programme	Typical length of the programme	Cumulative years of education at the end of the programme	Minimum entrance requirement	Programme specifically designed for part-time attendance	Reported in the UOE	Enrolment 1996-97	Other relevant information
0					Nursery schools and classes		2-3	2	1-2						Non-compulsory, not specifically designed for part time attendance but 95% of pupils attend part time.
0					Playgroups and day nurseries		2-4	1-3	1-3				No		Non-compulsory, contains educational content (inspection system), data currently coming on stream.
0					Reception classes		4	1	1				No		Includes first year of primary in Northern Ireland.
1					Adult literacy and numeracy	Varies but often no certification on completion	16+	Varies	Varies	11+		Yes			
1					Primary school		5	6	6	6					
2C				2C, 3C, 5B	Employer supported off-the-job	Varies but often no certification on completion	16+	Varies	Varies	11+		Yes	No		
2C				2C, 3C	Employer supported on-the-job training	Varies but often no certification on completion	16+	Varies	Varies	11+		Yes	No		
2B	P				Skillstart (Scotland only)	National Certificate Skillstart 1 and 2	16+	1	1+	11+			No		Designed as the basic point of re-entry to education for those with special needs or no qualifications.
2A	G				Secondary school (age <14)		11	3	3	9					
3C	P				GNVQ (GSVQ) Foundation Level	General National Vocational Qualification Foundation Level	14+	1	1	10+					
3C	G				GCSE courses/SCE standard grades	GCSE/ SCE Standard	14	2	2	11	2A				
3C	P				SCOTVEC National Certificate Modules	SCOTVEC National Certificate Modules	14-17			11	2A				
3C	V				Work-based training for adults	Varies but often no certification on completion	18-63	Varies	Varies	11+		Yes			
3C	G				GNVQ (GSVQ) Intermediate Level	General National Vocational Qualification Intermediate Level	15+	1	1	11+	3C				
3C	V				Activities leading to NVQ Level 2 and equivalent	Various qualifications equivalent to National Vocational Qualification Level 2	16	Varies	Varies	11+	3C				
3C	V				Activities leading to NVQ Level 1 and equivalent	Various qualifications equivalent to National Vocational Qualification Level 1	16	Varies	Varies	11+	3C				
3C	V				Traditional apprenticeships	Varies but often no certification on completion	16-18	0.5-4	0.5-4	12+	3C				
3C	V				Work-based training for young people (including national traineeships)	All participants must work towards a vocational qualification	16-17	2	2	13	3C				
3A	V				Activities leading to NVQ Level 3 and equivalent	Various qualifications equivalent to National Vocational Qualification Level 3	16+	Varies	Varies	11+	3C				Government supported training so must involve vocational qualification.
3A	G				SCE Higher Grade	GCE A/AS equivalence	16	1	1	12	3C				
3A	G				Scottish Certificate of Sixth Year Studies	Certificate of 6YS	17	1	1	13	3C				Mostly in school but some in FE.
3A	V				GNVQ (GSVQ) Advanced Level	General National Vocational Qualification Advanced Level	16+	2	2	13	3C				Taken in comb with A/AS or NVQ3.
3A	G				GCE Advanced Level	GCE A/AS	16	2	2	13	3C				
3A	V				Modern Apprenticeships (MAs)	All participants must work towards a vocational qualification – NVQ Level 3	16-19+	3-4	3-4	14	3C			No		
4A	G				HE Access Courses		18+			11+					
5B					Activities leading to NVQ Level 5 and equivalent	Various qualifications equivalent to National Vocational Qualification Level 5	21+	Varies	Varies	11+	5B	Yes	No		
5B					Activities leading to NVQ Level 4 and equivalent	Various qualifications equivalent to National Vocational Qualification Level 4	18+	Varies	Varies	11+	3A		No		
5B	Short				Higher National Certificate (HNC)	HNC	18+	1	1+	14	3A				
5B	Short				Higher National Diploma (HND)	HND	18+	2	2+	15	3A				
5A	Medium	1st			Diploma in HE (including nurses training)		18+	2-3	2-3	15-16	3A				
5A	Medium	1st			Bachelor's degree, 2 years (accelerated)	Bachelor's degree (BA, BSc, etc.)	18	3	3	15	3A				
5A	Medium	1st			Bachelor's degree, 3 years	Bachelor's degree (BA, BSc, etc.)	18	3	3	16	3A				
5A	Medium	1st			Open University (Bachelor's degree)	Bachelor's degree (BSc, BA, etc.)	18+	3	3	16	3A	Yes			
5A	Medium	1st			Bachelor's degree, 4 years	Bachelor's degree (BA, BSc, BEd, Beng, etc.)	18	4	4	17	3A				
5A	Long	2nd			Master's degree (taught)	Master's degree (MSc, MA, MBA, etc.)	21	1	1	17	5A (1st, M)				
5A	Long	2nd			Professional post-graduate on-the-job training	Many professional qualifications in various fields (accountancy, law, audit, etc.) e.g. CIMA, Articles	21	1-3	1	17	5A (1st, M)	Yes			
5A	Long	2nd			Post-graduate diplomas and certificates	Post-graduate diplomas and certificates (post-graduate certificate of education, etc.)	21	1	1	17	5B				
5A	Long	1st			Bachelor's degree, 5+ years	Bachelor's degree (MB, BDS, BV, etc.)	18	5	5	18	3A				
5A	Long	2nd			Master's degree (by research)		21	1-2	1-2	17-18	5A (1st, M)				
6					Doctorate	Ph.D.	21	3	3	19	5A (1st, M)				

United States

ISCED-97 level	Programme orientation	Cumulative duration at ISCED 5	Position in the national degree/qualification structure (intermediate, First, Second, etc.)	Notes on programmes that span across ISCED levels or sub-categories	Descriptive name of the programme	Main diplomas, credentials or certifications	Typical starting ages	Theoretical length of the programme	Typical length of the programme	Cumulative years of education at the end of the programme	Minimum entrance requirement	Programme specifically designed for part-time attendance	Reported in the UOE	Enrolment 1996-97	Other relevant information
0					Preschool or pre-Kindergarten		2-5	3	2					8400000	Education "takes place" in schools or other instructional institutions, although these may be housed in churches or private residences. The majority of the funding of this programme is provided by households. Enrolment includes enrolment in Kindergarten.
0					Kindergarten		4-6	1	1						
1					Primary education		5-7	6	6	6				24500000	
1				A, B and C, Levels 1 and 2	English as a second language		18-30	1	0.5	9		Yes	No		Not a separate level of education.
2	G			A, B and C, general and vocational	Secondary education (grades 7-9)		12-14	3	3	9	1				
3	G				GED or H.S. Equivalency Programme	High School Equivalency Diploma or General Educational Development (GED) Award	18-30	1	3	12		Yes	No		No enrolment in a course is necessary in order to take the GED examination and earn the high school equivalency certificate. It is not a separate level of education but an alternative route to completion of an ISCED 3 certification.
3	G			A, B and C, general and vocational	Secondary education (grades 10-12)	High School Diploma	15-17	3	3	12	1			21500000	Enrolment includes enrolment in secondary education (grades 7-9).
4C	V				Vocational Certificate (< 1 year)	Occupationally specific vocational certificate	18-30	1	0.75	13	3		No	500000	Inclusion in UOE is partial, enrolment in 2-year colleges is included. No completions are included (about 1/3 of enrolments are included in 1997 UOE). Enrolment includes Vocational Certificate (1-2 years).
4C	V				Vocational Certificate (1-2 years)	Occupationally specific vocational certificate	18-30	1.5	1.5	14	3		No		Inclusion in UOE is partial, enrolment in 2-year colleges is included. No completions are included in 1997 UOE).
5B		Short	1st		Vocational Associate's Degree Programme	Associate of Arts or Associate of Science Degree (A.A. or A.S.)	18-30	2	3	14	3			5500000	Enrolment includes Vocational Associate's Degree Programme.
5A		Short	Intermediate		Academic Associate's Degree Programme	Associate of Arts or Associate of Science Degree (A.A. or A.S.)	18-30	2	3	14	3				
5A		Medium	1st		Bachelor's Degree Programme	Bachelor of Arts or Bachelor of Science Degree (B.A. or B.S.)	18-30	4	5	16	3			7000000	
5A		Long	2nd		Post-graduate certificate programme (e.g. teaching)	Post-graduate certificates (e.g. teaching credential)	22-30	1	1	17	5A (1st, M)			90	
5A		Long	2nd		Master's degree programme (short)	Master of Arts, Science, Fine Arts, etc. (M.A., M.S, M.F.A)	22-30	1	2	17	5A (1st, M)			1700000	Length of programme varies by field of study. May or may not require a written thesis or project. Enrolment includes Master's degree programme (long).
5A		Long	2nd		Master's degree programme (long)	Master of Arts, Science, Business, Public Administration, etc.	22-30	2	2	18	5A (1st, M)				Length of programme varies by field of study. May or may not require a written thesis or project.
5A		Very long	2nd		First Professional Degree Programme	Juris Doctorate (J.D. – Law), Pharm.D. (Pharmacy), Master of Divinity Degree	22-30	3	3	19	5A (1st, M)			295000	Length of programme varies by field of study. May or may not require a written thesis or project. Enrolment includes 1st Professional Degree Programme – Medical.
5A		Very long	2nd		1st Professional Degree Programme – Medical	Doctor of Medicine (M.D.), Doctor of Dentistry (D.D.S), Doctor of Optometry (O.D.)	22-30	4	4	20	5A (1st, M)				Must pass exams administered by professional boards in order to practice. Additional training in a speciality area often follows degree completions – this is usually on the job training.
6		Very long	3rd or +		Doctorate (Ph.D. – Research)	Doctor of Philosophy (Ph.D.)	24-30	5	11	21	5A (1st, M)				Length of programme varies by field of study and intensity of participation.

OECD PUBLICATIONS, 2, rue André-Pascal, 75775 PARIS CEDEX 16
PRINTED IN FRANCE
(96 1999 04 1 P) ISBN 92-64-17037-5 – No. 50591 1999